Soutie
And
The Big Crocodile

By

Sapper Soutpiel

WARNING:

There will be a lot of swearing in this book.
If the following sample offends, please hand it to one of your skollie friends. If not, please pour yourself a massive Klippies and Coke and enjoy the ride.
Vasbyt troepie!

Bossiespruit, Kroonstad, 1987

Sixty terrified pairs of eyes peered out into the dark as the screech of the truck's tailgate being lowered signalled our arrival.

The corporals circled like a pack of hyenas sniffing out their prey. The screaming flared up and we leapt out like a herd of startled dassies. We gathered around the corporals who'd send us off to our designated bungalows. Eventually, it was my turn.

"*Wat's jou van*?" demanded the corporal.

"Er, Kaapstad," I replied in my best G-grade Afrikaans.

"*Nee, jou fokken doos*. What's your name?"

"*Jammer*. Mike Bardsley."

"Mike Bardsley what?" he barked.

"Just Mike Bardsley, I think."

"It's Mike Bardsley, *Korporaal*, '" he snarled.

Brilliant, I'd been promoted already. This was going to be easy.

"*Baie dankie*, Korporaal."

"*My fok. Jy's 'n dom bleddy soutpiel, nê*?" he said as he led me off.

Seeing as we were both corporals I was a bit hurt that he didn't even offer to help carry my gear but somehow I balanced my balsak, trommel and tog bag on my skinny body and staggered after the rapidly disappearing form of my fellow corporal. Two minutes later we were in front of a structure they called a 'bungalow'.

Now in my experience, bungalows were cute little homes with sweet-smelling rose bushes, garden gnomes, manicured lawns and inhabited by genteel old folks who'd invite you in for tea and gingerbread cake. Not this one.

"*Welkom by u nuwe huis*," the corporal smirked.

"Baie dankie, Korporaal, " I replied.

I fumbled in my pocket for some money to tip him but he'd left by the time I found ten cents. His loss.

Dedicated to

Private Colin Bardsley
Corporal Harry Bardsley
Leading Seaman Colin Bardsley
June Bardsley
Every troop who served in the SADF, especially the ones who weren't assholes.

Acknowledgements

My amazing editor Aimee Dyamond who has now fled to Kuruman.
Dave and Unda at Myebooks for all the invaluable help
Lieutenant Beetge
Lieutenant Pete Wainwright for the photos and the input.
Bianca, and the staff at Tiger's Milk Muizenberg, for allowing me to steal their electricity to write this.
Lloyd Ross and Shifty Records for allowing me to use 'Hou my vas Korporaal' by the late, great Bernoldus Niemand aka James Phillips.
Rex Sumner
and
my very own Guardian Corporal

Preface

Muizenberg, Cape Town. October 2017

After moving into a small flat, with limited cupboard space, I had to throw out some of my gear. Top of the list was my army *balsak* (kitbag) that I'd been dragging around for thirty years. As I pulled out my old boots and uniform, the smell and dust of the Free State hit me and army memories came flooding back.

I still have the occasional nightmare of being called up again and frantically searching for my missing beret. I couldn't throw my kit out but hopefully writing about those surreal army days will be therapeutic but if not, I'm still in the market for a second-hand sappers beret.

The army was mainly Afrikaans in personnel and language so there are a lot of Afrikaans words in the book. It is a language that originates from the Dutch settlers who arrived in South Africa during the 1600s and has its roots in Dutch, French, German, Malay and anger.

Basically, you change every C to a K, put 'nie' at the end of every sentence: V sounds like F, and you never speak below 240 decibels. It's impossible to whisper in Afrikaans but it does have some amazing words like *spookasem* (ghosts breath) meaning candyfloss.

Now, that Afrikaans isn't being forced down my throat, I love it. After a few Klippies and Coke my vocal chords turn Afrikaans. It's also the best language to gossip in, especially when those *bleddy* foreigners are hanging around.

There is a glossary at the back of the book to help you translate. So even if you don't enjoy the book at least you'll be able to get into a fight in Bellville.

Soutie

English-speaking South Africans were often called *soutpiels* or *souties* – especially in the armed forces. Allegedly, we had one foot in Britain and one foot in South Africa with our *piel* (Afrikaans for penis) dangling in the *sout* (salt) of the Atlantic Ocean.

Initially, I took this as a compliment. Obviously, they thought we had long willies, but it soon came to my attention that this was not the case; maybe there was still some lingering resentment after the British Lions slaughtered the Boks in 1974.

One day I checked out a world map and worked out that if I'd had one foot in my hometown of Huddersfield, England and the other one in Cape Town my willy would have ended up in a cocoa plantation just outside Abuja, Nigeria.

We should have been called *sjokoladepiels*, which might have enticed a few more girls to dance with me at the local *sokkie* (dance).

The Big Crocodile

During my time in the army, Pieter Willem Botha was the President of South Africa. An angry man, with a nice hat, an overused forefinger and a petulant pout. He declared the State of Emergency and, along with the State Security Department, promoted the idea of a communist 'Total Onslaught' on South Africa.

His Afrikaans nickname was *Die Groot Krokodil* – the Big Crocodile. He was probably proud of it.

National Service

During the mid-sixties, the majority black population of Southern Africa got *gatvol* (tired) of being covered in dust as whiteys hurtled past them in their huge Mercedes Benz's. They also wanted big German cars and holidays in Plettenberg Bay and Lourenco Marques. Over some Sorghum beer, they realised that the first step was to get the vote so they could also have a say in their country and maybe get some of the spoils. They asked whitey but he wasn't too keen so they got angry and then some Commies got involved and that's why we had to do National Service in the armed forces.

Early excuses

It's been thirty years since I finished the army. In that time I've consumed over a thousand bottles of Klippies brandy, a swimming pool of beer, a large Jojo tank of wine, plus some dodgy stuff used to preserve a dead snake in a glass container at a Shanghai nightclub – so there might be some lapses in memory.
Some names have been changed and I might have mixed up a few as well. Sorry.

There are a few sections in italics, about my early life in England and Cape Town. I hope they don't bore you but if they do flick the page over – just make sure you aren't on Tinder.

Soundtrack :Salty and the Big Crocodile

https://open.spotify.com/playlist/0Ftmuizzc2ANICKLCu5cjP?
si=fosA5tV_Rn6WtsddqjeXCw

Inspiration :

Hou my vas Korporaal by Bernoldus Niemand AKA James
Phillips.
Copyright Shifty Records

Hou my vas, korporaal
Ek's 'n kind skoon verdwaal
Gaan ek weer my tjerrie sien
As ek van die trein afklim?
Ja, sowaar, korporaal
Dis mos swaar, korporaal
Ek speel oorlog met my beste dae
Ja ja ja, ek en al my maatjies

Bymekaar
Bymekaar

Sal so doen, kolonel
Sal nie weier alhoewel
Elke dag is deurgekruis
Een dag nader aan my huis
Hot en haar, korporaal

(Hold me tight, Corporal
I'm a child completely lost
Am I going to see my girlfriend again
when I get off the train?
Yes, indeed, Corporal
It is hard, Corporal

I play war with the best of my days

Yes, yes, yes, all my friends and I

Together
Together

Will do so, Corporal
Will not refuse although
each day is checked
One day closer to my home
Here and there, Corporal)

At Victoria Station the R.T.O. gave me a travel warrant, a white feather and a picture of Hitler marked "This is your enemy." I searched every compartment, but he wasn't on the train.

Spike Milligan: Adolf Hitler my part in his downfall.

Chapter One
A Call to Arms

South Africa, 1977

My first encounter with the army came shortly after emigrating from England to South Africa. I was in Standard Eight when my mates Suttie, Slys, Sandro and La received their official SADF (South African Defence Force) identification number and a wad of forms to fill in. This was my introduction to National Service.

All white South African males had to serve two years in the Defence Force. Foreigners like me weren't required or wanted. My first feeling of FOMO: Fear Of Missing Opvoks.

One section of the form asked prospective *troeps* (troops) which arm of the Defence Force they'd prefer to join: Army, Navy or Air Force. Even at the tender age of fifteen, my mates knew that you *kakked* off more in the Army and it was bloody dangerous for your health.

The Navy and Air Force were more English speaking while the Army was heavily Afrikaans. Nobody at Pinelands requested an Army posting except one dyslexic, whose form Suttie helped fill in – it was funny at the time.

The SADF could have crewed a hundred aircraft carriers with all the budding sailors and pilots out there. Lads whose only marine experience was going down a waterslide on the Breede River claimed to be master yachtsmen – okes whose only flying experience was a captain's invite to the cockpit

on a flight to Durban brazenly claimed they were potential chopper pilots. The SADF posting board must have laughed their heads off reading all the requests.

When the postings came out, it seemed that the SADF strategy was to give recruits the exact opposite of their request and post them as far from home as possible. All my classmates who'd applied for the Navy or Air Force were sent to the Army except Slys, who got a Navy posting but still ended up kakking-off in the marines.

Then, in 1979, during our Matric year, my mates started receiving cunningly worded invitations to do their two years for the Fatherland at various unheard-of parts of South Africa. As I was still a British passport holder my participation still wasn't required. My mates weren't too bothered about my exemption although my repeated requests for their girlfriends' phone numbers were met with uncalled-for abuse.

After years of avoiding the school library, my mates finally had to wander through its hallowed portals to research their military designations. They spent hours paging through encyclopaedias searching for info about Middelburg, Bloemfontein, Saldanha and Bourke's Luck. It wasn't encouraging – they were all shitholes with very few redeeming features. Once they realised the *shit* they were in, they fled the scary confines of the library and the swots nervously crept back in to peacefully resume their pursuit of knowledge.

Now if I'd been the Minister of Defence (Still waiting for a reply to my job application), I would have set up training camps in Clifton, Umhlanga, Hartebeespoort Dam, Plettenberg Bay, the Drakensberg and Mauritius (South Africa still had nukes then, which might have persuaded the

Mauritians to allow us a base or two).

Having training bases in *kiff* places would have totally neutralised the End Conscription Campaign and even the Commies and Pinko-Liberals would have joined up, but oh no — Magnus Malan and the other SADF geniuses knew best, hey. They put the training bases in the *kakkest* parts of the country. Cue the exodus and Luxavia flights to Europe full of potential Rambos being sent overseas by mummy.

As the end of Matric hurtled towards my schoolmates, the grim reality of military service became imminent and scary. To quell their fear my mates hurtled over to the grim reality of the Pig and Whistle for a few thousand-farewell drinks.

Chapter Two
Bats, Bokkies, Dogs, Rum and the Lash

Cape Town. 1980.

So my schoolmates finally headed off, leaving me in tears – the selfish bastards hadn't left me their girlfriends' phone numbers.

They did, however, teach me some valuable lessons that I'd need when my army time came around:

Suttie

After a lifetime of inciting trouble and causing the nervous breakdowns of several teachers, Suttie's extended school career finally came to an end. His teachers were desperate for him to pass Matric and move onto greener pastures – any pastures really, just so long as they were far away. Some teachers were rumoured to have filled in Suttie's exam papers. He still almost failed.

Suttie did his basics at 4 SA Infantry Battalion in Middleburg, up in the old Eastern Transvaal. Then, somehow, in its infinite wisdom, the army sent him to Infantry School in Oudtshoorn to be trained as an officer. He began to think that he was the reincarnation of Alexander the Great. He began to quote Winston Churchill, and flush with gung-ho fervour, he volunteered for the Parabat course.

Luckily for the civilised world he tripped over a devil thorn, dislocated his ankle and any chance of a distinguished military career flew out of the window.

Suttie's well-advanced military plans of conquering the rest of Africa fell apart and sanity prevailed. Somehow, he hobbled around enough to be promoted to rifle platoon leader and was shipped off to Potchefstroom to train troeps and take them up to the border.

Suttie: demonstrating the art of smuggling a bottle of Coco-Rico.
Wayne, Jillian, Suttie, Caroline, James, Andy and Dolly.

Upon arriving at Potch he scored a luck; the admin troep *klaaring* him in was Dougie Craythorne, a good mate from Pinelands and after hearing Suttie's sob story about going to the border, he shuffled some papers and, hey presto, Suttie got a job in the stores.

Suttie thrived in his new environment and realising his good fortune became a conscientious worker, often working late into the night after everybody had left. It came as a major shock when a surprise audit revealed massive losses in the stores. Fortunately, none of this could be pinned on Suttie

due to his blanket denials, bald-faced lies and burning the CCTV tapes.

A couple of months later he heard that army Kosher food was better and Jewish troeps got more holidays so he went on his own 'Road to Damascus' experience in reverse. He claimed that after downing a few Stroh Rums during a drinking game with a Rabbi in the Voortrekker Hotel, he had seen the light and was now a prodigal son of Zion. They believed him. *Oy vey.*

Lesson: Circumcision, although painful, can result in better food and more leisure time.

Slys

When Slys got his call-up to the Navy, he was rather pleased with himself. He high-fived the whole of Pinelands, drunk a case of Red Heart Rum and memorised the entire script of *Mutiny on the Bounty*. He'd hit the jackpot – no army bullshit for him, just a happy life on an ocean wave. Off he joyfully skipped to Saldanha where, due to a momentary lapse in concentration, he stood in the wrong queue and accidentally volunteered for the recently created Marine Corps. The Marines are basically the Navy's version of the infantry, except you train on sand dunes and you never step on a ship. So, instead of singing sea shanties and knocking back bottles of rum in the rollicking pubs of Simonstown, Slys spent most of his service flat on his face on the border, getting shot at by annoyed Namibians. Luckily he's not a bitter person. I hope.

Lesson: If you want to drink rum in Simonstown, don't stand in the same line as troeps who want some 'action'.

Sandro Baccari

Our token Italian was well loved for his quick wit and even quicker fists, but mostly because he possessed a Suzuki 50cc motorbike. This was put to good use every Friday transporting Old Brown Sherry and five-litre Autumn Harvest cellar casks from Raapenberg bottle store in Mowbray back to our parched lips in Pinelands. (Our suburb was a 'Garden City' which meant an abundance of pretty gardens but no bottle stores and pubs. Not the ideal situation for a bunch of *skollies* hell-bent on some alcohol-inspired debauchery).

Sandro got quite a weird call-up – the dog unit in Bourke's Luck, in the old Eastern Transvaal. Sandro wasn't exactly a dog lover and most dogs preferred biting him to licking him. Unfortunately for the dogs, he wasn't averse to biting them back but eventually a détente was established which allowed all parties to concentrate on the real job: hounding the enemy.

Lesson: A dog is a man's best friend unless it's hanging from your throat.

La

Laurence was the sarcastic one in our mob. Any attempt at reasonable and logical discussion would swiftly be shot down with snide comments and incisive putdowns making him a perfect candidate to be a training corporal, which is what he became after completing his basics and Junior Leadership course at 1 SA Infantry in Tempe, Bloemfontein. He spent a year abusing troeps before returning home to be abused by his wonderful wife Tracey. Whenever I got back home on army leave, I'd give him kak about being a corporal. He'd laugh and order me to buy the next round.
Lesson: Stripes make you look fat.

Chapter Three
A Moment of Madness

Pinelands, 1980

Because I was a team player, a full-blooded patriot and a bit of a *doos,* I decided that I needed to do my bit, so I and fellow Brit and schoolmate Andy vowed to volunteer for the South African Navy. Our dads had been sailors, and somehow, our Old Brown Sherry-soaked brains thought it would be a good idea to continue the tradition; a bit stupid as I'm not exactly Vasco Da Gama – I get seasick running a bath. But when duty calls there will always be fresh idiots ready to prove their manhood. So, while nursing the traditional *babalaas,* we headed to the Castle.

Built by the Dutch East India Company from granite rocks mined from a quarry on Signal Hill, the Castle is an iconic pentagon-shaped structure in the middle of Cape Town. It is also, the oldest existing colonial building in South Africa and symbolic of Afrikaner military history. Most SADF military insignia feature its pentagonal shape. A comforting place for some – a reminder of untold horrors for others.

After parking on the Grand Parade, we strolled over to the imposing façade of Cape Town's SADF Headquarters and asked where we could sign up for National Service. After some confusion and unexpected laughter they pointed us towards an office at the end of a cold, dank and dark corridor in the bowels of the Castle. By this stage, our gung-ho fervour was cooling off rapidly and then we took a wrong turn into a medieval-looking torture chamber. Enclosed by stone walls, with a high sloping ceiling, it was claustrophobic and eerie in its silence. Rusty iron shackles jutted out of the walls and a contraption that looked suspiciously like a gallows hung from the ceiling. A scar of a window shed a sliver of cold light into the room. The interior designer had done a fine job although it might have needed a couple of throw cushions to pull it together. It was a room specifically designed to inflict pain and death. My visions of heroic deeds on the high seas began to wane drastically. As we scrambled out we slammed straight into a brick wall, otherwise known as Sergeant Swanepoel.

"*Ja, mense.* Is you the two heroes who are going to save our country from the infidels?" he bellowed through his gigantic bushy moustache.

"We want to join — Navy," I stammered.

"Our dads were in — want to do a bit, —" said Andy.

"Follow me," he bellowed again, a glint in his Aryan eyes. And follow we did.

He stomped down the corridor, blocking out the sunlight with his massive frame and trampling over any unsuspecting troep who wasn't quick enough to get out his way. He was built like a Casspir armoured vehicle and moved almost as fast. Finally, we got to his grim office. I soon noticed that there wasn't a massive queue of enthusiastic volunteers begging to join the Defence Force. It looked more like a queue for voluntary Tabasco enemas. The corridor was empty. Surely we weren't the only idiots keen on a fun-filled two years of action and adventure? Maybe those sniggers had been aimed at us?

After ushering us in and triple-locking the door behind us, Sgt Swanepoel sat at his battered desk and slid over some Xeroxed army application forms and a badly chewed Bic.

"Right. Just sign here and here and we'll have you on-board in no time," he proclaimed.

Through the smudges, I realised that the form was in Afrikaans and even my alcohol-soaked brain knew not to sign something I couldn't understand. It could've been a Sun International timeshare application or even worse, an Old Mutual retirement annuity policy.

"What does *weermag* mean?" I enquired nervously.

"Navy," the sergeant muttered under his breath.

"Why would the Navy have a training base in Oudtshoorn?" Andy correctly pointed out.

Sgt Swanepoel looked a bit flustered and shifty-eyed. He nervously stroked his moustache. He'd have to be patient and use all his animal cunning and strategic know-how to seal the deal.

"Just sign the *bleddy* thing!" he screamed.

"Erm. Do you have one in English?" I squeaked.

After growling at us and rooting through his solitary desk drawer filled with *Scope* and *Farmers Weekly* magazines (I was slightly disturbed that the pages of the *Farmers Weekly* mags also seemed to be stuck together. Must have been the humidity down there), he found some English forms. He proceeded to Tippex out 'Army' and crudely replaced it with 'Navy', before handing them over.

"What does Permanent Force mean?" Andy asked warily.

"*Fok, manne,* " he exclaimed.

He snatched the forms off us and using the gnarled Bic pen, started filling them in.

"You first." He shot me an angry glance. "Name?"

"Michael Bardsley, but you can call me Mike," I grovelled.

"Just pass me your *bleddy* ID books." We handed them over. As he scrutinised the details, he started looking us up and down.

"It says here, you is non-South African citizens." Sergeant was on the ball.

"Correct, but we are happy to fight for the cause," Andy exclaimed.

"So long as it's in the Navy," I quickly pointed out.

"All our mates are going," Andy implored.

"*Nee, nee, nee, fok*," he sighed. "*Meneers*, you have to be South African citizens to join."

"What — why?" I protested. "Surely you must have read Hemingway's account of the International Brigades in the Spanish Civil War?"

"*For Whom the Bell Tolls*," Sergeant replied swiftly. Evidently, the sexy heifers in the *Farmers Weekly* weren't his only literary interest.

"Exactly," I said. "Foreign heroes who went to defend the rights of the Spanish patriots."

"Fucking Commie bastards," he spat out.

"I think you'll find that they were more along the lines of Democratic Socialist Republicans," I explained. His massive fist slamming into the desk put a full stop to that conversation.

"We can't allow *bleddy* foreigners in our armed forces," growled Sgt Swanepoel, "You could be Russian spies."

"You mean British spies," I muttered.

Luckily he didn't hear me.

"Once you become South African citizens we can reconsider, " he pronounced.

The manic rage in his eyes subsided as I squeaked, "How do we do that?"

"Well," he said. "You need to be born in South Africa, be mainly white and understand Afrikaans."

Ah, well, one out of three wasn't going to crack it.

As the door gently slammed shut behind us, we shuffled out.

"Fuck! What do we do now? We can't take this lying down," Andy said.

"What day is it?" I asked.

"Monday"

I had a cunning plan. Glancing at my watch and rapidly working out our coordinates, I made a swift strategic decision. Forty minutes later we patriotically shared a case of warm Castle Lager at the infamous happy five hours at the Pig and Whistle.

Ah, well, it was the South African Navy's loss. Those bastards in the Botswana Navy were lucky.

I could've been a modern-day Nelson. Not that Nelson, the other one – Admiral Horatio Nelson. The one who's on top of that big pole in Trafalgar Square – the scourge of the French. The man, who defeated their Navy at Trafalgar, got shot and then bravely came out of the closet in his dying moments.

I'd escaped the clutches of The Big Crocodile for now, but he was still lurking in the shallows.

Chapter Four
Tears for Scabies

A sunny day in 1984. Thornton (AKA: Lower Pinelands or Upper Goodwood)

After my folks got divorced, my old man moved to a neighbouring suburb called Thornton. A couple of rungs down the social ladder from Pinelands, but not too bad. Living there gave you street cred. Thornton was Etzebeth territory, ruled by the infamous clan who spawned Eben, our feisty Springbok lock. Eben is a hippy liberal tree-hugging pacifist compared to the rest of his brethren. You didn't mess with them.

One day, sitting in my bedroom, listening to the funky-punky sounds of The Stranglers and feeding kudu biltong to my pet rat Scabies, Dad pushed an official letter under my door and scurried away. Assuming it was my long-overdue Unemployment Insurance Fund cheque, I dropped Scabies like a hot rat, ripped open the letter with my remaining teeth and started salivating. But, instead of some beautiful numbers with a big 'Rand' in front of them, there were loads of letters which, when my eyes finally focused, created words.

It was from our glorious government and was congratulating me on becoming a fully-fledged citizen of the Republic of South Africa. Brilliant. What a pleasant surprise and I hadn't even applied for citizenship. They'd obviously heard of my noble efforts in bringing Punk Rock to Africa. However after a bit of research I discovered that my new citizenship might have been due to an increasing demand for fresh troeps. The Big Crocodile had brought in a new law to ensnare all us girlfried stealing foreigners. So if you were under twenty-five, had lived in the country for five years and had a penis you automatically became a naturalised citizen and once you became a citizen, you were eligible for military service.

Sadly, the euphoria of becoming a citizen soon wore off. My unpatriotic mates ignored my requests to sing *Die Stem* before every baseball match at Clyde Pinelands Club and then I started receiving suggestive letters from the Minister of Defence. For some strange reason, Magnus Malan thought I'd like to spend two years in Kimberley. Now, I've got nothing against Kimberley but I was quite enjoying the *jol* in Cape Town, and The Pig and Whistle pub was relying on me to keep their profits healthy. Luckily I was still at college so I declined the invitation.

At eighteen, I'd been young and impressionable, the perfect candidate for brainwashing but at the ripe old age of twenty-three, I'd already succumbed to the deadly perils of Mainstay cane, Russian Bear vodka, Coco Rico and the occasional white pipe (even the drugs were racist). I was still a fighting machine but only at one o'clock in the morning and fuelled by plenty of double cane-and-cokes.

I also realised that the government were in deep, deep kak if they needed a *suipgat* (drunkard) like me to help win the war. Although I'd been called up to the army, I was still studying Construction Supervision at the Cape Technikon so I was exempted until graduation. I'd escaped the jaws of the Big Crocodile again but prehistoric predators never give up.

In January 1985 the first 'immigrant intake' began their two years of military service for their newly adopted country. PW wasn't kidding.

After years of getting call-ups for Intelligence in Kimberley (they'd obviously not seen my Matric results), I started getting call-ups for The School of Engineers in Kroonstad. Evidently, my Construction Supervision marks at the Cape Technikon combined with my skills in putting bricks on top of each other had caught their eye. I was being headhunted for greater things.

Many immigrants and some South Africans had already fled overseas to escape national service; some because of their opposition to Apartheid, others because they didn't fancy two years of being shouted at by idiots. Now I had to make my choice.

I carefully weighed up my options:

1. Fleeing overseas
This would've made sense but I was broke. I'd just finished my three-year Construction Supervision Diploma at the Cape Technikon and my savings weren't enough to get me a third-class rail ticket to Houjoubekfontein, never mind a flight to London. I could have asked my folks for money but they were already battling to afford the golf club fees, the weekly twenty gallons of the finest Chardonnay and their divorce.

2. Conscientious objection
It was a noble option but being abused for six years in a prison run by Apartheid's foot soldiers wasn't much of an incentive. I wasn't too keen on Apartheid, but I wasn't keen on martyrdom, either.

3. Doing my time

I'd be based at The School of Engineers, and that didn't sound too bad: a little bit of running around, some rifle practice, then into the nice school to learn some engineering;

my type of army. I started talking myself into going. Surely I could survive two years? So, instead of sneaking off overseas I prepared myself for national service.

With a month to go, I realised I might need to up my fitness regime. I started running every day and brought my daily alcohol consumption down to single figures. With a week to go and no sign of the Border War ending, I started packing. I'd been warned that I could only take the bare minimum; luckily, I only possessed the bare minimum.

Luggage list:
Football boots
Squash racquet *(Optimistic)*
Chains and locks *(So your laundry didn't get stolen. Not for S & M)*
Walkman and cassette tapes *(Sex Pistols, The Jam, Rodriguez, Pink Floyd, Sonja Herholdt,)*
Brasso
Omo washing powder and clothes pegs
Iron *(With step by step instructions from Violet our long suffering domestic worker)*
Sewing kit (*For buttons and head wounds*)
Electric shaver *(Saved me a lot of time and blood)*
Boot polish and brush
One set of civvies
Three *Scope* magazines *(June, August and November 1986)*
A poster of Anneline. (Tastefully done)
Condoms – Banana flavour *(Extremely optimistic)*

My last week of freedom involved lots of tears — or was that beers? — yeah sorry, probably just beers, although I'm sure I saw one of the bar ladies at the Pig wipe a tear from her remaining eye although that could've been after a bouncer demonstrated his new mace spray. It was all a bit of a blur.

> *At the ANC's seventy-fifth anniversary, President Oliver Tambo rules out negotiations with the South African government and declares 1987 'the year of advance to people's power'.*
> *8 January 1987*

Chapter Five
Citizen Cane and Coke

Cape Town. January 1987

Finally, the dreaded day arrived. After dragging me, screaming and kicking, from under my bed, Dad drove me down to Wingfield, the local SADF base where I would board the train for Kroonstad. The place was full of jittery young men heading north to Bloemfontein, Kroonstad, Bethlehem, and Pretoria. Our *Groot Trek* or *Groot Afkak* was about to begin.

Looking cocky. Just before for the train to Kroonstad. With Moose, Dougie (Air force cap), Dolly, me, Wayne and Vanessa.

Assorted loyal friends had generously taken time off work to come and see me off on my epic journey. I was genuinely touched by their sacrifice. My good mate, Moose, was particularly inconsolable. I'd never seen this giant of a man so distraught and his tears flowed uncontrollably – it had finally dawned on him that he had nobody else to go drinking with on Tuesday mornings. He married soon afterwards.

As the minutes ticked by I desperately scoured the crowd for the flowing blond locks of my soul mate Anneline, but obviously that bastard Sol had locked her up in their sumptuous one bedroom en-suite cabana at Sun City. Our passionate love for each other would have to remain a tragic secret for a while longer.

We stood around, in the crotch dampening heat, until an officer gathered us around and gave us a rousing speech about the Corps and the pride of becoming a sapper. He was a lovely chap who assured all the folks that we would be safe in their hands and that they should be extremely proud of us. If we had any questions he'd be happy to answer them. My dad asked "what time is the bloody train leaving?" – he had a thing about punctuality.

My mates glanced nervously at their watches as they realised that various 'happy hours' were beginning at pubs across the Cape. They started making weak excuses and quietly drifted off. As the clock inched towards the top of the hour, the soldiers followed suit and we were kindly asked to make our way to the train station.

So far, so good.

This wasn't as bad as my mates had said. Their horror stories about the cruelty of the army had been grossly exaggerated. I gathered up my kit and gave my Dad a manly handshake. He stared into my bloodshot eyes, wished me

good luck and shaking with raw emotion, sprinted to his car – he was late for his tee-off time at Westlake golf club.

I turned and strolled along the hot tarmac, every step taking me further away from my past life. This was it, this was what I needed – adventure, action, excitement and camaraderie. I looked around for my mates Peter Wainwright and Ross Petersen, Pinelands *ous* who'd been at college with me and had also been called up for Kroonstad. I couldn't spot them. No worries, I'd find them on the train and we'd have a laugh as we headed north to our shared destiny.

As I got to the corner, I took one final glance behind me, turned and saluted proudly; a bit dramatic maybe, but I'd seen it in a John Wayne movie and I'd never have the opportunity again. Although the crowd had thinned out, my heart suddenly leapt as I spotted Anneline's shimmering golden locks behind a Port Jackson tree but then I realised it was just a Checkers bag caught in a branch. I sadly trudged on.

As we turned the corner and lost sight of our loved ones, the temperature plummeted twenty degrees, the sky went dark and an ominous growling sound filled the air. The smart, chilled-out corporals, who were there to escort us, had been transformed into wild-eyed, rabid savages who were trying to break the World record for swear words used in one breath. One impressive contender reached one hundred and seventy-two before pausing for some fresh air. It was later discovered that he was a dominee, so he was disqualified for being a professional. It was mayhem.

The corporals lunged at us, screaming in our faces and gesticulating wildly. We panicked like canned lions spotting a group of drunk trigger-happy Yanks but eventually the corporals herded us back towards the train.
In the distance, I spotted the mild-mannered officer who'd

given us the welcome speech, a sadistic smile lit up his face. We'd been ambushed – by our own army.

After a while, long lines of trembling recruits formed, waiting to board the train. I was about halfway in the queue when I noticed that the recruits at the front were being rigorously searched. Moose had assured me that they'd only give our bags a quick glance before throwing us on board but these bastards were pulling everything out. They looked in every nook and cranny, even inspecting the steam irons to see if there was any liquor hidden in them.

Oh shit!

While packing my luggage, I'd accidentally slotted in a quarter-jack of Klippies brandy, two mini-bar bottles of Mainstay Cane and a banky of the finest Malawi Gold.

The queue got shorter and a couple of guys got caught with booze and dagga and were dragged off by the military police. I was now *kakking* bricks assuming that I'd be next. We were out in the open surrounded by corporals, so any attempt at throwing away the offending merchandise would have been spotted. I needed a plan. I bent down and started untying and then re-tying my shoelaces. A couple of impatient recruits, eager to get a good seat on-board, pushed passed me, then with a subtle bit of moonwalking I was soon near the back of the queue. Thanks to Jacko's favourite dance moves, my first strategic retreat had succeeded.

By the time I got close to the search squad, the train driver was demanding that they leave on time. Feeling rushed, the corporals only took a cursory look in my bag. They had a good laugh at my squash racquet but failed to detect my illicit goodies. Relieved, I scrambled on board. I'd barely survived my first ten minutes in the army.

Once on board, I was shoved into a cabin with a bunch of terrified *laaities*. After the initial shock of army life, I was just happy to grab a seat and get my breath back.

After the last recruits had boarded we had to wait as they did the paperwork. Presumably, a shitload of guys had chickened out at the last moment because the corporals kept sticking their heads into the cabins and counting us. Eventually, they cut their losses and with a sudden jolt we were off.

A few minutes later, as we chugged through the picturesque suburbs of Elsies River and Vasco, I went to find Pete and Ross. Before I'd even stepped into the corridor, two aggro corporals charged at me, screaming and pushing me back into the cabin.

What the fuck was happening? I tried again but this time they just looked at me and then at their rifles. Who were these psychos? It was slowly dawning on me that my rose tinted view of the army might have been a bit naïve.

The train was the Trans-Karoo Express. It usually carried civilian passengers between Cape Town and Jo'burg via Laingsburg, Kimberley and through the Karoo, but on this day it was reserved exclusively for us troeps.

Lucky us.

There were about ten carriages in the traditional South African Railway dark red attached to a large locomotive engine. Each carriage contained cabins that were designed to house six people, furnished with six thin beds that folded out from the cabin wall, with the bottom ones used as seating during the day.

My Scope magazines, NikNaks and biltong soon covered the small table that protruded from the wall. One of the laaities

tentatively put his Bible on the table, but when I started reading it and asking him what Sodom meant he quickly snatched it away.

Ten minutes into our journey, the train stopped. That was quick, I thought, as I grabbed my gear. Unfortunately, it was just Bellville station, where we picked up even more victims before steaming off through the innocent scenery of Stellenbosch, the Hex River Valley and the Boland. The colourful patchwork of vineyards dotted with little whitewashed workers' homes blinking in the sunlight already made me homesick.

My babalaas kicked in and I realized I might need a little sleep so I nestled up to the window and started snoozing.

Just as I was busy impressing Anneline with a radical roundhouse cutback at the Valley of Waves an ear-shattering explosion shattered my dream. A red gooey mess dripped down the window where my head had just been. Bloody hell, twenty minutes into my army career and I'd already been shot; not exactly the World Record I wanted. I quickly probed my skull for bullet-holes but found nothing. Clutching my heart, head and wallet I stood up, looked outside and saw a bunch of young farm kids running alongside the train hurling ripe guavas at the windows. The *bliksems*.

After barely surviving my first contact, I was shaken and badly in need of emergency medical help. Luckily, I'd watched Doctor Zhivago so I diagnosed myself a therapeutic double Klippies and Coke to sooth my trauma symptoms.

After failing to break the ice with my prepubescent cabin mates, I thought they'd also appreciate a little tipple.
I pulled out the quarter-jack of Klippies and saw their greedy little eyes opening wide.

"Okay, boys," I announced. "Time for a little beverage."

"You aren't allowed to drink on the train," said a voice of reason.

"Says who?" said an angry voice of unreason. Me.

"The Sergeant Major, the lieutenant and all those corporals with the rifles," added the acne-blighted face of the laaitie across from me.

He had 'Prefect' written all over his forehead, literally.

"Bloody hell, how do you even know their ranks?" I asked.

"Didn't you read that pamphlet the army sent us?" Prefect scoffed.

"Of course not, it could have been propaganda," I lied.

What pamphlet? I thought. Shit! My Dad must have thought it was a final demand from the taxman and burnt it.

Five teenagers, clutching their Bibles and Liqui-Fruit cartons, smugly faced me. Bollocks to you lot, I thought as I cracked open my can of Coke, took a sip and with fine precision, poured in some Klippies. As soon as that golden elixir hit the back of my throat I calmed down and after a few more sips the fear subsided; but just as we were passing Snotklapfontein, disaster struck – my Coke was finished. After hours of ignoring the accusing glares from The Brady Bunch, I couldn't hold out any longer.

"Anybody got some Coke?" I pleaded.

"No!"

"No!"

"No!"

"No!"

"No, only Crème Soda."

"That will do," I cried triumphantly. "Name your price"

The little capitalist bastard knew I was desperate. It was a vicious case of supply and demand: lots of demand, very little supply. After some bitter and hostile negotiations I

knocked him down to three rands and was soon sipping on my first Crème Soda and Klippies cocktail. I formally named it The Green-Eyed Monster and soon understood why it wasn't featured on the Mount Nelson cocktail menu but it did the trick. I was soon beaming like a baby who'd just shat its pants; obviously, I hadn't, but after the guava incident my sphincter had been a bit unpredictable and I was ready for any eventuality.

We chugged through the bone-dry Karoo towards the exotically named Beaufort West, De Aar, Kimberley and finally, Kroonstad. All the while off-loading the cannon fodder as we went. The gentle rhythm of the train eventually lulled me back into a deep sleep and I was soon dreaming of that fateful day which put me on the path to Kroonstad.

May 1977. Huddersfield, England

One day, Dad shocked us by coming home before midnight. Mum immediately sprang into action, filling up a bucket with water while phoning the fire brigade and giving mouth-to-mouth resuscitation to my Dad's sand wedge.

"Good Lord, has the golf club burnt down?" Mum screamed hysterically and possibly with a touch of sarcasm. "Don't be bloody stupid, woman," replied dear Papa, ripping his beloved sand wedge from my mum's puckered lips.

He stood majestically in front of the TV and announced .....well, he would've done if his timing hadn't been so disastrous – Top of the Pops was just starting on the TV.

(The greatest music show in the UK. Think Noot vir noot *times ten. Think the* X-Factor *times a hundred. The world's best bands, the countdown to number one, disc jockeys famous for their great taste in music, witty banter and wandering hands)*

And Dad was stood in the bloody way

"What are you doing? It's Gary Glitter!" I yelled, trying to get him to move.

"Bugger Gary Bloody Glitter," Dad retorted.

Prophetic words, but we weren't listening.

In despair he turned off the TV.

This must be serious. I didn't even know the TV had an off switch. It wasn't just a television set: it was our primary source of entertainment, doubled up as a heater and was our only piece of artwork. That telly was the very glue that held our dysfunctional family together.

Then my granddad, sneaked into the room, plonked himself in his favourite chair and tried to look past my dad.

"Shift your bloody carcass, it's Top of the Pops!*" Granddad yelled at him.*

"We are moving to South Africa," Dad replied in exasperation.

"But Gary Glitter's on" Granddad was a big fan even though his hearing was going.

"Bloody hellfire. I said we are emigrating to South Africa," Dad repeated.

"About time we got out of this shithole," Granddad chirped, leaping up to go pack his stuff.

"Oy. Not you," Dad called out.

"What?" Granddad exclaimed.

"It's either you or the dog."

It was a close decision, but unfortunately for Granddad the dog had the deciding vote and after years of bitter winters

spent in the back garden, Gypsy, our border collie, fancied the warmer climate of Africa. Granddad took it surprisingly well, apart from cutting us out of his will and leading the international boycott against South Africa.

In June 1977, we boarded our flight in London and flew out to sunny South Africa via the island of Las Palmas and Blantyre in Malawi (due to sanctions they were the only airports that would allow South African flights to refuel).

It was a long journey and Mum kept the airhostesses busy with her frequent requests for gin and tonics, wine and beer and brandy and vodka and another wine, please.....
"Why are these bottles so small?" Mum asked. "Maybe just give us a big bottle or you're going to be very, very tired," Mum was always thinking of other people. Eventually, they left the drinks trolley next to her.
After twenty-four hours of travelling, we landed at DF Malan Airport in Cape Town. As we clambered off the plane, a gentle drizzle greeted us and Mum melodramatically went down on her knees and kissed the sweet black soil of our new home; spitting out a mouthful of steaming tarmac she started singing Toto's 'I'll Bless the Rain Down in Africa' which was amazing because she was tone-deaf and the song was only written five years later. Mum was always way ahead of her time.
As we elbowed our way through hordes of bawling relatives we started searching for Dad. We couldn't find him, so Mum courageously volunteered to search the bar. When we realised we'd lost mum too, Andy and I set out to find her. We eventually found her perched precariously on a barstool, trying to flirt with the terrified barman and swooning about the cheap prices.

Beer was about a third of the price compared to England, they were practically giving away spirits and some psycho genius had recently invented the five-litre wine box.
"Wine in a box! Look, it's wine...in a box. Hallelujah!" Mum repeated excitedly.

Mum was beginning to fit in but where was dear Papa? Had he been impaled by an angry Zulu impi? Mauled by a lion? Or even worse, been caught in rush-hour traffic on the N2?

As Mum ordered another triple Mainstay and Stroh rum mixer, I made my way back into the arrivals hall. By this time the crowds had thinned out and the cleaners were mopping up the tears and lost children. Then I heard that wonderful sound I always associated with my Dad, a chronic post-nasal hacking cough and the clack-clack of golf shoes on tiles. Grabbing my hand, he smiled his gentle smile and asked me what my name was.

"Mike," I replied earnestly, realising that he might have been testing my memory. (He still owed me seventeen pounds and twenty-seven pence, about four million Rands, that he'd borrowed off me in England.)

His hands, which I'd always found quite rough and calloused, were now smooth and gentle. What wild African magic had transformed his skin? Had he been to the local witchdoctor? Had he been bathing in elephant's milk? I looked down and as my eyes focused through my tears, I could just make out a strange tattoo on his wrist – 'Titleist.' He'd forgotten to take his golf glove off. Another case solved. We walked over to the bar.

Instinctively dodging Mum's right uppercut, Dad paid the bill and dragged our measly possessions off to the car park. In those days Samsonite was just a Biblical theme evening,

but due to our severe lack of money/credit/dignity, we'd only been able to afford cardboard suitcases. Yes, you heard correct. 100% cardboard except the metal locks. I was still using one of them to travel up to Jo'burg ten years later. They just don't make cardboard like that anymore.

We trooped off to the car park to find Dad's shiny new second-hand Datsun 130 – the car of choice for most sales reps unrelated to the boss. As we drove into town he began pointing out the landmarks and famous natural features of Cape Town.

"Directly in front of you is the world-famous Table Mountain", he trumpeted.
"Where?" I asked.
"Just behind the thunderstorm."
"And coming up on your right is the world-famous Groote Schuur Hospital where Christiaan Barnard performed the first-ever heart transplant."
"Where?" Andy demanded.
"Just through the mist," Dad explained.
"And here is the world-famous city centre and the world-famous Castle of Good Hope."
"What bloody Castle?" Mum had woken up.
"It's on the right. Wait till the floods subside and you'll see it," said Dad.
I was getting a world-famous bloody cold. Bugger this. We'd immigrated to a place wetter than Huddersfield.

We'd left home in the searing fifteen-Celsius heat of an English summer and now we were bloody freezing and soaked in Africa. We'd been conned. After three weeks of accusing Dad of taking us to the African version of Manchester and ignoring his PowerPoint presentation

proving that it was winter in the Southern Hemisphere, we grudgingly relented and ventured outdoors.

The rain clouds had lifted and finally, we could see Table Mountain and the rest of Cape Town. It was mightily impressive. Forty years later, I realise that we'd scored a massive luck landing up there.

Chapter Six

Drowned Horse Town

Kroonstad, 1987

After a night of erratic sleep punctuated by farts, snoring and dribbling (mainly me), we pulled into Kroonstad railway station.

Ninety-five years before our bunch of terrified passengers arrived, the first train had steamed proudly into the Boer Republic's fancy new station. At its peak in 1955, there were seventy trains passing through Kroonstad each day, making it an important railway junction on the main line from Cape Town to Johannesburg. Clearly, international sanctions had begun to bite because hardly any trains carrying goods bound for the overseas market headed past us. Not a good time to be in the export business, clearly.

It was a typical, stinking hot day on the veld and even the scorpions had scuttled into the shade for some homemade lemonade. We, on the other hand, were met with a typical warm Free State greeting as hordes of manic corporals tried to outdo each other in pushing and screaming at us. Once the yelling had subsided we were hurled onto a fleet of Bedford trucks and we had our first attempt at an obstacle course. It wasn't easy climbing up the tailgate while holding onto your kit bag and nursing a massive crème soda and brandy babalaas. It was also the first taste of camaraderie as we started helping each other and some eye contact even broke out. We were in the shit together so we'd better look after

each other.

We sat down on a row of benches inside the enclosed truck and clung onto our bags. Fuck, and fuck but it was hot. Within seconds, we were all sweating our asses off and with my perspiration being eighty-percent alcohol I wasn't too popular. After a few minutes the truck was full but still the corporals kept on screaming, "*Skuif op*, shift up". Sardines were sending sympathy letters. Was this some kind of magic trick? How to get a whole brigade onto one Bedford? Incredibly, they *skuifed* even more troeps up. David Copperfield would've been well impressed but when they realised that the disgusting smell from the truck might be the early onset of decomposure they swiftly sent us on our way. And off we did *skuif* to The School of Engineers, Kroonstad.

Once out of the railway station car park, we got our first glimpse of the town we'd soon call home. It had a modest town centre with the usual shops (Seven Eleven's, OK Bazaars etc.), wide roads with trees and attempts at lawns, some of which were successful. The housing was mainly single-storey bungalows, nothing too fancy but nice enough and plenty of church spires dotted the landscape.

Kroonstad is the third-biggest city in the Free State after Bloemfontein and Welkom. Nowadays it has a population of over a hundred and sixty thousand. It seemed a lot less when we arrived in 1987 probably because 90% of the population were out of sight in the black township on the outskirts.

Located on the N1 highway, it's one hundred miles south of Johannesburg, a hundred and fifty miles north of Bloemfontein and a million miles away from sanity.

It's close to the gold mining towns of Welkom and Virginia with the agricultural town of Bethlehem to the east – which was the other main Engineer Corps training base where they trained the poor buggers who were destined to sweep for mines on the border.

The town was established in 1855 by an Irish pioneer Joseph Orpen, who stumbled on the area during his search for a decent pint of Guinness. *Kroonstad* is an Afrikaans word and literally means 'Crown Town'. The name hadn't come from Orpen's allegiance to the British Crown (*Kroon*), but was in honour of an unfortunate horse named *Kroon* that Orpen witnessed drowning in a nearby ravine after it had broken it's leg. Orpen's love for animals clearly trumped his love for the Empire, and he named his new town after the doomed horse, in Afrikaans, *nogal*.

They definitely kept that info off the tourist brochure. Imagine the road sign as you entered the town:

Welcome to Kroonstad
A great place to drown your horse.

For about two months during the Second Boer War, Kroonstad became the capital of the Orange Free State, and later the site of a British concentration camp, where between April 1901 and April 1902, more than a thousand Boers were murdered by the British Empire. Not a great surprise that many Afrikaners justifiably hated the British. I kept my 'England' tattoo well hidden.

It's well known as an agricultural centre surrounded by farms producing wheat, maize, meat products, dairy and wool. It also has a massive prison.

We'd often have gangs of prisoners (*bandiets)* working in the main base and as we passed each other we'd exchange sympathetic looks. Even the bandiets felt sorry for us. They thought we'd committed a crime.

One quietly asked me what I was in for?

"For being a complete doos," I replied.

He nodded and wished me luck.

Ten minutes after leaving the railway station we clattered through the gates of The School of Engineers' main base. I was pleasantly surprised. It was large, with nice red brick buildings, green lawns, females and an absence of gallows. Things were looking up. The trucks shuddered to a halt on the main parade and we clambered out of the back, rubbing our legs to try and get the circulation going again.

The South African Army Engineer Corps is an offshoot of the British Corps of Royal Engineers, created after William the Conqueror invaded Britain in 1066. King William had brought with him his own engineers whose job was to maintain the King's siege equipment (*insert your own dirty joke here*).

'Engineer' stems from the Latin word *ingenarius* and originally meant 'genius' or 'a person skilled in the art of constructing defences'. So, I was going to the School of Geniuses, finally, some recognition for my obvious mental superiority. Unfortunately our military title was Sappers, not exactly a heroic sounding title but somebody had to sap for the country?

We soon learnt that the Engineering Corps had an inferiority complex and were desperate to prove that they were just as tough as the Infantry, Parabats and Special Forces. As a result, they overcompensated a bit.

We did full-on infantry training plus engineering add-ons. I was going to be a busy boy.

Soon after disembarking, I found my Pinelands chommies Pete and Ross in the crowd. We were all in shock.

"What the fuck was that?" Pete whispered.

"That was a taste of our future" I replied

"I'm sure it will get better," Ross chimed in optimistically.

It did – two years later, when we klaared out.

After another screaming session we were led into a big hall where we were met by admin staff and the famous Dankie Tannies, who would assist us to enrol. With loads of civvies involved, the corporals were now restricted to snarling and glaring at us.

The Dankie Tannies were part of a nationwide group formally known as the Southern Star Fund that was comprised mainly of elderly civilian ladies who provided assistance to the troeps. They helped with admin and sent parcels to the troeps on the border. They were nice to me.

After filling in most of the forms, I hit a slight problem. The form was asking what my religion was. I was agnostic but still brainwashed enough not to go full atheist. A couple of Dankie Tannies tried to help me find my church but after ten minutes searching for the local agnostic church they were stumped. I tried to explain that we didn't have a church but they were tenacious.

"Is it like the Hebrews?" one asked, helpfully.

"Not really, it's actually —" I started.

"There's a synagogue in Welkom," another pitched in.

"No, I'm not Jewish."

"You're not one of them Islam's, are you?" another piped up.

"No. Agnostic means I'm not sure if there is a God or not. I'm sort of undecided," I explained.

I was met by two blank looks. The Tannies were clearly determined not to give up on me. They started looking at their list of churches again.

"Baptist?"

"No."

"Methodist?"

"No."

"Pentecostal?"

"No."

"NGK?"

"Isn't that a spark plug?" I laughed with a twinkle in my eye.

She steamrollered on.

"Buddhist?"

"What? Is there a Buddhist temple in Kroonstad?"

"No," she sniggered, with a twinkle in her eye.

Touché.

Eventually a corporal who'd overheard the conversation shuffled over and gave me some advice that saved my bacon. He told me that if I didn't nominate a church I'd have to do guard duty every Tuesday and Sunday. Not a good idea. Then he gave me some even better advice. The Anglicans had a *braai* and served beers at their Tuesday evening sessions.

"Hallelujah, praise the Lord. Where do I sign up?" I asked.

The Dankie Tannies were ecstatic that I'd been born again and was now a fully signed-up member of the Anglican Church, which is like the Church of England, I think.

I never saw that corporal again. Maybe he was a guardian angel or, as I prefer to think, my very own Guardian Corporal.

After we'd completed the paperwork, we were marched over to the barbers. This squalid salon was tastefully decked out with the hacked off ponytails of hippy recruits nailed to the wall and *Scope* centrefolds featuring girls with their nipples discreetly blacked out so as not to offend all us perverts ogling the poor girls chest ornaments. I've always found it strange that they would allow you to see ninety percent of the breast, but the little nipple part that was quite essential until powdered milk came along remained banished to our fertile imaginations.

Most young South African males in the 1970s and 80s needed counselling for years, after unearthing nipples instead of black stars during their first real-life cleavage experiences. I remember *Scope* magazine doing an April Fools edition in which they claimed that if you used a coin you could scratch the censors black stars off the centrefold girl's chest to reveal the sauciness beneath. They sold a record amount of copies. Luckily, a combination of cynicism and a lack of funds saw me give up after ruining seven copies.

A sharp shove in the back woke me from my erotic daydreaming and I was propelled towards the chair of pain. Being a proactive citizen I'd already semi-shaved my head. Thought I'd save them a bit of time. I'd been a skinhead back in my punk days so losing my bouffant didn't bother me and I thought it'd make me look harder.

"Just a trim please, good man," I chirped as my turn in the chair came along.

As he jerked my head back, cutting off my air supply with the bib, I sensed that his sense of humour only went as far as hanging forlorn bouffants on the wall.

At least I didn't need to start a conversation about the weather or Western Province's chances in the Currie Cup. (Army barbers. What kind of useless, unambitious *doos* do you have to be to decide your future lay in being an army barber? You required only one skill – that of doing the same haircut for every head that comes your way for forty years? Not that I'm bitter or anything.)

After gouging a couple of bald patches into my skull and nicking my ear I was hurled out of the chair and back into the terrified herd of shaven inmates outside. I tried to find Pete and Ross but it was impossible, everybody looked the same. We'd become anonymous, all part of the master plan.

Off we shuffled to our next stop, the medical: our last chance to get out of the army.

Chapter Seven
Last Chance Saloon

For some odd reason our first medical took place after we'd arrived at camp. Not sure why they didn't do the medicals in our hometown, as it must have cost them a fortune returning all the lucky bastards diagnosed with fatal medical conditions.

But the army wasn't going to let the new cannon fodder go without a fight. Most troeps deemed unfit for basics could still be of some use and were usually sent off to Pretoria to serve as admin clerks in the Personnel Service Corps. There, they patriotically shuffled papers and kept losing my request for a transfer back to Cape Town, or to Pretoria, or anywhere but Kroonstad.

Once you'd passed your medical, you were in for the duration, so this was the final chance to escape the army's clutches. Many recruits had spent plenty of time devising plans to fail their medicals. Now was the time to put it into practice.

Ways to Fail the Medical

1. **Psychological problems**

1.1. Claiming to be homosexual

This was 1987 South Africa and most gay troops were terrified of coming out. Most served with distinction and heroism, however, a few straight recruits, desperate for an exemption, went for the old "I'm gay" manoeuvre.

Scene 1: Army doctor's office.
Doctor: What do you mean gay?
New recruit: I prefer men to women.
Doctor: Well, seems like it's our lucky day then. You'll have a choice of six hundred and forty of them. G1K1

It was never going to work but looking back on it now, it was probably a good ploy because many of the *faux* gay troeps ended up as cooks or medics. A cushy gig unless you ended up at the border or boiling bacon at our training camp.

1.2. The "I'm befok *in the head" manoeuvre*

There were three variations of this one.

i) Speaking in tongues and rolling the eyes to the back of head.
With the recent increase in evangelical churches in the Free State during the eighties, this behaviour was already regarded as normal and they'd just klaar you in and send you to the happy-clappy church on Sundays.

ii) Running around screaming and urinating on yourself.
Not really an option as they'd just chuck you in with all the other loonies in 35 Battalion, our next-door neighbours.

iii) *The silent treatment*
Acting mute to get an exemption.

Doctor: Don't worry, troepie. We have devised a wonderful new drug that will cure you. Amazing what a combination of Tabasco, Mercurochrome and mercury can do to loosen the tongue. We'll have you chatting away in no time at all.

Doctor pulls out an injection with a twelve-inch needle. Recruit passes out and wakes up in his bungalow holding his G1K1 papers.

2. Physical problems

2.1   The Fake Limp

Word soon got out that flat feet would get you an exemption.

Scene 1: A limping, waddling troep enters the doctor's room with cries of, "Don't worry doctor! I'm sure it will heal soon."

Doctor: Looks pretty bad.
Recruit: Yes, and it seems to be getting worse, doc.
Doctor: I don't think you're going to be much use in the army.
Recruit: Shit! I was really looking forward to serving my country.

Doctor pulls out a shotgun and starts loading it.

Doctor: Any last words?
Recruit stops limping.
Recruit: It's a miracle. I'm cured.
Doctor: Hallelujah. G1K1.

2.2 Have a break, have a Kit Kat

The old diabetes trick. Just before klaaring in, some troeps would scoff buckets full of chocolates, sweets and sugary drinks until their blood sugar went through the roof. This often worked until word got around and the doctors started putting them in quarantine for a week.

No more Kit Kats and Jelly Tots – blood sugar down.

"G1K1. Next!"

Many troeps who'd been gung-ho before going into the army realised that it wasn't quite their cup of tea and devised intricate plans to be thrown out. But once you klaared into the army it was a mission to get out.

The army had seen all the tricks in the book and were naturally very cynical about requests for exemption or transfers to a base close to home. But it could be done, as long as you maintained the act for months on end.

Many stories circulated:

1.   A troep who started walking around with a brick on a dog lead and called it Magnus. He'd tell the others troeps to be careful of the brick, as it would bite. He kept it up for a few months and finally got sent home. Hopefully Magnus the Brick found a good home as well.

2.   Another troep would run out into the local farmers fields and manically stab a scarecrow, screaming that he wanted to kill black people. Within a couple of days he was heading home.

3.   A troep came back from leave with a gleaming samurai sword.

"Why do you need a samurai sword?" his corporal asked him.

"Killing with bullets is too clean, corporal. Follow me," he whispered as he started leopard crawling through the bungalow. He didn't last long.

Act like a bloodthirsty maniac and the army didn't want you. I missed a trick there.

By the time I got into the army doctor's room the poor bastard was struggling to maintain his belief in the Hippocratic oath.

After looking down countless Chesterfield inflamed throats, prodding multitudes of stinking feet and inspecting over two hundred pairs of hairy balls, he was ready for the golf course and a few triple whiskies.

Luckily, he was English-speaking and from Cape Town so we had an almost-normal conversation, my first one since coming to the army that didn't involve shouting. He took my temperature, weighed me and checked my height. Then he started slapping his stethoscope all over my quivering torso.

"Sounds good," he pronounced.

Spotting my England tattoo, he said, "You might want to keep that well-hidden The Boer War hasn't finished here."
We both laughed heartily.

As he checked my tattoo he spotted the scar just above it.

"What's this scar from? Car accident, rugby, ski slalom?" he asked.

"No. A gang sort of stabbed me," I replied.

He backed away nervously.

"And this one?" pointing at a wound in my back.

"Also a stabbing, but I was the innocent party, honest."

As he inched further away to the safety of his desk, I could see the humanity fade from his eyes.

"Do you smoke?" he asked.

"Yes, about fifteen a day."

"And drinking?"

"About the same, especially on Mondays."

By now he was shaking his head and making copious notes.

"What cigarettes do you smoke?"

I emptied out my pockets, revealing a crumpled packet of Chesterfield, some Lion matches and my asthma pump.

"What's that?" he demanded.

"My asthma pump."

"What the hell. Are you asthmatic?"

"Only when I can't breathe." I joked.

"Shit man, that's not good. Why didn't you tell me?"

"I thought I'd surprise you."

"I've got to classify you as a G3K3."

"What does that mean?"

"No running during basics."

"That sounds like a good thing."

"Don't bet on it." He replied.

He stamped my papers and sent me on my way. Not wanting to scare him, I walked out slowly.

Bliksem! I'd hoped that my knife wounds might give me a little escape route out of the army but no such luck.

Such a waste of a good stabbing.

'Steek Hom'

Newlands, Cape Town. 1985

Cape Town is a bit like Rio de Janeiro – stunningly beautiful, but with some major dodgy areas. It is well known as one of the murder capitals of the world.

I experienced my first dose of ultra-violence attending a cricket match in the normally non-dodgy area of genteel, upmarket Newlands. I was part of a crowd of Clyde-Pinelands baseball players who'd converged on the lawn at the cricket ground to watch a one-day match featuring the great Western Province side of Le Roux, Jeffries, Kirsten, Hobson, Ackerman etc.

Suddenly, a fight erupted in front of me. One of our youngsters, Clint, was grappling with another laaitie who'd taken exception to Clint pissing on his leg. Being a bit of a pacifist, I jumped in with Dougie Curran and a couple of others and broke it up.

To a smattering of applause (which might've been for a quick single by Ackerman), Dougie and I strode back to our place on the lawn to find that his sports bags and my leather jacket had been stolen. Shit, shit, shit. In those days, my prized possession was a black leather jacket punked up with hand- painted logos of The Sex Pistols, The Stranglers and The Jam. I had to get it back.

After receiving a description from an undercover informer (the ice cream vendor) we headed to the exits looking for the bastard thieves. Dougie spotted one of them and after grabbing him, we found he'd already handed the loot over to his mate, who was making a beeline for the exit. We handed thieving bastard number one to a security guard, and told him to detain him until we got back.

We dashed through the exit but we'd lost thieving bastard number two. Never mind. We had one of them and he was bound to spill the beans.

Back inside, we found the sheepish-looking security guard. who'd let thieving bastard number one go because – well, because he was a fucking idiot who didn't even have the brains to be a security guard – which we might've mentioned as we stormed off.

Having given up on finding our gear, we watched the end of the match then headed off to the Sportsman Bar at the nearby Newlands Hotel to drown our sorrows. It was one of our favourite drinking holes and luckily we'd been unbanned after Dougies boet, Speedy had sincerely apologised for ripping a beer keg off the bar the week before. Once our sorrows had been drowned, rescued, resuscitated and then re-drowned, we staggered out and headed in the general direction of Dougie's car. As we got to the far corner of the car park, we passed a bunch of youths who were milling about.

Suddenly, through the alcoholic mist, Dougie spotted the distinctive squirrel badge on his Clyde Pinelands jacket that was now being worn by one of the gang. It was easy to be suspicious, since our emblem, a cute little squirrel gnawing on an acorn, was not something most hard-core gangsters preferred to have on their bitchin' gear.

"Where the fuck did you get that jacket from?" Dougie demanded.

The gang of about fifteen youths, suddenly alert, started inching away.

"Hey, that's my fucking jacket!" yelled Dougie.

Now we were in their midst, they were looking a bit jumpy. Dougie was going ballistic.

The next thing I knew, a fist smashed into my face and Dougie had taken a couple of smacks as well.

The gang sprinted off towards Main Road, with Dougie on their heels. Dougie, unlike me, was an athlete specialising in sprints, so he was quickly onto them. I followed behind, resetting my nose and hoping Dougie wouldn't catch them.

I heard one of them shout, "Gee my die mes, gee my die mes!" (Give me the knife!)

Dougie went flying into them and then I heard, "Steek hom, steek hom!" (Stab him!)

Not sure why they kept repeating things. Might have been a hard-of-hearing gang out on the prowl. Anyhow, Dougie went down under a storm of blows and stabs.

Shit, this might mean I'll have to get involved, I realised.

Luckily, my natural persona, Cowardly Mike, had been usurped by Still Cowardly but Drunk Mike, who went charging in like an epileptic Bruce Lee; kicking, punching, chopping and completely missing any contact with flesh – although I might have head-butted the tarmac. Fortunately, the sight of a vodka-sozzled whirling dervish made the gang pause and then scarper up the road. As I staggered up off the tarmac Dougie lay crumpled on the road. So did our sports bags and, more importantly, my leather jacket.

"Help. They've fucking stabbed me," Dougie groaned.

"Hold on, mate," I replied

I tried to pick up our bags, my jacket plus Dougie, who was now covered in blood, sweat and my tears. He kept slipping out of my grasp. Fuck, what do I do? I panicked. Dougie is my best mate and he might be dying but on the other hand, I'd spent days painting that jacket. It was iconic, my most prized possession. I wore it everywhere, even played baseball in it.

"Aaaaaaargh," Dougie gurgled through the frothy blood he was coughing up.

Jacket or Dougie? I thought. What kind of man had I become?

Finally, I came to my senses. I flipped a coin for it. I always call tails. Came down heads. Shit. Okay, best out of three I persuaded myself.

"Aaaargh, I've been stabbed" Dougie repeated unnecessarily. I'd heard him the first time.

"Hold on, Dougie, nearly there." I flipped again.

Fuck, heads again.

After checking that I hadn't been slipped a double-headed coin, I dropped my leather jacket and our bags and hauled a still-dripping Dougie into the car park.

Luckily for us, but not for them, a young couple had been sitting in their car, watching the action. They'd assumed it was a gang fight. Next second, I'd opened the cars backdoor and thrown a soggy Dougie inside. I also dived in.

"Quick, take us to Groote Schuur, my mate's been stabbed!" I yelled.

The woman just stared at me angrily. I suddenly clicked.

"PLEASE," I added.

"That's better," she humphed.

Obviously, a Herschel girl.

There was blood all over the car, two possible gangbangers in the mix, and she wasn't moving until I said please. That's strong parenting skills. Respect. So Miss Daisy and her shocked blind date drove us to Groote Schuur.

Making sure I said "thank you" to our rescuer, I dragged Dougie out of the car and into Emergency, passing gunshot wounds and various heads with axes in them; the usual Friday night victims from the greater Cape Town area.

Strangely, many families, including children, accompanied the injured: clearly cheaper than taking them to the movies. Once I'd filled in the paperwork, Dougie was taken away, making faint gurgling noises.

Now I had to make 'The Call'. So I found a tikkie box and phoned Dougie's mum, Pam. Dougie and Speedy weren't exactly the studious types. They were more free-spirited – vodka or brandy usually. Pam had already received quite a few heart-stopping phone calls before, regarding her sons. It was late when I called so she knew it wasn't the Nobel Peace Prize Committee calling.

"Hi, Pam."

"Which one?"

"Dougie this time."

"What happened?"

"Nothing too bad, he's going to be just fine. Just a light stabbing."

"Where are you?"

"Groote Schuur..."

"On my way."

As I was sitting in Emergency, a young nurse came over and suggested I come with her to a little room down the corridor. Wow. The night was definitely improving.

We strolled down the corridor and as we turned a corner Dougie came wandering along in a hospital gown, his hairy ass displayed to the world.

"Where the fuck are you going?" I asked.

"I'm looking for a pillow."

"They didn't give you a pillow?"

"It's too lumpy, I can't sleep," he moaned.

"We should've gone private. I'll be sure to send in a strongly-worded complaint to the Health Department tomorrow," I promised.

Minister of Health:

"I've just received a strongly-worded complaint from a Mr Bardsley of Thornton, Cape Town. He's asking why we don't have a wider variety of pillows in our hospitals. Why aren't there any soft downy ones or hard well-packed un-lumpy ones, and maybe some without blood stains all over them.? Says he's asking for a friend."

Chief Medical Officer at Groote Schuur:

"Sorry, Minister, unfortunately we seem to have spent all our budget on bandages, medicine and doctors."

As we got to our romantic lair, the nurse turned to me with gentle, bloodshot eyes.

"Don't worry, this shouldn't take too long," she panted.
Shit! My ex-girlfriend must have been gossiping again.
A woman scorned, hey. Although come to think of it, she'd broken up with me.

"No, you don't understand – erm," I glanced furtively at her name badge. "You don't understand, Penny, that was long ago and I've been practising. I can last for up to two minutes now."

She looked at me with that same confused look I'd encountered so many times. She opened the door to reveal another female nurse, an operating table and a nervous-looking male intern putting on a pair of latex gloves. I'd heard all about kinky nurses before but this was getting ridiculous.

"Whoa, whoa, whoa." I started backing out. "Listen, I'm as kinky as the next man but I'm playing midfield tomorrow and we need the points."

But Penny had already put me in a stranglehold and a quick nudge from her well-padded knee propelled me back into the room.

"We're just here to stitch you up," said the male intern.

"I'll bloody stitch you up, mate," I warned.

"Now me and my girlfriend..." – I glanced down at her badge again – "erm, Penny, need a bit of privacy, so if you wouldn't mind buggering off. I've had a rough night and I'm badly in need of some tender loving..."

"But you've been stabbed," the other nurse pointed out.

"No, nurse, that was my mate, Dougie. He's stable now and apart from pillow problems I'm sure he'll recover, so if you don't mind, me and – erm – Penny really need that operating table for about seven minutes, ten at the most."

"Look at all the blood on you," Penny chirped.

"That's just from Dougie, he tends to spill a bit."

"Then why is it still dripping off your fingers?" she pointed out.

"What?" I exclaimed.

Glancing down at my right hand and a pool of blood that was forming on the floor, I realised they might have a point. Now I'd watched all three Godfather movies and from what I recalled, getting stabbed usually implied a bit of pain. I'd felt nothing. I'd made medical history, my folks would be proud.

My new girlfriend – erm, Penny – left me and the other nurse gently hacked off my blood-soaked shirt. Once they'd mopped up the blood, they found a wound in my upper right arm and a smaller one in my back. Bastards! Who stabs people in the back, literally? Leather-jacket-stealing bastards, evidently.

It was the intern's first night in Emergency and as I was his first patient, he was understandably a bit nervous.

I tried to calm him down with some old medical jokes but it didn't help. As I closed my eyes, everything went quiet except for his heavy breathing and the nurse's sniggers. I realised things weren't going well as I heard words you don't appreciate when you are getting stitched up: "Oops," "Shit," and, "Let's try again."

Fourteen attempts later and Doctor Frankenstein got the first stitch in, the nurse had nearly finished her Huisgenoot *and my seventeen Castle Lagers and four double Klippies and Coke were beginning to wear off. I hoped they weren't charging by the hour. After twenty minutes and two stitches, the pain began permeating through the alcoholic mist and I was desperately looking for an escape route. Finally, the first wound was stitched up, the nurse gave a sarcastic round of applause, I whimpered a little and then Doc attacked the back wound with renewed gusto. Eventually, he finished, slapped a bandage over the wounds, ordered a Lamborghini and groped the nurse. He'd make a fine surgeon one day.*

As I staggered out and headed towards the waiting area, Pam came out of Dougie's ward.

"Home?" she said.

"Good idea," I replied.

A lady of few words but always the right ones.

Sadly, after months of stalking the nurses' residence, I never found, erm, Penny again. She's probably still out there, wandering the corridors looking for her slightly punctured lost love.

I still see Dougie occasionally. I'm a bit disappointed that after bravely saving his life he didn't name his first-born after me, but I try to be humble.

And somewhere in the Cape some lucky bastard is proudly wearing an old leather jacket with 'Anarchy In The UK' emblazoned on the back. Punk's not dead. Oi Oi Oi.

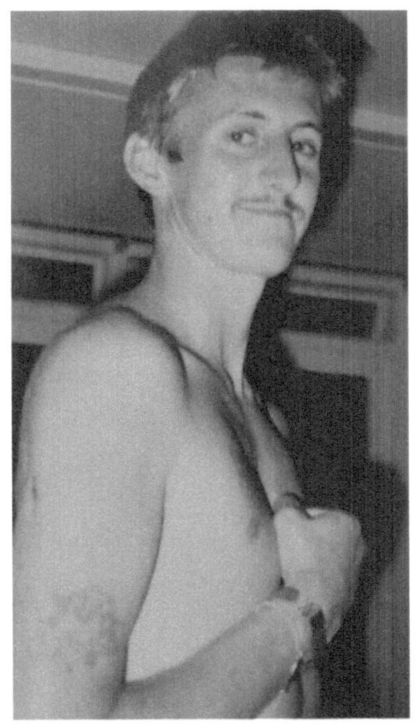

The England tattoo that caused all the kak; the stab wound that wasn't enough to keep me out of the kak; and the kakkest moustache in the army and maybe the World.

In the army, there were three medical classification indicators: G, K and W. We never heard about the W classification; it was a mystery then and remains a mystery now.

<u>G stands for *Ground Duty Factor*</u>

G1 and G2: Total fitness for ground duties *(You can fuck them up.)*.

G3: Physical activities are limited and clearly defined by relevant restriction codes. *(Find out what their excuse is, and then devise other ways to fuck them up).*

G4: Troop is only fit for admin duties. *(Lucky bastards)*

<u>K stood for *Geographic and Environmental Factors*</u>

K1: Member is suitable for service in all geographical areas. (*Border/ townships/ Pig and Whistle*).

K2: Unfit for active operations in the field and unfit for foreign deployment. May render service in temporary unit base areas and may do routine border patrols. *(Caddie for the brigadier).*

K3: Unfit for active operations in the field and unfit for foreign deployment (*No wonder my transfer request to Hawaii got denied*).

K4: Member is only fit for restricted service in a base area where both a specialised and general medical service is available. *(Guarding 1 Military hospital and the nurse's flats).*

These classifications were usually combined into the following:

G1K1: Superior soldier: shiny white teeth, flashing blue eyes and rippling muscles. (*Not me*)

G2K1: Looks good on the surface, but lots of niggles like poor hearing, dodgy eyes or bad breath. (*Physically dodgy but could be deployed to guard a pothole or take a bullet for the President*)

G3K3: Perfectly healthy specimens except for the occasional tendency to roll around on the ground gasping for breath and trying to find their asthma pump. (*Attention -seekers and cowards who should be forced to work hard during the day and stand guard duty every night.*)

G4K4: Medically buggered up. Troops who should have been in bed at home supping on mums chicken soup. *(Con artists and pilferers. Coughed a lot but this didn't stop them selling stolen kit, food or your army file)*

GT: Temporary deferment: based on medical grounds. (*Just waiting for their missing limbs to grow back*).

G5/GP: A complete waste of time: Troops who had one foot in the grave. Medically discharged. *(The gold medal of classifications)*

Troeps who were classified as G3K3 wore badges to identify themselves, so they didn't die at the hands of the corporals. Basically, it was a badge of shame that allowed all corporals to give us shit but not to kill us, like having a large red target on your back.

All troeps were given metal dog tags engraved with our force number, name and blood group. We also wrote our blood types on our belts in case we got shot or blown up and they needed to put a few extra pints into us.

The Escape Route

If you didn't get a medical exemption, the next option was to be transferred to an easy camp: Cape Town, Durban, Pretoria, Monte Carlo, or one close to home. This usually entailed having a relative high up in the armed forces, being a junior member of the Broederbond or being Anneline's

brother. I sent Anneline a letter inquiring if she'd ever misplaced a brother but she was obviously too busy building Sun City to reply. I've forgiven her and moved on, but still love her.

It's a familiar story in the history of the world. Those in power look after themselves. You'll notice that the main warmongers never go to the trenches or send their loved ones: Bush, Blair, Kim Jong-un and al-Assad. How can you become Commanders-in-Chief if you've never been shot at? Many modern leaders facing war duty came up with the best excuses: bone spurs (Trump), excessive cocaine use (George W. Bush), being a dictator (Saddam) and pant wetting (Tony Blair).

After the unexpected news of being classified a medical loser and coward, I headed over to the stores to complete my ensemble.

Chapter Eight
Boots, Jocks and Plastic Helmets

All my mates had warned me to stay focused when I got to the stores. Getting the wrong gear would cause blisters, rashes and two years of shame. Most importantly, I had to get the right-sized boots or I'd be crippled within days.

With that thought ringing in my ears, I resolved to be strong in the face of adversity as I entered the valley of death. Two steps in and a pair of army issue underpants hit me in the face. What the hell? It was chaos in there.

The storemen's approach to dressing us for battle was simple: assess every troep in one quick glance then hurl whatever was closest at us. As we tried them on, the panicked rush of troeps behind us propelled us forward.

"*Roer jou gat, troep!*" screamed a corporal.

Within a minute I was trying to cram all my badly fitting gear into my new *balsak* (kitbag): bush hat, jacket, big jacket, socks, trousers, belts, underpants. To complete my new fashion wardrobe I received a plastic helmet called a *doibie*, which made me look like a used matchstick.

Our last stop was at the boot emporium. All around me troeps were valiantly attempting to cram wrong-sized boots onto their feet. Everybody had been advised to get the right boots. The store men were having great fun insisting that the boots would either expand or shrink to fit our hooves. A huge troep in front of me was almost in tears as he tottered around like a prima ballerina in a pair of size sevens.

He could barely get his toes in, never mind the rest of his foot but the storemen insisted, "they were a snug fit and they'd be fine in a week". He begged for a bigger pair, but these were hardened store men, trained to ignore logic and skilled in the dark arts of crippling troeps. It was David versus Goliath and Goliath was still a *roef*, he finally pirouetted out of the door with a whimper. Now it was my turn.

"I'm a size 9," I pleaded as the zombie behind the counter hurled a pair of size thirteen's at me. My feet barely touched sides as the hard red leather swallowed them up, Louis Moolman, the Springbok forward would have struggled never mind yours truly. I gave the store man a look of despair as I waddled around like Charlie Chaplin. They weren't just big, they literally flew off my feet when I walked – I'd be a danger to passers-by if I ever tried to march.

"Don't worry," one of the store men smirked. "Just leave them in the rain overnight and they'll shrink nicely or wear twelve pairs of socks. That usually does the trick."

Next step was to get our *trommel* (trunk), which we filled with our blankets and pillow. We were now hauling around our tog bag, a balsak full of army clothing and a big metal box stuffed with blankets and pillows. The whole lot weighed about fifty kilograms – I was only sixty kilograms of skinny gristle and two kilograms of muscle so I was rapidly gaining respect for pack mules.

Unfortunately, even though I was stumbling around and in obvious difficulty, not one Good Samaritan popped out of the crowd and offered to carry my burden.

"Thanks, God." Obviously, not an Anglican. Once we'd finished our shopping spree, the store men drew a huge sigh of relief and got back to their normal routine of selling everything on the black market. Capitalism doesn't stop just

because of a little war.

We gathered outside and carried our ill-fitting clothing back aboard the Bedford trucks. Once on board, I took another look at my new fashion wardrobe, I wasn't inspired. At least the Nazi's had been dressed by Hugo Boss – we'd been dressed by The Croc and Tannie Elize. It was crumpled and faded, the colour best described as diarrhoea brown or nutria brown as the army called it. My overall was so large it could have hosted a Gupta wedding reception.

I'd never been known for my sartorial elegance but now I looked like a midget in a tent, like back in my old school days in Pinelands.

August 1977: The Land of Pines and Squirrels
Our first three months in the Cape, was spent at the Hotel Elizabeth in Sea Point, commonly known as The Liz. It was the main jol in the area. Dad had done his homework.

When I say that we stayed at a hotel, what I mean is that we lived in the 'budget-friendly' block of flats at the back.

One of those cheap transit places where the desperate diaspora from Britain, Rhodesia, Zambia, Ireland and Mozambique converged, looking for work in sunny SA. It was full of wonderful characters from around the world. It was great. I'd have happily stayed there forever. It was knocked down a few years later and replaced with a non-descript block of flats. Another unique part of Cape Town tippexed out by the soulless developers and brain-dead council.

As laaities, Andy and I had the run of the Liz and we soon became firm friends with the staff, especially the waiters. For some reason there were quite a few Durbanites working there and they loved betting on the horses – especially Raj, who would become a firm friend and mentor.

I was short, skinny and corruptible – the perfect dimensions for a jockey and once Raj heard that I could ride a horse he began working on my future jockeying prospects...and his future gambling profits.

"Watch your weight. Put that potato down. Have some lettuce. Don't run by the pool. Stop growing," he'd gently berate me as he filled in his two rand place accumulator.

Maybe I should've mentioned to Raj that the only horse I'd ever ridden had just had the plough taken off him and was so knackered that he could barely stagger around the Welsh potato field they'd called a riding school. I still managed to fall off him so many times my folks called it quits and demanded half the fee back. Unfortunately, the Welsh farmers were almost as tight-fisted as my folks, so they only got a 28.364% refund less VAT.

The Liz Hotel was the entertainment Mecca of Sea Point, full of bars, bands, comedians and a late night disco. The place rocked and many of the touring entertainers stayed in the same block as us. It was a non-stop party. This was my first taste of the entertainment industry and I was enthralled by their lifestyle, especially the lazing in bed in the morning part. They'd perform late into the night, party afterwards then stagger out of bed for lunch. Sometimes they taught me songs or tried their jokes out on us, other times they'd teach me card games and as my pocket money dwindled I soon learnt some valuable maths lessons – don't twist on twenty. Happy days.

Our extended holiday in Sea Point couldn't last forever and soon, reality struck. A hotel flat wasn't a suitable family home and Andy and I needed some more schooling.

My folks went flat hunting and eventually found a place that suited both their budget and lifestyle: cheap and with the

local bar next door. Although Pinelands was a dry suburb, the loophole was that sports clubs and members-only clubs could run bars. The Pinelands Club stood within staggering distance of our new home, Garden City Heights, and was known as the spiritual home of the local barflies. It was also the epicentre for teens learning the ancient rituals of getting hammered. The Club had a swimming pool, tennis courts, pool table and badminton courts, which nobody used because we were all in the pub swilling down the ridiculously cheap booze.

Two minutes after moving into our new home my folks dashed over to sign up. Problem was, you needed a member to nominate you and then it had to be passed by the committee. A delay of a few days, Mum and Dad were shocked. Dad hadn't charmed snakes for the Royal Navy just to be denied his basic human right to get pissed, so he swung into action. He skirted their outer defences, brazenly marched into the bar, bought a few rounds for everyone and promised many more in the future. Their defences stood strong until a rapid-fire charge of Jagermeister shooters won the day. In record time the Bardsley family were nominated, passed and warmly welcomed into the Club.

Mum's cheers could be heard for miles around.

The folks had done well, but to realise this dream of suburban bliss, Andy and I needed to be accepted into the local school, Pinelands High.

In England, you just got shoved into your local school. No interviews, no tests and so long as you hadn't stabbed anybody popular, you were in. Pinelands, on the other hand, wasn't exactly a hotbed of radical liberal socialism like Huddersfield, and so they insisted on a little chat before allowing us into their hallowed prefabricated classrooms.

I was nervous, as the only other interview I'd done was when I got a job delivering newspapers in Huddersfield. However, after solemnly swearing on the Quran that I wouldn't steal anything from our loyal customers, Mr Patel bestowed on me the holy delivery bag. Easy.

My first job in journalism; delivering the Huddersfield Examiner. Back, on a visit in 2016.

Pinelands High School sits proudly on Forest Drive, the' main thoroughfare. A single storeyed, face-brick structure with an impressive courtyard and posh main entrance- it had pillars. Its Latin motto is 'Fides, Prudentia, Labor': Trust, Foresight and Toil. It was never going to be a good fit, especially the toil bit. My Latin motto was more along the lines of Fido, Prudence and Lassie.

As family Bardsley traipsed through the echoing corridors toward the headmaster's office Mum administered a quick clip around the ear to make it abundantly clear that we should be on our best behaviour. Shit, they were serious about this deal.

The headmaster Mr Goss, swept in, his black academic gown billowing dramatically behind him. He implied with a brisk nod of his head that we could be seated in his presence – I thought I'd been transported back to the 1950s. Goss was a tall, proud, curly haired, man imbued with a vision to steer his pupils in a certain liberal Christian direction. Unfortunately his liberal caning sent most of his victims into a different direction.

The interview started off well. Our folks had given us the green light to blatantly lie about our academic and sporting achievements. We happily obliged. Admittedly, they got a bit jittery when Andy mentioned being on the Cambridge University rowing team but a quick kick to his shin and a timely amendment explaining that he was just the cox brought Goss's raised eyebrows down enough to get us over that hurdle.

After complimenting me on my reign as the junior mayor of Huddersfield and Andy on his invention of the microchip at the age of fourteen, Mr Goss got onto sports.

Finally on safe ground, I excitedly told him about the years representing my school in the football first team. He coughed unenthusiastically but I continued to wax lyrical about my admirable goal-scoring record and tactical skills in exploiting the 4-4-2 formation.

By now, Goss was looking confused. I needed to up my enthusiasm so I hit him with a rousing re-enactment of my overhead bicycle kick that resulted in a match-winning goal against Almondbury School. I paused and waited for his thunderous applause.

"We don't play football here," he announced.

I checked to see if he was taking the piss, or whether my hearing had finally gone after years of full-volume Deep Purple and Led Zeppelin but he seemed pretty serious.

What the hell? Every school played football.

Maybe my folks had enrolled me in an all-girls school. Not a bad idea as I'd be happy playing netball with a load of buxom beauties although wearing a short dress might be a bit draughty and wearing a sports bra might cause some nipple rash issues.

"Pinelands High is a rugby and hockey school," Goss boomed proudly.

What the hell is hockey? It wasn't a big sport in Huddersfield. Any sport that used potential weapons was never going to last long there. Not even the girls played it – their main sport was toying with the emotions of teenage boys and getting pregnant.

Goss then gave us the added bad news that apart from no footy we also had to wear a school uniform. (Back in Huddersfield, our uniform was whatever hand-me-down clothes Mum could scrounge off her friends and relatives. My folks were in complete shock. Now they'd have to spend money on us.

Mum wasn't too keen on splurging money on a new school blazer, so she found one at a local second-hand shop. Knowing that I would grow quickly, mum tactically bought a blazer three times too big for me, it already had three leather patches sewn onto the elbows. It would have to last me for the rest of my school career.

Mum made sure of that every year, she added another elbow patch until my blazer ended up with so many patches that when I tried to sleep during accountancy, my elbows were six inches above my school desk. Every time the teacher asked me a question, they thought I was surrendering.)

Our interview came to an end and we filed out. He'd let us know. I wasn't optimistic. A week later, I walked into my new school, Pinelands High. I think my hands were trembling but

I couldn't see them as I was wearing a blazer the size of a two-man tent.

Garden City Heights, Pinelands, Cape Town. 1977

(Gypsy, our Border collie, sniffing for sheep. She was sadly disappointed but made a valiant attempt at herding the local squirrels.)

Chapter Nine
Bossies

With the gentle grind of the Bedford's gears, we headed out of the main camp through the dry, deserted streets of Kroonstad. After crossing the N1 highway, we found ourselves heading away from the suburbs and going deep into the veld. Where the hell were we going? Was the driver drunk? Had they finally realised that we'd be a liability to the army and decided to drive us back home? Were they taking us to a secret army boots store where we'd be custom-fitted with the latest military footwear?

We looked at each other with growing terror. It was getting dark and our insane driver was hurtling around corners, engine screaming, sending us flying into each other. The infamous *roefie* ride.

Being in the back of the truck, we could only see what we were leaving behind – civilisation. The suburbs rapidly faded away. Things weren't looking good. Twenty minutes later, Sarel van der Merwe swung the overheating Bedford onto a dust road and we came to a shuddering halt.

The only sound was the cold wind blowing and a truck full of thumping hearts. We sat waiting in the Free State bushveld, on the fringe of nowhere, waiting for instructions. Surely they had made a mistake. We'd been promised the delights of The School of Engineers, not Count Dracula's Castle.

Sixty terrified pairs of eyes peered out into the darkness as the screech of the tailgate being lowered signalled that we'd arrived.

The corporals circled like a pack of hyenas sniffing out their prey. The screaming flared up again and we leapt out of the back like startled dassies. We gathered around the corporals as they sent us off to our allocated bungalows. Eventually it was my turn.

"*Wat's jou van*?" Demanded the corporal.

"Er, Kaapstad," I replied in my best Afrikaans.

"*Nee, jou fokken doos*. What's your name?"

"*Jammer*. Mike Bardsley."

"Mike Bardsley what?" he barked.

"Just Mike Bardsley, I think."

"It's Mike Bardsley, *Korporaal,*" he snarled

Brilliant, I'd been promoted already. This was going to be easy.

"*Baie dankie*, Korporaal."

"*My fok. Jy's 'n dom bleddy soutpiel, nê*?" he said as he led me off.

Seeing as we were both corporals I was a bit hurt that he didn't offer to help carry my gear. Eventually, I balanced my balsak, trommel and tog bag on my skinny body and staggered after the rapidly disappearing form of my fellow corporal.

Two minutes later we were in front of a structure they called a 'bungalow'. Now in my experience, bungalows were cute little dwellings with sweet smelling rose bushes, garden gnomes, manicured lawns and inhabited by genteel old folks who'd invite you in for some tea and gingerbread cake.

Not this one.

"*Welkom by u nuwe huis*," the corporal smirked.

"Baie dankie, Korporaal, " I replied.

I fumbled in my pocket for some money to tip him but he'd left by the time I'd fished out ten cents. His loss.

I walked inside, warily nodding to my fellow inmates who were busy offloading their gear onto the bunk beds that lined the walls. The bungalow was about thirty metres long and six metres wide. It had pre-cast walls, plastered on the outside, a screed floor and an asbestos roof. Inside were eight cubicles containing four double-bunks each. Ten bungalows at sixty-four occupants per unit housed about six-hundred-and-forty troeps in total. A battalion of kak-scared *roefs*. I claimed a bunk, dropping my bags onto its thin foam mattress. I'd made my bed and now I'd have to lie in it, or so I thought.

A few minutes later, one of the roving corporals, dragged us over to the next bungalow and took great delight in showing us a big red stain on the ceiling. He smiled as he retold the story of a troep who'd stolen a bullet during rifle practice, loaded it into his R4, put it under his chin and blown his brains out; all because he hadn't made it onto the Commissioned Officer course. Not quite the same quality as Mum's bedtime stories but at least he'd made an effort.

It finally dawned on us, that our training camp wasn't going to be at the semi-civilised main base in Kroonstad, but at this derelict old farm called Bossiespruit, fondly known by its guests as Bossies, or *Poesplaas*.

I'd never heard of it before, but whenever I mentioned it, children squeezed their mums' hands a little tighter,
grown men spilled their beers and atheists hurriedly made the Sign of the Cross and blessed me.

That night, as the lights went off in Bossies, six hundred and forty humans clambered into beds that weren't theirs. Bodies twisted on the shitty foam beds, pillows were hugged and only muffled crying broke the terrified silence.

Our old lives had ended and our new ones were beginning. They were going to make soldiers of us, or we'd die trying. I wondered what my ancestors would think of me now. And where the hell was my teddy bear?

England.

My Dad, Colin Bardsley, was a good man, but a product of the thirties. Looking after the kids was the wife's duty, even if Mum also had a job. Playing golf and buying rounds of drinks for thirsty strangers was public relations. Basically, his aim in life was to live it to the full. He succeeded. During World War Two, he'd lied about his age and sneaked into the Royal Navy to catch the last bit of the conflict. Luckily, he'd ended up in the warm waters of the Indian Ocean rather than the icy expanses of the Atlantic and North Sea.

Looking at his lovely sepia photos he was a lot bloody happier than I was during my national service. Snake charming in Ceylon, frolicking in the turquoise sea, haggling with the local food vendors. Bliksem, I'd chosen the wrong bleddy war. I'd have to write to my MP.

Dad annoying a snake in Ceylon during World War Two.

After the War, Dad became a textiles sales representative travelling around the world and visiting exotic destinations like Scandinavia, Eastern Europe, America and Bolton.

When he finally found his way home, he always had exciting tales of his travels. Eating reindeer steaks with Laplanders, being followed by the KGB in Berlin, driving down a cul-de-sac in Bolton and being mugged while driving in New York. The drugged-up mugger had simply staggered into the middle of a six-lane highway, aimed a big gun at my Dad's hire car and hoped for the best. Luckily for him, Dad was a law-abiding citizen who devoutly followed the Highway Code – which frowned upon knocking pedestrians over. He slammed on the brakes and was promptly relieved of his wallet and passport.

However, faced with fighting a heroin-fuelled, homicidal jaywalker or the prospect of having to deal with the pasty-faced wankers at Heathrow immigration, my Dad started a life and death struggle for his passport in the middle of the highway.

A week later Dad passed effortlessly through passport control at Heathrow and a New York junkie dined out on his tale of the mad Pommie who was willing to take a "cap in the ass" for his little blue passport.

Dad was away for most of our lives, but when he came back he was happy to pay for our love with presents. We gladly accepted the deal. Fortunately, just when the reindeer biltong and East German sawdust-infused bratwurst got boring, he started heading over to the good old USA, life started looking up.

After his first trip to New York, and feeling the full weight of our well-orchestrated guilt trip tactics, he brought back a pair of shining six shooters for Andy and me. Two toy handguns with belts and holsters; my first military hardware.

They didn't feel like toys. They were realistic, made of heavy, solid metal. No plastic bullshit. My scrawny little arms even struggled lifting them and you had to put some real effort in just to pull the trigger. You could've robbed a bank with them. Even the caps worked better, making a bang that even pensioners could hear. The piece de resistance, though, was that a big piece of the cap would shoot out of the barrel and sting any unsuspecting grandparent who'd naively asked you to shoot them in the head. You'd have thought that after four years in the trenches of the Somme, Pop would have learnt not to play with guns.

Mum in Monte Carlo. Trying to work out how much a pint of Chardonnay would cost in French Francs.

Mum was like most mums: a brilliant multi-tasker: nurse, bookkeeper, burner of food and the expert wielder of a torture tool known as 'The Slipper'.

Now, this wasn't one of those flimsy, break-on-impact cheap imitations. Oh no, this was the .45 Magnum of corporal punishment. What it lacked in accuracy it made up for in impact damage. As it smashed into our buttocks, a tsunami of intense pain went shooting through our bodies, telling every nerve ending that it better tune the brain that there was some heavy kak coming. Vital organs shut down and neighbours clutched their children closer as our screams rang out.

'The Slipper' was made from some kind of satanic, vulcanised blue rubber alloy, innocently decorated with yellow daisies and designed for 'a more comfortable walk' while crushing any dissent from toddlers. It didn't look like much of a weapon, but when wielded by Mum it felt like you were being smacked by, a just dismissed, Lance Klusener on crack cocaine.

Pop
We called my Dad's father, Pop. Not sure why, since our other granddad was simply called Granddad. I think it was a middle-class thing. Pop was small in stature, but a giant in life. His wife Annie, my gran, had died before I knew her. Annie was Scottish and from what I've heard she was a beautiful and caring lady. Pop never recovered from that body blow and never remarried.

Pop joined up as soon as World War One began and had endured the whole of that terrible war. He'd fought at The Somme, Ypres, Verdun and many other bloody battles. He'd started in the cavalry until the generals realised that charging machine guns on horseback wasn't a bright idea. After that he was in supplies, which meant hauling ammo and food with a four-horse power wagon. As he approached the

sniper areas he would crawl in between the four horses to shield himself. Somehow he survived but his younger brother Colin was killed mere months before the end of the war. They'd been close and that tragic loss had torn Pop apart.

When the war ended he was given a medical before he went home. The doctor clapped his stethoscope over Pop's skeletal body and pronounced that he was in better health than when he'd joined. Pop told him he was a bloody idiot. He was charged with insubordination and lost his pension and rank.

I've still got a cassette tape of Pop chatting to a military historian about his service. Hearing his voice brings me to a tearful standstill. It instilled in me a hatred of war, and an even deeper hatred for the warmongers and chicken hawks that send young folks off to die while they sit at home, profiting from the wars they created.

Pop trying to teach me how to be a jockey.
During the First World War, his horse reared up and took a bullet in its chest. Saved Pop's life and mine.

Chapter Ten
Chicken Parade

Bossiespruit 1987

As the early rays of the Free State sun peeked through the curtain less windows a gang of sneering corporals barged through the doors abruptly waking us. They shook our beds violently, reminding us that we were in the "fokken army now". We got up without a murmur and meekly climbed into our shapeless overalls, pulled on our wrong-sized boots and followed them through the door.

Having arrived in the dark of night meant that we hadn't seen the landscape of our new home. Bossies was, to be blunt, a bit disappointing. It was a derelict farm that had been converted into an army base. The khaki vista was barren except for a few thorn bushes, gaunt trees and some shrubby grass clinging onto the ground. The local stream was very nice; especially during the two months there was water in it. Otherwise, it was just another *donga*. Bossies was flat except for the occasional rise in the distance that couldn't even be classified as a hill. Bloemfontein-born JRR Tolkien had obviously based Mordor on Bossies: desolate, crawling with Orcs and everybody trying to evade the Eye of Sauron, otherwise known as Major Rabid, our Commanding Officer.

Once outside the corporals started screaming at us.

"What he's saying?' I asked in frustration.

"Something about a loop that's hard," Suggsy, my new *maatjie* suggested unhelpfully.

Finally, after much swearing and gnashing of our honourable corporals teeth, we worked out that instead of us strolling around, they actually wanted us to run everywhere. Bloody hell. The corporal was obviously a Liverpool fan. You'll Never Walk Alone or again as was the case. And we didn't for the next two years. Running or marching was the order of the day. But wherever we ran, some other pissed-off corporal started screaming at us. What had we done now? I checked to see if my fly was down but those shitty overalls didn't even have flies. One of the troeps, whose brother had been in the army, eventually told us that we needed to *strek* the corporals whenever we passed them. I misheard him and promptly went out to 'strike' one of them. Luckily for me (and my teeth), someone hauled me back for a quick explanation. Whenever you passed somebody with a stripe on his arm or a pip on his shoulder, you had to slow down to a walk and straighten your arms by your side. After a few steps in this position, you could start running again. We felt like dressage ponies on cocaine. Finally, after *strekking* some commissioned officers and receiving another round of abuse, we worked out that we had to salute anybody with scrambled egg on their shoulders. We'd spent a whole three days working out the saluting and strekking system. Why hadn't they told us when we arrived, or given us a nice instruction manual to read on the train? We could've used all that wasted time to defeat Lenin and his mates.

Our first important job for the Big Crocodile was to pick up all the *stompies* (cigarette butts) and litter in Bossies. It was called Chicken Parade because our bobbing up and down resembled chickens plucking seeds off the ground. After four hours of this I realised why chickens celebrate when they end up covered in the Colonel's special spices at the KFC.

We soon realised that we were now prisoners of the SADF. You couldn't walk out to the shops, or go to a pub, or see your girlfriend. Your opinion no longer mattered and if you stepped out of line you were soon klapped back into it. They owned us – lock, stock and trommel.

The next step on our military journey was a bit more interesting. We finally realised that *"tree-aan"* wasn't some weird horticultural term but a command that meant we had to line up as a unit. As those words echoed through the bungalow, we dropped everything, dashed to the front of our bungalow and tried to form ourselves into a squad. We formed up in three lines, stuck an arm out, and then shuffled around to make sure we were an arm's length away from the next troep. Once in position we swivelled our heads to the front; a bit like synchronised swimming but without getting wet and tying your hair back to resemble a shell-shocked alien.

We soon learnt that our sleeves had to be neatly rolled up two inches, or four finger widths above the elbow. This was a close call, as my England tattoo was just on the edge. The army doctor had already pointed out that if the corporals discovered it, I'd be well and truly fucked up. My early morning sleeve rolling-up became very precise.

After some light abuse and gentle jogging we had our first official visit to the ablution block. It soon became obvious that basics wouldn't include percolating in lavender-infused bubble baths with yellow ducks floating around. There were no baths and only about eight showers for all of us. The inspection might've gone quicker but the first eight troeps wasted ten minutes trying to find the hot water taps.

The inspection might've gone quicker but the first eight troeps wasted ten minutes trying to find the hot water taps.

There was only one tap per shower and it didn't have a lovely 'H' embossed on it, cold water only. Unlucky.

One minute to wash your body, one minute to dry. As we only had a tiny drop of hair we only required one drop of shampoo; when I finally *klaared* out I still had the same shampoo bottle that I'd gone in with.

It had been drummed into us that if you accidentally dropped your soap you risked being buggered by one of your fellow troeps. Ridiculous, of course, but we all held onto our little scraps of soap like they were Krugerrands. If you did drop it, everyone went quiet as you performed an outrageous yoga pose to clasp it with your toes and get it back into your hands without bending over and risking sodomy.

I did notice that one troep seemed to have very poor handling skills and spent a lot of time slowly bending over, like an arthritic giraffe at a shallow water hole. I've heard rumours that he is now an ordained priest teaching rugby to vulnerable children in the Philippines; obviously he's been practicing his ball handling skills.

The army generously provided us with absorbent brown towels to dry our drenched bodies: thirty percent polyester, twenty percent cotton, fifteen percent dirt and thirty-five percent holes. They were like hand towels, designed for pygmy jockeys; you can often recognise former troeps as they emerge from showers, pools or puddles, because we tend to brush the water off our bodies with our hands before using a towel. Of course, if you do encounter a hairy apparition flicking water off his body as he exits the shower you'd better hope you're either married to him or you're at the local Virgin Active.

Some troeps simply refused to shower. Not really sure why, but even after hours of sweating in the sun, being covered in filth, they'd still stay out of the showers. It didn't take too long for a fruity aroma to develop and soon the rest of the bungalow was offering not-so-friendly advice to the smelly ones to meet up with Mr H$_2$O. The smell in the bungalow was bad enough as it was, with rotten feet, bad breath, boiled bacon farts and fear and by drawing attention to themselves they'd put a target on their backs. After a few choice words and threats they usually got the hint and scrubbed up or they were thrown into the showers and scrubbed clean by the rest of the unit.

By the end of day one we'd seen enough of Bossies to wish we were somewhere else. Even a sweet-talking real estate agent would have struggled to market the place.

Downmarket Kroonstad Resort for Sale.

Do you love blasting out your latest Ge Korsten single, abusing troepies or shooting at shadows?

Tired of nosy neighbours reporting you to the police for domestic abuse?

Within marching distance of nothing. Nowhere near any schools.

Thinking of upsizing due to the arrival of a new child or six hundred troeps? Then this one's for you.

Structurally-sound. Open plan. Thirty toilets – some that work.

Your very own wet-room with refreshing, freezing water.

Low maintenance. No pesky lawns to mow; just good old-fashioned dirt, thorns and dust.

North facing as well as south, east and west facing; great for lovers of sunstroke and pneumonia.

Loads of potential but might require a lady's touch or two.

Quaint red fire buckets. Well-polished brass.

Earn extra income; rent it out for filming westerns and horror movies.

Good security (So long as the roefie *guards are awake).*

Small bloodstain on the ceiling.

Specifics:

10 bedrooms. 640 beds. 5 bathrooms.

Modern kitchen; slight boiled bacon aroma.

Asbestos roof to assist in getting cancer

Extras:

Communal pool (shared with the pigs)

Handy 2,4 km trail including a little hill to burn off that excess fat.

Extremely negotiable.

Bungalows at Bossies. The sandy patch is where they buried the garden gnomes.

The French already have a lot to answer for but inventing the beret is top of my list. It doesn't deflect a bullet, it's useless in hand-to-hand combat, and has no fashion merit. The moment my new dark blue sappers beret was placed on my head, I looked like a complete *doos*. I have a small head and the beret didn't sit right. In fact, it flopped over my cranium like a large sloppy blue turd. To look stylish you had to give your beret *houding*, which entailed wetting it and putting it on your head, moulding it to the shape of your skull. Then you had to attach clothes pegs to the edge, to make it sharp. Just before sunset I soaked my beret in one of the fire buckets, slapped it on my head, strategically attached the clothes pegs and sat outside waiting for a fashion miracle.

One of the few good things about Bossies was the spectacular sunsets. The red veld dust blew into the sky fusing with the blazing African sun, painting an intense, saturated masterpiece that shocked the eyes and pushed all thoughts from your mind. Sitting against the warm wall of your bungalow with a toasty Chesterfield in your mouth, a cup of Ricoffy in your hand and the sunset in your eyes gave us a glimmer of hope and inspiration. I dozed off and woke with a soggy blue cowpat stuck to my head; I was condemned to look like a *roef* for the rest of my two years. I just couldn't give that bloody beret any style.

On the front of our berets we had our Engineers Corps badge: a bursting grenade. Our motto was *Ubique*, which means 'everywhere' in Latin. I wish I'd known Latin in those days – maybe I could've persuaded them that I could also serve the nation 'everywhere', preferably in Cape Town. Unfortunately, I was way too busy learning Army Afrikaans to try and fathom the language of the Holy Roman Empire.

Chapter Eleven
Hotel, India and Juliet

Each bungalow at Bossies was named in alphabetical order according to the military alphabet: Alpha, Bravo, Charlie, Delta, Echo, Foxtrot, Golf, Hotel, India and Juliet. I ended up in India Bungalow with the other invalids, asthmatics and, oddly, the top rugby and football players.

Our bungalow had a mixed bunch: Souties and Dutchies, kids straight out of school, men who'd finished college and some who already had families, plattelanders and city slickers, Commies and AWB: all of them trying to survive and keep their sanity. In the evenings we'd sit on our trommels, polishing our boots, talking kak and getting to know each other.
If you didn't have great mates, you wouldn't survive the army.

Half the battle was psychological: the corporals picking on you, other troeps getting in your face, a terrible feeling of isolation mixed with dread. If you had nobody to confide in you'd soon lose your mind. Your *maatjies* encouraged you when you were down, pushed you when you wanted to give in and shared your grief or laughter at the end of another scary day. I was lucky to have top *maatjies*.
Warren was my first mate, and I immediately nicknamed him Suggsy from the British Ska band Madness.

Suggsy and me.

Some people just aren't meant for a life of soldiering, me included, but Suggsy was the poster child for pacifism. Tall and lanky with a pronounced slouch, he made me look like a State President's Guard.

He was anything between five-foot-four and six-foot-two, depending on his mood. With a gentle soul and an inquiring mind, the army probably wasn't going to be a good fit but

despite lacking any co-ordination and military bearing, he gave it a good crack.

With unbounded enthusiasm he climbed into the task of becoming a soldier; running, jumping, pushing, pulling, sweating, groaning and stealing socks, but with a look of increasing disbelief at the stupidity of it all. It slowly dawned on Suggsy that this charade might continue for a little while.

Suggsy was from South Johannesburg but hadn't been in jail – yet.

Sneezer

Sneezer was from a well-respected family in Pretoria. His mum was an educator who had dedicated herself to a project that assisted black adults get their Matric while they were still working; one of the first such schemes in the country. Privately funded, of course.

His old man had stood in the general elections for the liberal Progressive Federal Party (PFP) that opposed Apartheid. Not an easy task at the best of times, but in the Afrikaans heartland of the Northern Transvaal, it was nothing short of impossible. Yet somehow he almost pulled it off, only losing by a few hundred votes. It would've been the biggest shock in South African politics.

Sneezer had been educated at Pretoria Boys High and the University of Stellenbosch where he completed his Civil Engineering degree and masters. Tall, lean and not so mean. He had a finely honed sense of humour and a face that was always a millisecond away from smiling. A good footballer and a team player, always there to help and encourage, a prime candidate for leadership.

Slab

Slab hailed from the sleepy city of East London and after receiving his Civil Engineering degree from UCT he'd ended up in Kroonstad. Slab was fairly liberal which was a bit of a surprise since his dad was a National Party councillor, although upon meeting the old man, he was equally as cool. Slab was also classified as G3K3 and ended up with me and the other invalids in India Bungalow. Due to his debilitating physical condition (still not sure what it was), he did fuck-all 2,4 km runs during basics until the last one, when in an act of immense bravery, Slab threw off his mental chains and joined us.

He got off to a slow, staggering start, his little legs getting used to running, but after a few words of encouragement he got into his stride. Within a few hundred metres, he was leading the pack; had he peaked too early? Surely he'd soon collapse in a heap or suffer a heart attack. Not a damn. The cunning bastard was a crack athlete. He sprinted into the distance, leaving the rest of us in his dust. Nine minutes later, he powered over the finish line with barely a sweat, beaming with delight at the corporals' shocked and pissed-off faces. Slab had beaten the army at its own game. I staggered in two minutes later.

We had troeps from all around the country and the nine provinces all created their own distinctive characters:

Western Province: Arrogant pricks who think they deserve a pat on the back for having a flat mountain and beaches that stink of sewage. Kak at marching but good at hiding in the bush.

Eastern Province: Make fancy German cars but drive Datsun *bakkies*. Don't lend them your car keys. Too friendly to be corporals but good at poaching crayfish.

Orange Free State: Miners, farmers and rugby players. Experts at kakking in the mielies, shooting buck and *langarm* dancing. Good snipers and carriers of cement sacks. Not so good at poetry.

Natal: Lazy dagga *rookers* who think surfing is a sport and steal all the best rugby players from the Free State. Hippies who still worship the Queen of England and refuse to speak Afrikaans. Not to be trusted with your daughters - or anybody's daughters. Good lieutenants.

Transvaal: A scandalous bunch of money grabbing, BMW-driving, thieves. Always with a project in the pipeline. Always in debt. Don't let them work in the stores.

Northern Transvaal: A load of nine-to-five civil servants who think rugby is a kicking game and Loftus Versfeld is the capital of South Africa. Good to have them as friends just in case they have broeders in a bond. Good at shouting. Corporal material.

Eastern Transvaal: Spend most of their time searching for Krugers hidden gold or trying to sell hidden treasure maps to German tourists who are lost. They all claim to be game rangers. Should be in the Recces or leading escapes from camp.

Border: English-speaking giants with Oxford accents and dark homoerotic secrets from their time in posh boarding schools. Never let them out of your sight. Watch your sons. Good at carrying small cows and machine guns.

Chapter Twelve
Bumfluff and Scowler

During the first few days, the training corporals hadn't been assigned their units so it was a free-for-all, every corporal ordered us around.

After a few brief and bruising contacts, we started a wish list for the corporals we wanted. At the bottom of the list was one evil looking Corporal, who oozed hatred and inspired fear; he was a Karate Springbok and full on pyscho.

They were all pretty nasty, except one who had some potential for decency. He looked like he was still in school – Junior School. Baby-faced, thin and lacking the default corporals swagger. His poor attempt at a moustache looked more like bumfluff. Our prayers were soon answered. Hallelujah. Corporal Bumfluff was assigned to be our corporal for the next three months. A few days later and our second corporal was assigned, this one looked like a real corporal: black moustache, permanent scowl and a face like a broken biscuit. God evidently had a twisted sense of humour as Corporal Scowler turned out to be just a run-of-the-mill bastard, but Corporal Bumfluff took it to a whole new level of bastardship. Because of his weedy stature and Standard Five looks, he was desperate to prove that he was a real man; which made him the meanest *bliksem* in town.

Basic Training officially started about four days after everybody had klaared in.

Our days of picking up stompies were coming to an end; things were about to get serious. The corporals built it up to sound like an impending apocalypse – they'd soon be let off their leashes to hunt; unsurprisingly, the prey didn't sleep well that night.

Before the crack of dawn had even yawned, all hell broke loose. Our corporals barged in, screaming and kicking us out of bed. Half asleep we stumbled in the dark trying to put on our overalls and boots as they yelled at us to get the hell outside. It was all in Afrikaans but I got the idea.

We lined up and Corporal Scowler asked who was G3K3, about ten of us raised our arms. He smiled. It wasn't a reassuring smile, more like the one The Undertaker gives as his opponent lies on the canvas, waiting for the *coup de grâce*. Scowler separated us from the herd and issued us with an invalids badge and red helmets – we were the Ambulance Squad. For the rest of the day, we walked around the camp making ambulance sounds: "mee-mah mee-mah mee-mah."

The thinking behind this abuse was to make troeps contemplating faking an illness fall back into line, and all us G3K3's got a nasty shock. It was fucking humiliating. I was fuming. I hadn't signed up for this kak but I didn't know what to do. Seeing the rest of my bungalow running around was horrible. I felt like I was being left behind. Halfway through day one, Corporal Scowler came over to me.

"What's wrong with you, Soutie?"

"Asthma, Corporal."

"What's that?"

"I have problems breathing, Corporal."

"So is your arms okay?"

"Proud to report that my arms, although a little skinny, are in perfect working order, Corporal."

With a nasty gleam in his eye he pointed at two metal buckets sloshing with water.

"Right, let's see how strong your little soutie arms are. Lift them up and hold them steady."

Now I was in the kak. I'd have struggled with them empty but now the bastard had added ten litres of water, which, if my standard-grade science was correct, meant they now weighed 223 kilograms. With tears streaming from my gentle hazel-brown eyes and my rectum tightly pinched, I slowly lifted them up. Shit, they were heavy. I finally got them up – sort of. I was looking like Schwarzenegger for a full thirty seconds, then gravity kicked in and I started trembling. As my teeth clenched tight, my arms started lowering.

"Hou jou arms, troep!" Scowler yelled.

Somehow I inched them back up but you can't defeat gravity. Soon the buckets were sloshing around as my arms gave way.

He gave me a minute to get my breath back before we started again but I had little strength left and the buckets were soon back on the ground. After twenty minutes of this, my eyes were popping out of my head and my arms felt like they'd gone thirty rounds with Kallie Knoetze. Though I was finished, I refused to give in and utter the shameful "*ek kan nie meer nie, Korporaal*-No more Corporal." I kept trying to lift them, even a couple of inches off the ground, fortunately Scowler got bored and after a few insults, sent me back to join the rest of our unit.

It dawned on me that being G3K3 wasn't going to be much fun. In fact, it was going to be worse than being G1K1. As asthmatics, we still got physically fucked up, endured all the usual humiliation and then had to impersonate a bloody ambulance. Bollocks to that, I wanted the challenge of doing full basics along with the rest of the camp.

I decided to get re-classified as G1K1. Easier said than done. I'd have to approach our not-so-approachable corporals.

Finally I plucked up enough courage to march up to Bumfluff during a refreshment break and, in a garbled mix of Afrikaans, English and Gibberish, I requested a reclassification. His weak attempt at a moustache trembled in the breeze as he kakked me out for taking the piss. He initially thought I wanted to downgrade to G5K5 but I finally persuaded him that I wanted to be a real man and do full basic training. Once his still-evolving teenage brain put the pieces together, he sent me off to see the officer in charge of us – Lieutenant Beetge.

A meeting with the Looty meant a visit to the HQ offices. This was a bit like Archbishop Tutu popping into the Randfontein AWB clubhouse, during happy hour, and asking them to keep the noise down - not for the fainthearted. So with a faint heart, I marched over to the HQ and entered with a wild flurry of streks, salutes and about-turns. It was a performance that had me saluting the cleaning lady and ignoring the RSM. He could've ripped me inside out, but instead, gruffly pointed me in the right direction. I made a sharp but polite military-sounding knock on my Looty's office door, and after the cue to enter, marched in like an arthritic zombie.

Lieutenant Beetge

Because the army is structured to mould soldiers into hard, unfeeling robots, it's rare to find one who maintains his own character and ethics. Lieutenant Beetge was a rare find. He actually listened to me. Though initially a bit surprised that I wanted to do full basics, he understood my reasons for reclassification and although he didn't have the authority to change it, he promised to sort it out. He was as good as his word and they soon removed me from the list of ambulance impersonators and I started proper basic training. I still had to wear the dreaded invalid badge, but being with the normal troeps meant I wasn't treated like an invalid. Either way, we were going to kak. It was tougher, but a lot more rewarding, and I maintained what was left of my dignity.

As I left Beetge's desk, another Looty, who shared the office stomped over and demanded to know who I was, where I came from and where I'd studied. As soon as he heard I was from Cape Town, Lieutenant Fat Fuck launched into a verbal tirade at my being a disgrace to the entire Western Cape and all its inhabitants. He wouldn't let up. I didn't know what had hit me. He was one of the few English speaking Looty's but I guess this didn't matter. He laid into me for no reason and I wasn't even his troep. I might've understood my own Looty giving me kak but this twat was just a bully. I don't like bullies. I swore that I'd get revenge on him one day. He was from Cape Town so I knew our paths would inevitably cross back home.

Heidelberg Tavern, Cape Town 1989

Shortly after klaaring out I was having a few dops at the Heidelberg Tavern in Observatory with Moose, Pik, Beans, Speedy and a few others. While seated at our table of lovable louts, I spotted the fat neck and porky ears of what looked like the Looty who'd abused me back at Bossies. He was sat, with his back to me, at the table in front of us. 'Oh sweet Lord, let it be him,' I thought. I got up and did a quick recce around his table. I wasn't very subtle about it; I glared at him as I passed. He'd already recognised me and the shock on his face was beautiful to see. The colour drained from his face. I went back to my table and prepared for some fun.

(I should note that I'd been thrown out of the pub a few weeks earlier, so as the red mist descended I had to be a bit careful.)

"Hey Lieutenant Fat Fuck, remember me?" I shouted over to his table.

He stared straight ahead but his friends were now aware of the impending peril. I could see them asking what was going on. His podgy neck was turning red.

"Remember when you called me a disgrace to Cape Town? Well, I'm back now. I survived your kak. You want to tune me again?"

Nothing.

My mates asked what the hassle was and I was happy to broadcast the tale of my dealings with Lieutenant Fat Fuck. They got ready to stomp him but I held them back. I just wanted the satisfaction of knowing he wasn't so tough without the pips on his shoulders. I could see his pals looking at him differently; he'd been caught out and without a peep he slinked off into the night. The red mist lifted. My dented dignity had received a little panel beating and I was so happy I even bought a round of drinks; it was happy hour after all, I'm not that stupid.

The Defence Force had a language policy that meant all orders and instructions should be fifty/fifty between Afrikaans and English. Nice in theory, but this was Bossies. The corporals assured us that they'd adhere to this policy but then claimed that because the last fifty years had been in English the next fifty would be in Afrikaans. I could hardly speak English never mind Afrikaans so I was completely screwed, sorry, *naaied*.

I badly needed to brush up on my army Afrikaans, so I started compiling a dictionary. Fortunately my maatjies helped me out.

Ek sal op jou kop staan en kak in jou nek: A traditional Afrikaans cough remedy.

Julle naaiers: Yellow sewing machines.

Hou jou bek, troep: Would you mind keeping the noise down? Many thanks.

Vasbyt: Something you quickly put on your fishing hook to catch *Geelbek* (Quiet Fish).

Ek kan nie meer nie, Korporaal: I can't build a wall, Corporal.

Gaan kak in die mielies: Would you like some butter on your corncob?

Moenie vir my loer nie: Can I borrow some cash for my insane child?

Ek is jou pa en jou ma en jou fokken meisiekind maar die enigste een kry naaied sal jy wees: Something about the whole fucking family getting together to indulge in some extreme sewing.

Moenie na my kyk. Dink jy ek is 'n hamburger?: Give me some money for cake and I'll throw in a hamburger as a bonus.

Corporal Bumfluff also taught us a few new Afrikaans words. From now on we would be called *roefs*. Anybody who still had at least eighteen months to go was a *roef*.

There was also terminology for the various levels of abuse we'd be receiving:

Rondvok: To fuck around.
General abuse suffered by the whole bungalow. Lots of running around the *perdestal*, press-ups and sit-ups. A daily occurrence after inspections, breakfast, lunch and anytime the corporals got bored.

Opvok: To fuck up (Confined to Barracks drill)
This usually happened to a troep or troeps who'd caused some major kak and needed *klapping* back into position. It was a vicious punishment where they'd be run into the ground for hours on end. They would have to stand inspection every couple of hours, even during the night, and they'd barely sleep. All the Bossies corporals took turns abusing the troeps and it could last a number of days – taking the troeps to the brink of mental and physical exhaustion.

The first *opvok* nearly started a mutiny in the camp. A troep in Hotel Bungalow had annoyed his Corporal and was targeted for an opvok. The rumour quickly spread. We'd all heard about this infamous punishment but the reality of it remained shrouded in mystery. The poor troep was led out into the space between our bungalows as they'd decided to show us the full extent of their brutality – a warning to stay in line. It started gently, with the troep doing repeated runs to the *perdestal* and back, followed by a gruelling series of press-ups and sit-ups. This was accompanied by abusive references to his mother, sister and his sexual preferences.

Other corporals arrived to share in the fun. By this time, the unfortunate troep was leopard crawling and rolling around in the dirt. A subtle sprinkling from one of the fire buckets added to the corporals' shared amusement. This went on for about an hour, until, just as the troep thought it was all over, they told him to prepare for inspection. He staggered into his bungalow. The corporals paused for a cigarette, after which they stormed in and dragged the troepie out again. He'd failed his inspection, so the corporals set about him for a second time. We crowded the windows, watching in silence. It carried on all night long. Seething anger permeated the air and some troeps had to be restrained from running out and stopping the assault. The troep, who'd hung tough, was eventually reduced to a blubbering wreck. Crying and staggering from the punishment and verbal assaults, he collapsed outside.

The brutal spectacle was intended as a warning not to defy the corporals. It worked in the short term, but left troeps in such a state of shock that many lost faith in the army and the cause we were supposedly fighting for. Why should we fight for people who were perfectly willing to sacrifice us to achieve their own goals? Their total onslaught had made them the enemy rather than the terrorists.

Two days later, the *opvok* troep created another stink; a sickly, burning flesh stink. While he was ironing his kit, his mate noticed some smoke and a certain gag-inducing stench. Coming over to investigate, he saw that *opvok* troep was ironing his thumb as well as his trousers. Following the brutality of his opvok, the nerves in his spinal column had freaked out, causing him to lose all feeling in his thumbs.

Using one thumb to create a straight crease in his trousers, due to the numbness, he'd ironed the shit out of it. By the time he became aware of it, he'd destroyed half his thumb. He was rushed to the medics. Unluckily for Major Rabid, the troep's father was a lawyer and proper procedures for the *opvok* had been ignored, as no medic was present. Somebody had to pay. While we sympathised with the troep, we also celebrated; now it was clear there'd be consequences for their actions, the corporals might have to back off.

As the storm gathered, we *tuned* the troep to demand an inquiry and stop the kak that was going on. Initially, he was keen but after they promised him rank without having to fully complete the course, the temptation was too much – he accepted their offer. The corporals and officers were off the hook and the abuse soon resumed.

The Food: Casa la Bossies

"An army marches on its stomach," Napoleon had famously remarked. Unlike most camps, we were lucky to have a Michelin-star chef – everything tasted like tyres.

With all the running, marching, carrying and pushing lazy troeps over the finishing line, our bodies needed as many calories as we could gobble down. However our culinary experience at Bossies was slightly disappointing, or as Suggsy said, "I've had better food out of waste bins." and he should know.

Bossies a la carte Menu

Breakfast
Boiled bacon, tortured tomato and battered beans
Powdered scrambled egg *a la* radiation seasoned with a hint
of dandruff.

Sides:
Stale mouldy white bread topped with a Sunshine Margarine
reduction.

Lunch
Roasted road-kill accompanied by badly bruised potato mash,
rotting vegetables and lumpy gravy

Dessert
A rusk

Drinks
Watered down litchi juice (1 part litchi concentrate-100 parts
water)
Almost-boiled chicory

Dinner
Meat surprise
(Pork, chicken, fish or steak: they all looked and tasted the
same)
Soggy French fries
Sad cabbage
Green kak

The food was shit and the cutlery wasn't much better. We ate out of dixies – two square aluminium bowls which fitted inside each other. It was a struggle to eat the slop they served up but that was nothing compared to trying to clean the grease off our dixies with cold water – ruined my fingernails.

We soon realised we'd have to supplement our diet or end up like ultra-fit skeletons. Food parcels from my folks, pals and Anneline were lifesavers: Biltong, Bar-Ones, Nik-Naks and timeshare brochures from Sun City. I was expecting some caviar from Anneline but, after weeks of waiting, I realised that filling an envelope with slippery fish eggs might be difficult, especially with long fingernails. Mum tried to make up for my disappointment by sending me a can of Lucky Star pilchards.

Chapter Thirteen
Gary Player and the crawling leopards

The physical side of basics was the toughest challenge of my life but at least it made sense; soldiers had to be fit.

One of the first things the corporals did was test our fitness to ascertain how much training would be required for each troep. The tests consisted of press-ups, pull-ups, sit-ups and the dreaded 2,4 km run – a course originally designed for the US Army to test aerobic fitness. Being a skinny bastard, I was okay. I only weighed about sixty kilograms, so not too much blubber to haul around. However the troeps who'd spent all their pocket money on *vetkoeks*, tubs of chocolate ice cream and litres of Crème Soda were in deep kak. Those poor bastards were in for three months of hell.

Once the corporals had assessed our fitness levels, they designed our daily schedule for the next three months.

The schedule for a typical day during basics:

05h00 Wake up
05h05 Stop crying
05h10 Iron, polish, dust, sweep
05h40 Shit, shave and shower
06h00 Fail inspection, uitkak and press-ups
06h30 Breakfast - sort of
07h00 Parade, uitkak and press-ups

07h30 Running, pushing, pulling, sweating

08h30 Lectures on how to do war
10h00 Rondvok
12h00 Lunch - sort of
13h00 2,4 km runs. Repeat till exhausted
14h00 Brainwashing
15h00 Running around in the bush
16h00 Military law and tactics
18h00 Supper
19h00 Canteen, relax, plan escape route
20h00 Clean rifle, iron bed, talk kak, polish floor
24h00 Sleep on floor

Most in our bungalow were fit and thin enough to deal with the demands of basics, but a few were overweight. One troep was so obese he'd been declared a national monument. Weighing over 140 kg, he had the perfect physique for pressing grapes and pulling ploughs but not for running around the veld. We'll refer to him as Baobab.

"Hee la fuckin troep terug in twalf minoots. Roo jou ghat!" Bumfluff screamed in what was commonly called 'Army Afrikaans'. Sneezer translated for me by running off into the distance. I followed.

Desperate to prove ourselves, we charged off on our first 2,4 km run. I'd always been a decent runner, but at altitude, I soon dropped back. This was the Free State, so it was as flat as a *pannekoek* until in the middle of nowhere we were confronted by a great big bloody manmade hill.

Some evil bastard with a front-end loader and too much time on his hands had built a little mountain in the middle of the veld; welcome to Bossies' very own Table Mountain. Unfortunately the idiot had forgotten the cable car so up we ran. Lungs were soon bursting and muscles we didn't know

existed waved the white flag but the corporals drove us on relentlessly. Most of the troeps were heavier than me and the climb slowed them down, temporarily bumping me into the top ten. I eventually finished in the middle of the pack, exhausted but happy. My time was just over eleven minutes – not bad for an asthmatic *suipgat;* however, when Baobab finally crawled over the finish line about twenty minutes later, the corporals freaked out and sent us off again. Most of us had put all our effort into the first run so our times were even worse. Baobab didn't even make it.

After Bumfluff sent us on our third run, we got suspicious that there was an ulterior motive to all this exercise. It finally dawned on us that they actually wanted the whole unit to finish in less than thirteen minutes; were they insane? It was a desirable idea but with Baobab and others holding us back we had no chance. The poor bugger tried, but his upper thighs rubbing together caused so much friction that the Kroonstad Fire Brigade was almost called out in case of a bushfire.

In desperation, Baobab appealed to the forgiving Christian nature of the corporals.

"*Moenie huil nie,*" they laughed as they sent us off for the fourth time.

Surely they didn't expect us to drag our man mountain around an obstacle course for the next three months? Baobab soon became the well-fed albatross around our necks. No matter what we accomplished, he dragged us back. There was one obvious solution but the ground was too hard to bury a body his size. The only alternative was to push and pull him around the course. This meant two of us taking off our belts, looping them around Baobab's belt and pulling him, while others pushed him from behind.

After a month of routinely collapsing from the exertion, Baobab's times started coming down. The Bossies Starvation Diet had brought his weight down to a point where he could perform a fast walk. Everyday he was getting faster, not fast enough to please the corporals but we were getting there.

Using a combination of blatant self-promotion and by being the loudest, most obnoxious voice extolling my fellow troeps onwards I made sure the corporals knew I was a team player and worthy of a place on the Junior leaders course. I'm not sure what they thought of my constant cries of; *vasbyt, min dae* and *gaan kak in die mielies* - I was at the very limit of my Afrikaans - but they couldn't ignore my enthusiasm.

Another fun exercise in the army was the old tree leaf trick. The corporal pointed at a tree in the distance and ordered us to retrieve a leaf off it. We charged off and brought back a single leaf, only for the corporal to kak us out for bringing back the wrong leaf – off we went again, backwards and forwards until we collapsed in frustration and exhaustion.

Before the sun had set, we'd caused more environmental damage than the mining companies in the Amazon. We were like a plague of locusts at an 'all-you-can-eat' evening. The few trees, that had miraculously survived hundreds of harsh Highveld seasons, were soon stripped of their foliage and the will to live.

Bossies was once a farm and it still had some pigs and pony's and our daily training involved running to the *perdestal* (horse stall) and back – repeatedly.

We'd gallop off like thoroughbred stallions and stagger back like arthritic carthorses. Each time we missed the cut-off time we'd be sent off again until we were knackered. The pony's seemed to enjoy the company, though, and after hearing a few equine snorts as we cantered passed, I think the bastards might've started betting on us. We'd become entertainment for livestock.

Then we came to the even tougher exercises:
Pull-ups:
Even skinny troeps like me battled with this one. We had to suspend ourselves from a metal bar and haul ourselves up so our chin went above the bar. We had to do at least ten in thirty seconds. Excellent training for boarding enemy tanks, scaling dam walls with explosives in your backpack or peeking over walls to perv at the girls in the pool next door.

Sit-ups:

Gary Player's favourite exercise and mine. (When I was a laaitie attending a golf tournament back in Huddersfield, he patted me on my head and asked how I was. My first contact with a celebrity, and he was a Saffa.)

Sit-ups were easy because I was skinny, but the fat guys struggled. Now that I've cultivated a beer *boep*, I feel their pain.

Push-ups:
The standard punishment in the army. To be used whenever required. Whenever we failed our inspection – which was every time – we heard *"Sak vir twentig!"* after which we dived onto the floor and smashed out twenty push-ups. Parades were always a good excuse for another thirty or forty.

When you received a letter from home, another thirty or fifty if the letter was dripping in perfume. I warned Anneline about excessive use of her Chanel No.3; she compromised by not sending any letters at all. Better safe than sorry I suppose.

Whenever the corporals got bored or ran out of ideas, we'd end up face-to-face with the dirt, doing pushups. We soon got accustomed to sweat in our eyes and red dust in our teeth.

Rifle PT:
I'd assumed that our rifles were meant to save our lives, but for the first few months they nearly killed us. Instead of being used to fire at the baddies they were used as expensive weights to give us a good workout. Rifle PT was extreme.

There were plenty of variations:

1. Extending our arms out and twisting our rifles around. The rifle weighed about five kilograms – not too much, but after a minute we were struggling. An exercise designed to make our wrists so strong we could even open an old jar of pickled onions.

2. Running on the spot while holding our rifles above our heads. Great practice for dancing the Can-Can while carrying your wife above your head.

3. Taking the end of the barrel in one hand, then slowly lifting it until it's parallel to the ground. Holding it there indefinitely, or until your arm fell off.

Hop, skip and a jump:
This involved climbing over walls by running over your mates who'd formed steps with their bodies.

1. A troep, on all fours, was positioned on the ground, forming step one.

2. Another troep stood hunched over so that his back formed step two.

3. You then ran up, strode over their backs, vaulted over the fence and ended with a parachute roll on the other side.

4. Then you'd run off, leaving the two battered and bruised staircase impersonators to their fate. Served them right for letting us walk all over them.

Fireman's lift:
This involved carrying a *maatjie* over your shoulder and running as fast as you could. After years of escaping bouncers, with Speedy passed out over my shoulder, I was well prepared, but the poor buggers who had to carry Baobab are still receiving chiropractic assistance.

Leopard crawling:

(If this is how leopards hunt, I'm amazed they haven't already joined the extinct species list.)

Basically, you lay down with your body pressed into the ground, stay as low as possible and crawl forward towards the enemy, or the camp security fence if you were sneaking out for the weekend. If your ass was too elevated you'd be spotted and might receive a piece of lead in your bum cheeks – not a pleasant feeling, so I've been told. You had to use all your limbs to propel yourself along the ground: feet, knees, and elbows, all while cradling your rifle.

The leopard crawl is great for sneaking up on the bad guys, but it does come with some downfalls, such as putting you into intimate contact with devil thorns, dust and the lingering farts of the troepie in front of you. The manoeuvre also caused my asthma pump to crush my balls, and my balls to crush my Chesterfields. The enemy would've heard me from miles away, as my every movement was accompanied by a

loud blast from my asthma pump.

(Not recommended for keen smokers with respiratory problems. On the flipside, my testicles never experienced any breathing difficulties.)

Loop en val (run and fall):
Again, I'd had lots of practice for this back at the Pig and Whistle, but now there was a rifle to carry and I couldn't hide under a car until the cops left.

The idea behind *loop-en-val* was that, when charging at the enemy, you hit the deck every ten seconds and rolled away just before they could train their rifle sights on you. Then, after a couple of seconds, you got up from a slightly different position and charged again.

The enemy wouldn't have time to get a good shot at you. Not as easy as it sounds and a bit dangerous because as you went down, you had to break your fall using your rifle butt, then spin your body to one side. Pete Wainwright broke his collarbone, twice – and he became a Looty. Maybe I should've broken my leg; I'd probably be a general by now.

Water PT:

This was a particularly sadistic form of torture practiced by Corporal Bumfluff and inflicted on us if we nodded off during lectures. He'd make us to drink litres and litres of water until our bellies were grossly distended, then force us to do press-ups, sit-ups, and leopard crawl until we threw up. I'd done plenty of drunken cotching in my time so it was a novelty doing it sober.

Chapter Fourteen
Protestant Voodoo and Dominee Squeaky

During our first week, all troeps had to attend the NGK (Ned Geref Kerk) church services on base.

I wasn't known as a big churchgoer. Once every couple of years I'd been dragged off by a potential girlfriend to attend a Sunday service or maybe a wedding. Baptist, Methodist, Catholics, they were all the same to me. Nice people, lots of smiles and the ostentatious displays of the finest ladies fashion were always a bonus. I'd enjoy the singsong and snooze ('deep prayer' as I used to describe it) and the temporary love of my life would be able to impress her friends with her newly devout boyfriend. Everybody was a winner but this NGK stuff was way out of my league.

The NGK couldn't really be mistaken for a compassionate church. Their style was to start off with screaming sermons of death, sin and destruction, followed by sermons of death, sin, destruction and guilt. It was like being subjected to a half-time team talk from Alec Ferguson when you're four-nil down against Liverpool at Old Trafford – not for the faint-hearted.

The Messiah himself wouldn't have stood a chance of entering a NGK church. With his long hair, dodgy dress sense and general decency our dominee would've had a fit and the bloodthirsty congregation would have thrown a confused Messiah out into the street with the words;

"Get a bleddy haircut, you bleddy heathen, and take your bleddy donkey and palm leaves with you!" ringing in his ears.

Naively, I'd thought that military service was about maintaining white supremacy and keeping the '*swart gevaars*' in their place. Within days, it was drilled into us that we were actually fighting for some *oke* from Bethlehem (not the one in the Free State) who'd ended up with some paraat corporals (disciples) who, with the help of the Army (Roman Empire), had spread his philosophy of love and peace around the world. Thus, attending church was extremely important. So important, that you had to attend or you'd be lovingly and peacefully klapped until you went. The Holy Spirit would have been impressed.

We were marched over to the hall where they'd set up the church. Berets quickly came off as we silently streamed in and took our seats. I looked around at my Afrikaans mates. The joy and celebration of Christianity wasn't exactly shining through their eyes. They looked pretty miserable and wary. What was happening?

The eerie silence was broken by the ominous drumbeat of heavy boots stomping into the hall. The army dominee strode to the front and ascended the pulpit. He was about forty, tall, well built with dark hair. He paused for a moment to set his sneer, then his intense eyes swept the hall x-raying our souls. What chance did I have, what chance did any of us have? He'd sniffed out our feral nature and he didn't *smaak* it, *fokol*.

He started his sermon in barely a whisper, and then started shifting through the gears, soon reaching third and up to eight thousand rpm (rants per minute). I couldn't understand a word of it but his tone made it pretty clear that he and God weren't too impressed with us.

Shifting up another gear, he was soon foaming at the mouth and rocking the pulpit. He screamed his sermon at the assembled troeps, impaling our sinful hearts with the truth of our deceitful natures. This guy was good. I was more used to doddering religious salesmen who just wanted us to worship God and be nice to each other. This crackpot was genuine Old Testament and was using *rooikrans and blitz* for his 'fire and brimstone' sermon. There'd be no turning the other cheek here – this was full on 'eye for eye'. A klap on the cheek would be met with deadly automatic fire and a *skop* on the *kop. Thou shalt not kill* was jettisoned for *thou shalt kill but it's okay because it's in the name of Jesus.* As evil sinners, he promised, we were all due to be hurled into the lava filled jacuzzis of Hell. When I dared to look around at those around me, it was like witnessing the terrified faces at a screening of *Halloween.*

The service carried on and on and on and on and on, and the troeps sank lower and lower and lower into their seats as our collective sins weighed down on us. After about an hour at the pulpit the Lord's Northern Free State regional manager ran out of steam and with a final fiery flourish wrapped it up. He stomped triumphantly out of the hall, while our sinful souls slithered out back to our bungalows.

The same dominee came to Bossies just after we'd come back from our one and only weekend pass. He walked around, cornering individual troeps.

"So, how was your weekend, troepie? Lots of drinking and fucking, ne?"

"Was your girlfriend happy to see your little piel again?"

Creepy.

At that stage, even if we'd ended up in the welcoming arms of Farrah Fawcett on her annual vacation to Kroonstad, pouring twenty-year-old cognac down our throats as we sniffed cocaine off her heaving bosom, we'd have been more interested in getting some sleep and a crispy bacon sandwich in the morning.

Eventually we were allowed to attend our own churches on Sundays and Tuesdays. After joining the Anglican Church, I was ready to have my soul nourished and christen my taste buds in lager.

On our first evening attending our own churches, the whole of Bossies assembled in our step-outs and headed down to the parade ground. There, we were instructed to line up in our respective church groups. When they called the NGK there was a mad surge as two-thirds of the troeps stampeded into position. Once the dust had settled, the rest of us took our turns. A horde of Methodists smugly shuffled into second place followed by about forty pious Baptists and thirty of us holy Anglicans. Last but not least were a bunch of motley Catholics who were roundly sneered and mocked – that would teach them for persecuting the Protestant Huguenots four hundred years ago.

I'd been hoping that there'd be some Buddhists, but saffron dresses and finger cymbals were frowned upon in Kroonstad.

Once they had worked out the logistics of transporting us to our respective places of worship, we were thrown onto various Bedford's before heading into town.

I wasn't sure what to expect with the Anglicans but the church looked cheery enough. Stonewalls topped with a red corrugated roof, the obligatory stained glass windows, green lawns and a few thirsty trees.

Army troeps constituted a sizeable percentage of the congregation and the faithful were eagerly lined up outside the church, keen to check out the fresh meat.

We disembarked as gracefully as possible off the back of a truck and made our way over. The priest introduced himself. I forget his name but I remember that he'd worked in some rough areas, including various Seamen's Missions around the world. He introduced us to the rest of the congregation. They were a mixed bunch – old and young, male and female, white and white, but all English-speaking. It was a relief not having to translate every word I heard.

They welcomed us into their church and we settled into our pews, waiting to be screamed at. Instead, the priest gave a lovely New Testament sermon about being nice and all that type of stuff. At least that's what I was told – most of us fell into a deep sleep within minutes. After so much sleep deprivation I'm sure God would've been cool with it. Having to deal with all those billions of needy prayers at all times of the day, I'm pretty sure He also struggles to get his regular eight hours of beauty sleep.

I've never told Anneline but there were some beautiful girls there. One especially caught my eye; Lisa, also tall, blonde and graceful. Although she sang in the choir, she didn't have the same vocal range as Anneline but the glow on her face as she "Hallelujah-ed" was a sight to behold.

We were all transfixed. Soon, she was surrounded by a pack of hopeful suitors. I'd seen this many times before and strategically backed off. I decided to play the long game – a very long game, as it turned out – thirty years later and I'm still waiting for her to make her move. Women, hey. After the service we shuffled into the back garden, where a couple of braais were already smoking away.

Lisa and her friends were busy with the salads (a foreign dish of grass, leaves, round red balls and stuff that makes you cry.) This was all good and fine but my prime motivation for joining the Holy Order of Angles was to treat my parched taste buds to the distinctive flavours found in a Castle Lager bottle. After a couple of not-so-subtle hints, they soon got the idea and asked us if we'd like some liquid refreshments.

"Yes, please," we replied, getting off our knees and wiping away the tears of gratitude.

"Only two each though," Lisa smiled.

I bought two more beers from a capitalist teetotaller and as soon as the first two beers had been consumed, the evening turned into a wonderful blur. After the next two beers I thought I was back at The Pig and Whistle.

Word soon spread around Bossies about the drunken debauchery at the Anglican Church and many not-so-brand-loyal Christians started requesting a transfer – mainly from the NGK.

At the next church parade, the Anglican contingent mushroomed to thirty-five, a week later another dozen joined. Before the NGK could get their act together we had about thirty thirsty Afrikaans Anglicans heartily singing along to British colonial hymns. So many joined that they were thinking of conducting bilingual sermons.

Eventually, the NGK dominee noticed the empty seats and a substantial dip in the collection and let fire with a sermon that implied converting to the English religion was heresy and would result in the demise of Verwoerd's dream of a separate but almost equal South Africa. As the deluge of Afrikaner converts dwindled, the dominee breathed a huge sigh of relief and reconfirmed his order for a holy Mercedes SLX.

To get onto Junior Leaders in Kroonstad you had to be religious. Arrogant, womanising psychos whom Satan would have crossed the street to ignore suddenly found God in their hearts. It was a miracle. Hallelujah. As if by some miracle, they could suddenly quote verse upon verse from the Bible. I wasn't too surprised to find that, after conning the army and being accepted into JLs most had a Paul-to-Saul reconversion and were soon back to their dodgy ways.

One Sunday, Corporal Bumfluff asked a few of us to join him on a research trip to the Pinkster Protestante Kerk, one of the first evangelical churches to open shop in South Africa. They were 'happy-clappies' whose services were rumoured to feature speaking in tongues, non-stop singing and wild-eyed cavorting females. They were the Nazi Punks of the Protestant religion. Bumfluff was intrigued but didn't fancy the idea of going there on his own. He enquired if I'd like to join him on a little research trip.

"I'd love to join you Corporal, but I'm a devout Anglican now and I don't want to mess up my chances of going to Anglican heaven," I lied.

He gave me his death stare. I still wasn't convinced.

"I'll buy you beers afterwards," he promised.

"Ja, I'll join you, Corporal," I yelled enthusiastically.

He gave me his 'Why the fuck are you yelling at me' stare. Surely I could survive some fundamental Christianity?

We pitched up just before the service started. The Pinksters church wasn't what you'd call uplifting – it looked like a derelict warehouse. As we piled out of the army bakkie, the greeting from the congregation milling outside wasn't too encouraging either. They looked like rejected extras from *The Sopranos*, not a smile or slice of *melktert* to be seen. The men wore blue or black corduroy suits, sported greased-back hair and had about three days' worth of beard growth. They all looked swarthy but more 'serial killer' swarthy than 'romantic hero' swarthy. The women, on the other hand, were either gentle or terrified – it was hard to tell. They were covered in layers of gaudy flesh-covering cloth; forty-nine percent polyester, thirty percent rags, fifteen percent sadness and six percent bitterness. Complimenting this ensemble was a forlorn hat with some plastic flowers stapled on.

There were about seven of us, nervously led by Bumfluff who was now wishing he was back at the liberal NGK. The sermon was predominantly in Afrikaans, and by 'predominantly' I mean 100%. It was like the NGK on speed; demented screaming, foaming at the mouth and slamming of the pulpit – a terrifying display of Protestant voodoo.

It was good exercise, though. No chance of a little nap with those crazies. We had to jump up every two minutes to start clapping and singing, then sit down again for more admonishment from the preacher, then back up again for more ritual clapping. By the end of the service we were exhausted, spiritually and physically.

When they came round with the hat for the collection, I reluctantly put in an extravagant fifty cents. After all, it had been a good show: a bit of comedy, plenty of drama and a sprinkling of horror. It deserved ten percent of my daily income, but the corduroy mafia enforcer wasn't impressed.

He leaned in until his God-fearing bristles were in danger of taking my eye out. With the sour smell of cheap brandy and homemade *boerewors* dripping from his pores, he looked deep into my soul and implied that I might need to increase my contribution.

My Yorkshire-bred fingers instinctively tightened on my wallet, but as I glimpsed a terrified Corporal Bumfluff I realised we'd been cornered by a pack of scavenging evangelicals screaming 'Onward Christian Soldiers', rolling their eyes and clapping dementedly. Terrible visions of cult massacres and suspicious suicides played through my mind. As the frantic beat accelerated and the wild-eyed *tannies* closed in I realised it was a battle I couldn't win. With tear-filled eyes I extracted a two-rand note from my wallet, and, as Jan van Riebeck gave me a coy wink, I handed it over to Al van der Capone, while I prayed that we'd get out of there alive.

We scrambled out bowing, scraping and genuflecting to the very Aryan-looking Jesus cable-tied to the wall. The Lord truly moves in mysterious ways.

Archbishop Desmond Tutu meets the ANC in Zambia and fails to convince the organization to abandon the armed struggle

22 March 1987

Rooi Gevaar

Cape Town. 1986
By the end of my studies at Cape Technikon, my tiny brain had developed sufficiently to realise that Apartheid might not be what Jesus wanted. I started questioning the whole National Christian facade and the official and unofficial answers didn't make sense. I was torn. I'd fallen deeply in love with this crazy, stunning, fucked-up country but I thought Apartheid wasn't a great idea and now I was expected to join an army that was enforcing it. Whenever I chirped about politics I soon got shot down by my mates tuning me " Jou moer, you only get a say when you've done your two years" I realised that I couldn't comment on politics until I completed my two years.

Back at our bungalow, political arguments were breaking out – not surprising in a country being torn apart at the seams. My fellow inmates had all kinds of political leanings, from right-wing AWB to communist ANC and everything in between. Although many of the troeps weren't convinced by Apartheid, any attempt at putting forward a one-man one-vote stance was aggressively shot down.

A few of the youngsters had embraced the white power philosophies of the AWB and its messianic leader, Eugene Terreblanche. They were mesmerised by his fiery rhetoric, painting visions of the Volk rising up to defend the Fatherland. The AWB were so right of centre that they regarded Apartheid hard man, former-president BJ Vorster, as a liberal and the Groot Krokodil as a traitorous commie.

I elected to adopt a Gandhi-like attitude to the discussions, and was polite and respectful of all the views, even the most idiotic ones. I found that this created an environment of mutual tolerance and free speech – plus I didn't get my *fokken* head kicked in.

After a week of boring military lectures, designed to keep us alive, they cunningly introduced the subject of 'Politics, Religion and Philosophy,' – also known as 'Blatant Nationalist Party Propaganda'. This was more like it. At last, something we could discuss instead of being shouted at.

This was obviously an important subject as they held it in a room with walls and a roof instead of saunas masquerading as tents. Evidently, they were quite keen on us remembering some of their gems of wisdom rather than us falling asleep like in all the other lectures.

As we gathered for the first lecture, we tried to work out who'd be lecturing us. Most of our military lecturers were PFs who thought Marxism was a self-help comedy book by Groucho and that Engels was just a kak language spoken by the soutpiels. Eventually a fresh-faced youngster peeked around the door and tiptoed into position in front of the virgin blackboard.

Without looking at us, he grabbed the chalk and started scribbling:

Communism
Socialism
Marxism
Humanism
Capitalism
Christianity

With an emphatic tap on the blackboard, he turned around and introduced himself.

He was a young NGK dominee fresh out of officers course and now tasked with helping our tiny, immature minds to understand the world a little better.

Being a dominee he was given the rank of lieutenant, so he had a bit of power, which was lucky because he looked even younger than Bumfluff. This was his first lecture, and he seemed a bit nervous. Unluckily, though, his balls only seemed to have dropped halfway, causing his voice to go from deep baritone to castrated pig in one sentence.

"Right. Who can tell me what Communism is?" he squealed.

The lecture room went deathly quiet. Our gazes averted downwards to our dirty boots.

Did he really want to know or was this a trick question to identify the evil Stalinists and Marxists who'd infiltrated India Bungalow? We'd have to play this one carefully if we wanted to qualify for Junior Leaders.

Slowly, a hand went up from the back.

"It's a theory or system of social organisation in which the community owns all property and each person contributes and receives according to their abilities and needs," some clever bastard piped up.

"What? *Nee, nee, nee.* It's a system that rejects Jesus and wants to kill Christians," Dominee Squeaky insisted. "Right, now, what is Socialism?"

"It's a political and economic theory of social organisation, which advocates that the means of production, distribution, and exchange should be owned or regulated by the community as a whole," piped up another clever bugger who'd swallowed his Politics 101 textbook at varsity.

"Hemel en aarde. Nee, manne, it's a bunch of *bleddy* atheists who want to force Satanism on us," the dominee explained.

"If they are Satanists, how can they be atheists?" Slab asked.

Suddenly, the floodgates opened and everybody started discussing religion and politics. Dominee Squeaky evidently hadn't expected his lecture to develop into a discussion. Propaganda was meant to be a one-way street, and now everybody was expressing their own opinions. Goebbels never had these problems.

The young dominee had prepared his lecture assuming he'd be brainwashing a bunch of fresh out of school teenagers, ready to be programmed into fighting the heathen commies and saving Jesus from being unemployed. The congregation he encountered was mainly made up of university or college men whose brains were a bit more developed and analytical. Even the NGK Christians were ready to rip into him and his rudimentary and naïve theories.

He was Daniel in the lion's' den, getting nailed by university boys. Over the commotion you could just hear him screaming.

"And what about Capitalism?"

"Fuck Capitalism!" That might have been me.

"Rich bastards screwing the poor!" Probably Suggsy.

"Capitalism is what Jesus supported," screeched Dominee Squeaky.

"A rich man going to heaven is as easy as a camel going through the eye of a needle," shouted somebody who'd actually read the Bible.

"It could have been quite a big needle," insisted the dominee.

He finally departed; shoulders slumped, to the sound of laughter. I felt sorry for him, poor bastard. You could see his heart wasn't in it but to rebel against the church and state was tantamount to treason.

Over the next few weeks, he soldiered on with his lectures, trying hard to re-educate us. A few laaities took the bait but most of the guys saw through it and simply humoured him. Hopefully his balls have now dropped to the required height and he's preaching nice things to a less-cynical flock somewhere in the Karoo.

Chapter Fifteen
Corporal Punishment

After chatting to Pete and troeps from other bungalows, we realised that Bossies was out of control. We were only a month into basics and it felt like we were in the movie *Full Metal Jacket*. None of the PFs and Looty's lived at Bossies, so every night, after they departed, the camp was left in the hands of a bunch of juvenile corporals who were either pissed or pissed off. They had free rein and often staggered into our bungalows late at night to mess up our inspection or give us a *rondvok* knowing that there was nobody to stop them. The daily inspections took us hours to complete, leaving us with four hours sleep a night, often spent on the floor. With the extreme physical training and inadequate food to sustain us, we looked like skeletons on a colonics retreat. It wasn't just us – at camps all around the country, the walking dead dreaded their daily wake-up call.

The corporals were barely out of their teens, and not professionally trained. Like us, they were national servicemen. How can an eighteen-year-old kid, straight out of high school, be taught how to mould other children into proper soldiers? You need professionals for that shit.

The SADF only trained its instructors once, and that was for just a few months unlike professional armies, whose instructors were just as ruthless, but were well trained, focused and experienced. For them, it was a career, and not just part of obligatory national service.

Professional training instructors know when to stop and how to get the best out of their troeps. In the SADF, it was the old case of, "I got fucked up, so I'm going to fuck you up." *Klaar*. Their incendiary attitudes were further fuelled by a commanding officer that encouraged their abuses by informing everybody that the army was allowed to kill two or three troeps during basics. So, obviously, the corporals went on the rampage. It was all part of a fanatical desire to become known as one of the toughest training camps in South Africa.

The corporals even tried to outdo each other in their abuse. As amateur soldiers, they weren't properly trained to see the signs that troeps were not only getting desperate, but more importantly, were realising that the enemy wasn't on the border, but in their own camp. There was very little oversight at Bossies since we were miles from any critical eyes. Our Commanding Officer, Major Rabid, was free to do what he wanted and what he wanted was to fuck us up enough to prove that Sappers were as tough as any infantry, parabats or artillery; a noble aspiration but the wrong methods and personnel.

Any corporal who was too soft was ostracised by the other corporals. They all stayed in one barrack, and so they, too, were under pressure but their pressure was different. Their task was to mould an entire bungalow of motley individuals into a united force that, by the end of basics, could perform tasks far beyond their dreams.

It was a dangerous game that put lives in danger. If they injured us during training they could even charge *us* with damaging government property. *We* were government property. They literally owned us.

For three months, the corporals decided what time you woke, ate, shat, showered and slept. We were part of an all-encompassing military machine, each one of us a disposable part. We were the dirtiest grease, the tiniest unnoticed cog, the lowest rung on a well-trodden ladder. We were nothing more than prisoners who were given a few days leave every couple of months. Freedom was a thing of the past. We were at the mercy of immature psycho corporals commanded by a lightweight major. The only buffer India Bungalow had was Lieutenant Beetge. Other bungalows weren't so lucky.

Pete was in Golf Bungalow, run by a truly unhinged corporal intent on nailing the whole bungalow. If the entire unit wasn't in pain, he was disappointed. He should've been a patient at Valkenberg Psychiatric Hospital, but the army had decided that his sadistic nature was perfect for training troeps. He worshipped the 'break them down' part but forgot the 'build them up' part that was supposed to come afterwards.

Even troeps who supported Apartheid's nationalist Christian ideology began questioning their beliefs after their experiences at Bossies.

I'd always said to my mates that I'd take on the corporals if they gave me too much kak but now I realised why they'd spilled their beer laughing so hard. I realised this would be impossible as soon as I discovered that the army used the 'Screw your *Maatjies* System'. Used by armies and parents around the world, The System is highly effective and followed a number of steps. If you defied the corporals they started off with insults and threats. If this didn't work, the 'Screw your *Maatjies*' system kicked into gear. Instead of punishing one stubborn soldier, the corporal punished the whole unit (your *maatjies*), while rewarding the offending soldier by letting him rest, have a Coke and smoke a cigarette.

When your exhausted, sweaty and bitter maatjies got back from the *rondvok*, they were not too impressed with their now lounging, smoking, Coca-Cola-sipping *maatjie*. This was graphically conveyed by: thumbs drawn across the throat, threats of mutilation and sustained glaring. The *maatjie*, realising he may be killed by his own unit, hastily un-stubborns himself and gets back in line – highly effective.

On the flip side, it's also human nature to innovate in times of hardship, to use deceit and manipulation to survive, and so we began working on our own system – The Gyppo System. After being told three or four times our time was too slow for the 2,4 km run, we all slowed down and as long as everybody stuck together, the corporals got bored with kakking us out and moved onto the next form of torture.

Another tactic was used during press-ups; as soon as the corporal wasn't looking, we'd only raise our shoulders and head off the ground and from a distance it looked legit. We were learning the ancient tactics of the *gyppo-gat*.

The corporals and other NCOs weren't allowed to hit us. You received the occasional klap on the doibie, your feet kicked and the occasional body slam, but they couldn't punch you in the face – much to their frustration. However, they had a nice little loophole with which to inflict a bit of pain.

If they really had it in for you, they stood in front of you, and slowly but firmly pushed one of your overalls' metal buttons hard into your ribs. Doesn't sound too bad, but with the force of an 80kg corporal pushing a 10mm-square piece of metal into your bones, it wasn't too pleasant – and you couldn't back away. It was one of those cruelties that made you fantasise about shooting the bastard, and reminded you that basics was more of a mental test than a physical one.

The corporals would get right in your face, daring you to fight back and it took massive self-discipline and the threat of months in DB to hold back a punch as they sneered in your face. It was like the weigh-in before a boxing fight, but with only one man trash talking while the other had to *"hou* his *bek" (shut up)*.

One day, the corporals got a bit bored and decided to have some fun at our expense. Just as I was falling asleep in the lecture tent while learning about the intricate composition of bridge parts, a tube, spitting sparks, suddenly appeared next to me. The next second, there was an explosion and I went flying back, crashing to the floor. Through the stars I saw two smirking corporals stroll passed. I couldn't hear anything except a loud buzz and distant laughter. Now I knew what a Thunder Flash was.

A while later they gave us a demonstration on the power of a Thunder Flash. They lit one, put it under a steel helmet and stood back. The helmet was blown fifty metres into the air – it was no firework. I still dive under the table every time a waiter drops a glass.

The first skill we learnt in the army was how to protect your gear from being stolen – the second skill was how to steal from others in case skill number one failed. Thieving was so rife at Bossies that we had to put locked chains through our washing as it dried on the lines outside our bungalows. It became a scourge.

For example: one troep loses a sock but he needs all his socks present and correct for inspection. The sockless victim sneaks out in the dark recesses of the night to steal one off the bungalows washing line. The next morning, another troep realises he's a sock short and in desperation and against all his morals, he steals somebody else's sock. Before long, the whole bungalow is caught up in a vicious cycle of sock pilfering. In extreme cases, the bungalow next door becomes a target, and soon the whole bloody camp was full of sock thieves.

One missing sock meant a whole camp was damned to eternal hell for breaking one of the Ten Commandments. I wonder if there have been any Biblical amendments lately, because it's pretty obvious that God never did His two years or He'd have gotten rid of that 'no stealing' bit and probably a few others as well. In fact, after two years in Bossies He'd have probably narrowed it down to one or two Commandments and Moses would've been saved the schlep of dragging those two big stone tablets down Mount Sinai.

"Kaserne, kaserne aandag!"
The call we all dreaded. Now I knew how the poor buggers on the coasts of Northern Europe felt when the church bells rang, signalling another Viking invasion. The Bungalow Bill had to call it out whenever anybody with rank entered our bungalow and first thing in the morning, it meant inspection; the most important part of the day, every day, every bloody day.

Inspections had been invented in ancient times by a select committee comprised of Beelzebub, Genghis Khan, Attila the Hun and chaired by Vlad the Impaler. An evil form of torture designed to instil cleanliness, uniformity and square beds. Now, imagine being a cleaner on your first day at a seven-star exclusive luxury boutique "yes-sir-and-can-I-please-kiss-your-ass" hotel designed for the most elite, rich, famous and condescending snobs in the Milky Way. Locate this boutique hotel in the middle of the Great Pit of Carkoon with a hurricane blowing red dust through the holes in the walls, gaps in the windows and underneath the doors. Add in a head housekeeper who can spot a fleck of dust from a hundred metres and you get the idea.

We had to keep our bungalow spotless. Bumfluff would stroll in, pick up a pillow and kick it down the aisle – if there was one bit of dirt on it we'd fail the inspection. It was an impossible task.

The army likes everything to be neat and squared off so our uniform needed to be crisp and ironed, the webbing starched and upright, and our bunk beds had to resemble matchboxes. As the Americans would say, "So you could bounce a quarter on it."

I'd never had much need for ironing seeing as I'd always been a right scruffy bastard and when Punk Rock came along, I could hide behind my newfound ideology as the perfect excuse to avoid ironing duties. Unfortunately, this meant that my ironing skills weren't up to scratch. In basics everything needed to be ironed, including your bed.

After burning my fingers a couple of times and making my shirt look like a street map of Manhattan, I realised that my ironing skills weren't likely to improve. Luckily I was better at shining boots so I swapped out my ironing for boot polishing duties.

Everything that could possibly shine in the bungalow had to be polished; brass window fittings, rifles, belt buckles and the floor which usually came last as you didn't want troeps messing it up as they did other jobs. We'd wrap pieces of cloth or strips of blanket around our feet (*taxis*) so as not to dirty the bungalow floor, as we walked, we polished.

Having to make our beds square was another story. The bunks had a ragged metal lattice on which the mattresses rested, so our beds inevitably sagged in the middle. This was remedied by strategically placing clothes pegs on the lattice work to help prop the mattress up and keep it level; another major engineering feat – maybe we were learning something.

I was used to getting my badly needed beauty sleep warmly wrapped in my slightly faded and badly stained Union Jack duvet so cover slips and blankets were a dark mystery to me.

The first step was to fit the undercover sheet and tuck in the corners at forty-five-degree angles in such a way that the wrinkles were smoothed out and the sheet stretched out nice and flat. Then you added the cover sheet with the same attention to detail, keeping it taut. Next came the blanket.

Once that was on, you had to make the whole thing square, like a matchbox. We'd apply a mixture of saliva and toothpaste or shaving cream along the top edges of the blanket and sheet, and then, using your wooden polish brush as a straight edge, you'd iron the edges until they were stiff and at ninety degrees.

To make the edges extra sharp we'd bite them. For months afterwards I'd find strands of blanket threads in my teeth, at least I think that's what they were.

Warning: Don't try this at home, especially if the wife is still sleeping.

Not only did we have to iron our beds but also the blue and mauve Engineering Corps stripes on our blankets had to stand to attention. Using a toothbrush we'd delicately flick up the bristles of the three stripes and once complete, it was a marvel of modern blanket engineering. My mum would have been proud – confused but proud.

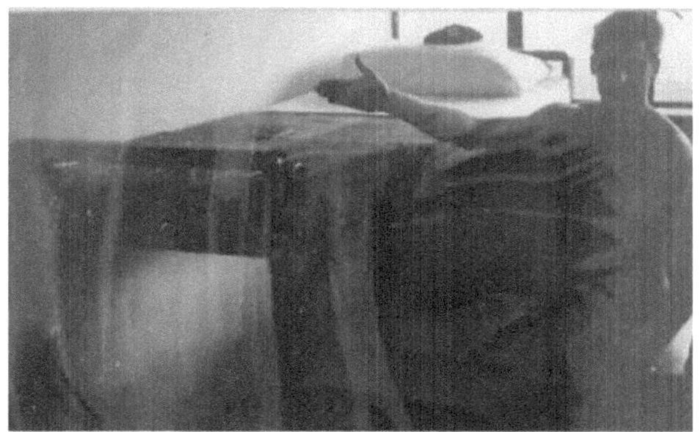

Rudi Pahl with a fine attempt at the matchbox bed. Having German DNA, he did have a slight advantage.

My pillow had been through some traumatic times. It was badly mangled and stained by the tears, sweat and drool of its many previous owners. It looked as though a Buffel, with Baobab on board, had driven over it – a few thousand times. Fully fluffed up, it was about two centimetres thick. It was more for decoration than assistance in snoozing and it's *slaapgat* attitude tended to ruin my inspection.

On top of our magnificent beds we displayed our shiny cutlery, gleaming rifle parts, berets, doibies, letters for home and toiletry items. Our kas contained our ironed kit while our webbing, squared off with cardboard inside, was placed on top.

At the command, troeps rushed to finish their inspections, and dived into place. The whole bungalow stood to attention in two lines and the corporals swaggered in. We glanced across the aisle at our maatjies, collectively kakking ourselves. Who's going to get fucked up this time? They tended to pick on one or two troeps before the rest of the bungalow got nailed.

Early in basics the corporals would tear everything apart, pushing bunk beds over and throwing kit onto the floor. In extreme cases they emptied the water and sand buckets in the aisles and for light entertainment they forced us to get into our pristine beds and act as if we were rowing a canoe, or swimming. Our fine works of boudoir art were soon destroyed as we thrashed around in our pristine beds. Linen went flying and our concealed clothes pegs popped off and lay scattered on the floor.

At first, inspections were soul-destroying until we realised they were just an excuse to mess us around and then we started finding the whole thing funny. By failing us for most of our inspections, the corporals had ensured the inevitable outcome: we stopped caring. What was the point of doing a good job if they just destroyed it?

After trashing the whole bungalow and reminding us that we were the scum of the earth, who didn't deserve to be in the glorious sappers, the corporals issued our punishment. We hit the deck to start our press-ups. If they were really angry or *babalaas*, they made us do it with our feet on our trommels or, one time, on our *kas*, which was like doing press ups while doing a handstand. When one troep slipped, gravity made him pay with a badly bruised face. Physical signs of abuse were frowned upon, so the *kas* press-ups were soon halted.

As with most of basics, we were *paraat* in the first few weeks so we did everything by the book – until we worked out ways to gyppo.

There were sixty-four troeps per bungalow, so the two corporals had a tough job watching us all. We got into position for our press-ups and would start off in fine fashion, but as soon as both corporals weren't looking our way, we'd stop moving but carry on counting and grunting. A few lads still tried to do all the proper press-ups but everybody else slacked off.

On the day we received our R4 rifles we became instant Rambos – strutting around looking for the enemy – which was a bit *dof* as we hadn't been issued bullets. And if they'd handed out bullets to pissed-off *roefs* there'd have been a lot less corporals around today.

At least the rifles were better than the useless whistles we'd been issued during guard duty, now we'd be able to point our R4's at the enemy and shout 'bang!' We were also issued bayonets for our rifle, which seemed a bit retro, as South Africa already possessed nuclear bombs.

The R4 rifle is based on the Israeli Galil rifle, which has an operating system similar to the AK47 – hardy and simple, a good rifle for bush combat. They taught us how to pull it apart and reassemble it – Jenga for soldiers. Then the corporals brought in a time limit, and the pressure was on. Nervous, sweaty hands started dropping springs and bolts. Some parts refused to go into their allotted slots, even when rammed. The puzzle soon fell apart, so at night we practiced amongst ourselves until we got it right, most of the time.

We had to carry our rifles almost everywhere: exercise, lectures, marching practice and out into the bush. If you took your eyes off it for a moment, the corporals stole it, and then you were in for an immediate opvok. It became your wife, your 'ball and chain'. Another downside of having your very own automated killing device was that you had to keep it squeaky clean. To do this you had to disassemble it into its various parts and then clean and dust them until they shone.

This added another thirty minutes to our inspection preparations. Maybe we should have stuck with the whistles.

"Vir inspeksie, hou geweer!"
"Present your rifle for inspection," the corporals yelled. We grabbed our rifles, lined up and presented arms.

This meant pulling back the bolt and holding the rifle with the barrel pointed at an angle to allow the corporals to peer down the barrel and into the open breechblock looking for dust and making sure there wasn't a round in the chamber. After a minute, your hand and arm began shaking and the sweat poured from your brow as you struggled to keep the spring-loaded bolt from zapping back into position. If you were last in line, you were soon gritting your teeth.

Any sign of dirt or dust in your rifle caused a rush of blood to the corporals' faces, triggering a bout of frenzied insults about planting potatoes in your rifle's dirt. A bit dramatic but we got the picture. However, no matter how many times we pulled our cleaning cloth through the barrel, there'd always be that one speck of dust to *naai* us.

Early one morning I was rudely awakened by the daily panic of terrified troeps polishing, sweeping, sweating and swearing. Inspection was in ten minutes and I'd overslept.

This was not a good situation.

"Why the fuck didn't you wake me?" I asked Suggsy.

You've been awake for an hour already," he mumbled as he chomped on his blanket.

"What are you talking about?" I tuned.

"You've been lying there with your eyes open for an hour. We just thought you were being lazy."

"When have I ever been…..never mind." Shit and triple shit. Now I'd started sleeping with my eyes open.

I had two options: panic, or claim I'd been abducted by aliens who'd just beamed me down and then pissed off back home to planet Ventura12fontbold. I panicked.

Fortunately, having perfected the art of sleeping to attention, my bed was still fairly square. With a quick drag of my toothbrush, the bristles of the three stripes on my blanket flared up and after a few adjustments my bed looked almost decent. Now I just needed to polish my boots, clean my rifle, iron my clothes, clean the windows, Brasso the brass, shine the floor, then shower, shave and have a shit.

Ten minutes later and still gagging for a shit I was nowhere near ready and had resigned myself to an *uitkak* and possible *opvok*. Then I heard the dreaded call of *"Kaserne, kaserne aandag!"* and I went into overdrive as the inspection began at the far end of our bungalow.

As Bumfluff sauntered down the aisle insulting everybody and ripping apart their hard work, I was frantically putting the finishing touches to my shambles of an inspection. My maatjies all stood to attention, willing me on and trying to indicate how close he was by using head and eye signals. When I looked up from my badly polished right boot and saw the frantic fear in Sneezer's eyes, I knew it was time to get back in line. I rapidly slid back into place with sweat on my brow and fear on my face.

I waited for the shit-storm to hit.

Corporals Bumfluff and Scowler stomped into our section and started checking our inspection.

After they'd finished with Sneezer and Suggsy they moved my way. Bumfluff took a cursory glance at my excuse for an inspection. His face turning red, he screamed in my face: "*Wat die fok gaan aan hier?*"

"*Jammer, Korporaal. Ek het a bietjie moeilikheid met my—*"

"*Nee, Soutie. Waar's jou fokken maatjie?*"

I glanced to my left and saw an empty place where he should have been standing. In my haste I hadn't noticed that my bunkmate had gone missing in action. What the hell was going on?

The corporals panicked, thinking he might have fled or been injured. I was off the hook. They charged out of the bungalow to search for him and I gave a small leap, punched the air and thanked my new best friend – the Anglican God. He'd evidently been impressed with my singing at the last Sunday service.

My bunkmate was finally found shivering on the floor in the showers with a bad fever. He claimed that he'd passed out and was taken to see the medics.

He was a terrified laaitie straight out of Matric. I forget his name, but I called him Snotneus. He was from one of the elite Cape Town schools: SACS or Bishops or Batavia. A nervous kid. Ginger-haired, small, pale and skinny, like a miniature Prince Harry. We were all scared, but he was petrified and no matter how hard we tried to ease his fears and include him in our slowly evolving circle of friends, he couldn't make the final leap. Maybe he was also scared of us. Snotneus never explained why he hadn't headed straight off to university after Matric with the obvious advantage of three or four years' army exemption. Although, in his defence, in 1987 there was no sign that the border conflict would soon end, the ANC be unbanned and national service gently fade away. The majority of school-leavers simply wanted to get

national service over and done with and then get on with their lives. We'd been programmed to serve.

After a few days at Bossies, Snotneus realised that he'd made a fundamental error and decided that he'd rather be home. Unluckily for him and for us, he became one of those troeps who dragged the whole bungalow down. He became the weakest link and was putting a shitload of strain on the chain. Humans are generally quite caring and decent but after a few *rondvoks* caused by my lazy bunkmate, the bungalow was losing patience.

After a month of abuse, lack of sleep and no mugs of hot Milo from mummy, he'd had enough and decided to take matters into his own hands (no, he didn't try to wank himself to death). In his desperation he went for the nuclear option: death, dishonour…or chronic disease.

I'm not sure if he had done any research, but he was truly dedicated in his quest for illness. Fully clothed, he'd soak himself in the cold showers, then stand out in the freezing wind and try to get the flu, or even better, pneumonia. He'd sniff the dust off the floor and even starve himself – not a difficult task at Bossies as we were all bloody starving. But he was so determined that he'd even ignore the buttermilk rusks, a sure sign of insanity. Initially, we thought he was trying to start a new cult because his chattering teeth and rambling speeches made him sound like a prophet or a loony. I think he even attracted a couple of disciples until he demanded that they sneeze on him as a form of worship. Then we assumed that this was a radical training method he'd devised to become the hardest bastard in the army and get into the Recces.

All night long he coughed, shook and spluttered. He was beginning to put me off my stroke. Something had to be done.

Within days of his drinking some of my contact lens cleaning fluid he'd ended up in the sick bay and suddenly he was gone. All that was left of him was a sweat-stained mattress covered in tissues and a lingering menthol smell. We were all truly shocked at the loss of our comrade ….for at least a minute.

As the initial shock wore off I realised that he'd been discharged in such a rush that he'd forgotten all his kit. Sweet child of the Himalayas, I was saved. Then the vultures began to circle.

"Who's taking his bed?" somebody asked.

"Can I have his boots?"

"I want his blankets!"

"Fuck off you, lot. The corporal ordered me to protect his stuff until he's back," I lied.

They backed off scowling. I swiftly commandeered all his gear and set it up in my kas and locked his kas with a triple combination lock. I'd pulled off the ultimate heist. From then on I always had a perfectly arranged kas ready for inspection, while my grubby gear was secreted away in his kas, which only I could open.

Sapper Soutpiel 1 – Big Crocodile 0
(I'm still disappointed that I never received a request from the Army Museum to have my immaculate kas put on permanent display for future soldiers to admire and worship).

The terror of inspections had got to the point where we didn't sleep in our own beds, as that would mean spending another thirty minutes making the bloody thing square again. We started sleeping on the cold floor.

What kind of insanity drove us to lie down for five hours on freezing, rock-hard floors rather than crease our linen? The fear was real.

Once the corporals realised our deception, they'd sneak in during the night to force us back into our pristine beds but thanks to Sapper Snotneus's recent departure, not only did I have a perfect kas, but I also had a bed to sleep in without worrying about making it up. Soon the corporals smelled a rat and would bring up the messy state of the bed above mine.

"It's not my bed, Corporal. It's that lazy, nose-blowing, ginger coward who fled our glorious camp," I replied. Corporal Bumfluff wasn't buying my bullshit and ordered me to makeup Snotneus's bed as well. Unfortunately the next day some thieving bastard stole Snotty's blankets and pillows and I couldn't make the bed up anymore. I wonder if they are still under the bush where I'd accidently dropped them.

I think I'm still making up for the lack of sleep during my army days. Thirty years later I still refuse to get out of bed before ten in the morning, unless I'm in a strange bed and her children are running around demanding breakfast from 'the uncle'.

Happy Birthday to Me

During basics it's easy to forget what day it is as they merge into one another. If you think life is passing you quickly, join the army. It rapidly slows down. Wednesday, 11 March 1987 was my 25th birthday. The corporals baked me a nice melktert, poured me a beer and the whole bungalow sang happy birthday as I blew out the candles and opened my presents. Then I woke up; my birthday was just another shitty day in the army.

I'm not sure if this is an army legend but I hope it's true.

Once upon a time, in a camp far far away a troep approached a corporal who'd been picking on him for weeks on end.

"Corporal, can I call you a poes?" he asked.

"Of course not, I'll fokking bliksem you."

"But am I allowed to think you're a poes?"

The corporal thought long and hard.

"Ja, I suppose so."

"Right, then I think you're a poes."

I'm not sure where that troep is buried now, but I hope there is a monument to him.

Chapter Sixteen
Cowboys, Indians and the Devil's saliva

After about a month, it was decided that the battalion was ready for its first, full-kit route march. Twenty kilometres, hauling twenty kilograms of gear and carrying our rifles. Proper border war training, minus the mortar attacks, landmines and extreme sun tanning.

The morning of the march found the camp in a state of panic as we scrambled to help each other put on full webbing; like dressing a greased pig in bondage gear. We filled our webbing with cans of food, equipment and ammunition and sleeping bags strapped on top. Water bottles attached to our sides, and doibies perched on our heads. We tottered out into the extreme heat and off we went.

It was tough getting used to an ever-shifting load on your back, but a few adjustments to the straps made it easier. The trick was to tighten the straps so that there was no gap between your kit and your body, otherwise it banged against you constantly. After a while I got into a rhythm: head down, deep breaths, a focused and determined mental attitude. The unit stuck together for the first few kilometres before spreading out as the fittest troeps powered forward. Baobab had been excused this one as he'd fallen sick. Or so they told us.

The march had a time limit and we were soon lagging behind but after the corporals gave us a bollocking we upped our speed to a gentle jog.

This was the furthest we'd done in our army boots. Blisters started developing until it didn't matter how your feet landed on the hard earth, it was agony. By halfway, most of us were suffering visibly in the intense heat, propelled forward only by the unrelenting stream of abuse and occasional words of encouragement. I remember one of the fitter corporals coming past carrying three rifles as he tried to help out the stragglers; the corporals would also be in the kak if we didn't complete the course in time.

The last few kilometres were a blur of misery. Every blister taunted me with repeated bursts of eye-watering pain. Soon, I was slamming my feet down just to burst the blisters, thinking this would somehow relieve the pain.

The twenty-kilogram kit now felt like fifty as we struggled on, drenched in sweat and dust. I finished the last drop of my water as my eyes battled to focus through the haze of fatigue.

The course took us around the perimeter of Bossies to areas we'd never been before so it was impossible to work out how far we still had to go. We pushed on through, then I spotted Bossies' very own mini Table Mountain and I realised it was only one kilometre left but that last km felt the longest. I glanced up to spot the finishing line, and saw another corner, then another – it was like climbing a never-ending mountain. Just as I thought I wouldn't make it, I cleared the last corner and entered the parade ground. Hundreds of exhausted troeps were hobbling around or crumpled on the ground. I soon joined them.

We'd done a decent time and Major Rabid seemed pleased, or at least not angry and we got the afternoon off to recover. By now, our blisters had hit full-throb level, making the stagger back to our bungalows look like Napoleon's retreat from Russia.

Back at India Bungalow, I delicately removed my boots.

It wasn't a pretty sight. My socks were caked in blood and blister goo. I slowly peeled off my socks. Both feet were covered in either fully-fledged blisters, or popped ones that revealed the raw bloody skin below. All around me, the little yelps, oohs and aahs told me I wasn't the only one.

I was faced with a dilemma: either accept the added pain of Merthiolate on my blisters, or hope that they'd miraculously cure themselves overnight. Maybe that famous Top Ten hit, 'Onward Christian Soldiers', was about blister redemption but despite the fact that I'd recently become a season ticket-holder with the Anglicans, I calculated that God wasn't going to waste one of His ever-rarer miracles on me.

Sneezer and his Merthiolated blisters came hobbling back from the medics looking as pale as a Scottish albino and sat huddled in the corner muttering about the perils of the Devil's saliva. Not the best encouragement but I knew it had to be done. I tiptoed over to the long queue that had already formed outside the medics' room. By the time it was my turn, half the camp was behind me – their blisters squelching in the heat. The Tampax Tiffie/medic hurriedly waved me into the procedure room and sat me down. He looked flustered. Faced with over half of Bossies demanding his skills and a diminishing supply of Merthiolate, he was in a blind panic.

He also confided in me that he had a date with a hot local *poppie* and needed to go "now-now" because he was already ten minutes late. I expressed my sympathy, but plainly didn't give a fuck. My poor feet needed the Devil's saliva and not just now but *now-now-now*, but the medic was desperate to shorten the queue of hopping soldiers outside and begged me to help him execute a cunning plan.

"All you have to do is let out an almighty scream when I inject the Merthiolate," he said.

He was hoping that the terrified troeps would flee allowing him to close up shop and go woo young Petronella. I agreed to play along. It would be my first taste of acting since playing a tree in the nativity play at Mount Pleasant Infant School (the reviews had been mixed), I couldn't wait. If Suggsy was impressed he might recommend me to his dad (an actor) and soon I'd be treading the theatre floorboards and starring in movies. As I warmed up my vocal chords to channel De Niro, the medic gently raised my swollen, blistered foot and with a swift motion, plunged the needle straight through the blister and an inch into my flesh, discharging enough Merthiolate to cure a regiment. Within a millisecond my Oscar speech was forgotten and I realised why we'd had to write a will. The blood-curdling scream, when it finally came out, was a fitting tribute to the strength of that innocent looking red liquid. A corpse in the Kroonstad mortuary rose from the dead and went home to a startled family, the great Serengeti migration started two months early, and most of my childhood memories were wiped out as the neurons in my head smashed into each other as they attempted to escape the loudest scream since Morne Du Plessis's infamous tackle on Naas Botha.

I finally regained consciousness, the doors banged in the wind, tumbleweed rolled down the main drag and an eerie silence hung over the deserted HQ. The queue had miraculously disappeared. So had the medic.

For a week afterwards, sappers staggered around on badly blistered feet, making the cross whenever they saw me. I never did get that casting call but I heard rumours that the sadist medic had got syphilis, so it wasn't a complete disaster.

There was a bit of swearing in the army.

Now, I enjoy the occasional swear word as much as anyone as I believe it can add some flavour to most conversations. Telling somebody to "go away" doesn't have the same emotion as telling someone to "Fuck off!" In the army, you learnt to swear in every sentence. It almost became a competition.

"Excuse me old chap, would you mind passing me the tomato ketchup?" suddenly became, "Jy, *poes, fokken* pass *die kak fokken* ketchup. Dankie, jou naai."

And that was just the dominee. Again.

I was already an experienced swearer when I got there, but life in the army takes you to new heady heights of filthy language. I soon began mastering some more Afrikaans curse words. They are simply in a league of their own. Nowadays I always revert to Afrikaans when I'm angry or spill my drink, thankfully that isn't often.

The first volley of profanities aimed at them, by the corporals, shocked some swearing virgins. These well-mannered boys staggered back in confusion, barely holding back tears of anger. This descent into vulgarity was the last thing they expected while defending the civilised world from the hordes of Communist heathens. Some never recovered, but most got into the swing of it and were soon conversing in sentences that barely had a decent word in them. English and Afrikaans swear words happily co-existed in an atmosphere of mutual vulgarity.

Now that we had our shiny new rifles, we had to learn how to shoot them. I'd never fired a rifle in anger or in happiness, and due to my kak eyesight, cataracts and DT's (Drinker's Tremble), I wasn't betting on becoming a sniper. However, I still needed decent shooting marks to progress to JLs.

While I'd been using my two fingers playing 'Cops and Robbers' back in England, many of my fellow troeps had grown up hunting and had been blasting holes in unsuspecting springboks since they were in nappies. My two fingers might've been deadly accurate, but they had no recoil so I found myself at a slight disadvantage.

For all the military nerds out there (cough, Suttie, cough), here's some info on the R4 rifle:

Weight: 4.3 kg: *In an amazing feat of science, the weight increased the longer you carried the rifle. By the end of rifle PT, it could weigh up to thirteen kilograms.*

Length: 1,005 mm stock extended – 740 mm stock folded: *The rifle stock was mounted on a hinge that, when hit in the right way, folded the stock inwards – shortening the rifle. Hitting it in the wrong way resulted in gales of laughter from your maatjies, a bruised arm and a shattered ego.*

Cartridge size: 5.56×45mm:
(Terrifying what damage that little piece of metal could inflict.)

Action: Gas-operated, closed bolt.

Rate of fire: 600–750 rounds/min: *(That must have been a very big magazine.)*

Muzzle velocity: 980 m/s: *(Almost as fast as a troep running to get a second dinner serving.)*

One afternoon, they shipped us off to our shooting range, just outside Kroonstad, where we were issued with magazines filled with real bullets. To protect our dainty eardrums they also gave us earplugs and I was amazed to read on the packaging that they'd been manufactured in Stockport, my birthplace; which might have explained why the neonatal nurses hadn't heard me screaming for milk.

For the next half hour, we learned how to shoot from various positions: standing, kneeling, sitting, and prone on the ground. We also got a thorough safety drill – the last thing the corporals wanted was an accidental bloodbath. The most important instruction was that, if you had a problem, to stay in position, raise your hand and wait for assistance. Nobody was permitted to turn around with a loaded rifle, point at the corporals and pull the trigger to show that it was jammed – no matter how tempting it was. Anyone who so much as slightly turned around was kakked out, thrown off the range and also risked getting a klap from an irate, kak-scared shooting range PF.

I didn't know what to expect from my first ever shot. There was complete silence, just the wind kicking up the dust and my heavy breathing. Our first position would be lying in the prone position. We were given the signal to start shooting and I soon lined up my sights and remembering the instructions slowly but firmly pulled the trigger. Fok!!!!!! The eruption of sound was deafening and the recoil so violent that it knocked me sideways. Adrenaline flooded my body and my mind tried to take in the sheer physics of the explosion and its kick. I took a deep breath and carried on firing but this time holding the rifle butt a lot tighter to my shoulder to diminish the klap from the recoil.

Shooting from a prone position on the ground was easiest as you didn't have to hold up the full weight of the rifle. The lightweight bipod folded out, allowing the rifle to rest on the ground aiding stability and enhancing sighting accuracy. Even without the bipod, our elbows supported by the ground kept decent stability.

Next up was kneeling position, also not bad, as you propped your elbow on your knee, a position which helped with the rifle's weight and kept it fairly stable.

Standing position was the most difficult for me. Lifting it into shooting position was easy enough, but attempting to hold it steady as you lined up the sights was tricky as the weight of the barrel caused my scrawny arms to tremble. The trick was to lift the rifle above the firing position then allow gravity to slowly bring it down to eye level, set your sights quickly, and pull the trigger. If you weren't quick enough, the trembles turned into shakes, and you'd be lucky to hit a Boeing 747 air hanger door, never mind a barn door.

We also had to remember to keep the rifle in single-fire mode and not automatic. It was quite easy to knock the lever into the wrong mode, expelling a prolonged burst of fire that sent the PFs running and your nerves jangling. It happened to the troep next to me; he let off a short burst but luckily this caused his trigger finger to jerk away immediately. The PFs heard it but couldn't identify the shooter. Lucky bugger.

Apart from the different firing positions, we also had different shooting distances, starting from a hundred metres all the way up to three hundred. At the further distances, I could barely see the targets, never mind hit them.

We had a few practice shots and the PFs in charge came around to adjust our sights. As we shot, the troeps in the *skietgat* (target area), controlling the targets, tallied up our scores.

Everybody had fifty rounds of ammo, and the maximum score was 250 points. You got five for hitting the heart area, three for the torso and one point for the rest of the body. I was just pleased when I hit the target at all.

Once our group had finished shooting, it was our turn to man the targets. They lowered the red flags to indicate a break in live fire and we marched over to the *skietgat*. Not only was this my first time shooting, it was also my debut for getting shot at. We were issued with a steel helmet and a pole for pointing out the bullet holes – very hi-tech. I took my position in the long trench and waited for the go-ahead signal, at which point we raised the targets using a pulley system.

There was a brief pause, and then the high-pitched crackle of gunfire accompanied by a hail of bullets whistling overhead and thumping into the sandbank behind the targets. I ducked instinctively yet was surprised by the innocuousness of the faster-than-sound bullets.

Admittedly my ears were still ringing from the ballistic shockwaves after my turn on the trigger, but now I was on the receiving end, the volume didn't quite match up to the grim destruction those bullets could inflict. After each session, we hauled down the targets, checked the holes, tallied up the scores, and then repaired them by placing stickers over each hole. On the command, we hoisted the targets up once again and the next round of shooting commenced.

It was a long day out on the range, hot as hell in the glaring sand and lots of troeps to get through.

Finally, the last bunch finished.

We hadn't been told our score but my target seemed to have taken a few hits. It looked like I was an average shot.

I was pleasantly surprised. Maybe all those childhood 'Cowboys and Indians' games had come in useful. I blew away the imaginary gun smoke from the ends of my middle and forefinger as we hitched up our wagons and rolled across the range back to the ranch. *Yee-haa*!

Our second visit to the shooting range was a bit more serious. This time, our scores needed to be good enough to get us onto JLs. It would be touch and go. We all wanted our pals to pass and one maatjie decided to help me get a decent score. He might've taken this act of goodwill a bit far, though. He made sure he shot in the row before me, then took his position in the *skietgat*, and commandeered my target. My group got into position and started shooting. It was difficult to tell from where I was standing, but I didn't feel confident. Luckily my maatjie was pulling some major gyppo moves.

It was easy to gyppo the result; you just poked a couple of extra holes in the target with a pen when the officer wasn't looking but my well-intentioned maatjie got a bit carried away. At the hundred-metre distance I ended up with twelve bullet holes on target, pretty decent, seeing as I only had ten shots. My final score was tallied up, and it was impressive – the bloody idiot had given me such a high score that I'd be ranked as a *skerpskutter* (sharpshooter). His subtle plan had now reached the point of getting me into kak. I scored about 190/250, which put me in the top five percent. Nobody would believe that a shortsighted, skinny soutie was a potential sniper.

At the next morning parade they started announcing the troeps who'd earned their sharpshooter badges. I prepared to walk up and receive mine; ready for the astonished looks I'd receive. But my name wasn't called.

The clever buggers must've realised I'd pulled a fast one: *"Soutie was nie a skerpskutter nie"*

While initially dismayed by this lack of acknowledgement, I was also relieved that the pressure was off. Another visit to the shooting range would've soon shown me up as a fraud.

Anarchy in Bossies

As we prepared for our inspections, we'd listen to punk and ska music on Suggsy's ghetto blaster. Then, one day, with the intoxicating Brasso polish fumes giving us a bit of a high, Suggsy put on a Sex Pistols tape and upped the volume. Soon, the wild punk demons of Johnny Rotten and Sid Vicious had entered our souls and taken control of our bodies. We started moshing around the bungalow. After weeks of abuse and humiliation, we'd found our souls again; snarling and glaring manically at the rest of the bungalow, we moshed through the bungalow, jumping on beds and screaming the incendiary lyrics of 'Anarchy in the UK'.

"I am an anti-Christ! I am an anarchist!"

We pogo-ed down the aisle, getting in the faces of the rugby players, daring them to have a go. The adrenaline was high octane and all fear was gone. We were ready to attack anyone.

"Don't know what I want but I know how to get it."

"I.........I want to beeeeeeeeee anarchy, destroy! Ha ha ha!"

As the song ended we swaggered back to our section, the marker had been laid down – *"those two are fokken crazy"*. We never got bullied – we were lucky.

Lack of sleep was obviously a contributing factor to our exhaustion. With only four or five hours sleep each night, we ran on empty most of the time. During the day, our bodies demanded more sleep, so as soon as we had a break we'd be snoozing within seconds. The toughest ordeal was
staying awake in a steaming hot tent while the lecturer droned on about forward defensive positions. Our sleepy heads rolled around and dropped, like lead balloons, before snapping back up, wide-eyed and confused. The corporals often klapped us if we ended up in dreamland during lectures.

By the time we'd completed our inspections and written our letters home, we'd collapse onto our beds. Sleep was short and sometimes disturbed by the sounds of young troeps crying. I didn't blame them, I was close a few times, but after a lifetime of supporting Huddersfield Town FC I had very few tears left to shed.

Chapter Seventeen
Deadly Potatoes and the Jukskei Jollers

Despite being up shit creek without a paddle (or a canoe), a little glimmer of hope lit up our lives: Sports day. Wednesday afternoons were reserved for sports activities; a welcome respite from the corporals.

I'd always been sport mad – playing and watching. I loved being in a team and the camaraderie it instilled. Football was my first love but I also enjoyed squash, baseball, golf, running, karate, and cricket. I even got into some extreme sports like darts, pool and carpet bowls. There aren't many sports I don't like, except that one where horses are forced to prance around by posh jockeys wearing tuxedos, Dressage, I think it's called.

I'd have been happy to play all sports but we could only choose one. I'd been heavy into karate back in Cape Town and wanted to get more belts, but most of my new maatjies were football players and football was still in my blood and soul. The Beautiful game it would have to be.

1970's. Crosland Moor, Huddersfield, England.

The 'backfield', as we cleverly named it, was just an unused field at the back of our housing estate but it was our Wembley. No fancy goalposts, lines or clubhouse – just a couple of jerseys thrown down to indicate the posts.

The field had two small hills on one side that made for interesting matches, good for altitude training. The left-wingers and right fullbacks often passed out from lack of oxygen and intense cramps so we'd throw water on them and abuse them for being soft twats. Alex Ferguson would have been impressed.

At that stage, my life consisted of playing football, watching football and dreaming of football. I played football every day. Our game was only interrupted at five-to-five to watch Tom and Jerry *on the TV while I attempted to finish one of Mum's inedible cheese sandwiches. Then we returned to the backfield to defend our 23 -17 lead.*

As I hit my teens, Mum started taking me to watch the local professional team every alternative Saturday. Our home team was Huddersfield Town, the Terriers. Back in the 1920s Town was the first team to win the Football League three times in a row. Unfortunately this was the seventies and now we were shit.

Mum had no idea about the rules of football, she hardly ever watched, anyway. While Town were in the midst of a nil-nil thriller versus Hartlepool, Mum would be gossiping with her close friend, Bridget. Meanwhile, my mates and I ran around, causing trouble and fighting with the opposition fans. The glory days.

I turned fifteen about three months before emigrating, so I treated myself to a ticket to the Bradford City versus Huddersfield Town match. At Bradford. A derby match. A grudge match. My first taste of urban warfare.

It later became known as the Battle of Valley Parade.

Bradford was one of our nearest towns and therefore a deadly rival.

Huddersfield Town football ground, with some of mum's toilet paper decorating the goals.

It was bigger than Huddersfield, making us the underdogs by default. An added incentive was that it was a top-of-the-fourth-division clash: we were top of the log and they were third. Points and reputation were at stake.

It was one of my first away matches and was planned like a military operation by the main hooligans. As the day dawned, we trooped down to our football ground where fifty coaches awaited us.

Several hundred cars and train carriages crammed with Town fans were ready to depart. It would be the largest ever attendance for a fourth division match.

The fans piled onto the buses and out came the cases of beer lovingly handled and gently positioned in the aisle. Most fans were already pissed and it wasn't even midday. The bus had no toilet, so, in an impressive show of improvisation, everyone just pissed in the aisle.

Forty minutes later, we entered the outskirts of Bradford and their fans ran out of alleyways and attacked our buses

with bricks and rocks, shattering half the windows. We were covered in broken glass but luckily no beer was spilt.

We got to the drop-off point and staggered off our demolished bus to join the thousands of Town fans who were now well up for a fight. (A lot of Saffers and people from civilised countries cannot comprehend football hooliganism. In hindsight I'm glad it's mostly been eliminated in the UK, but in the seventies it was our drug. It was tribal; fear, elation, adrenaline pumping through your body - like Play Station but without the head-butts.)

Cops surrounded the frenzied crowds. I remember one cop smashing a Town fan's head into a car's front windscreen after he'd hurled a brick towards the Bradford fans. Local cops were usually fans of the local team and many would have been hooligans if they hadn't been given a uniform, whistle and a strange pointy helmet. The cops were known as the biggest, baddest gang in Yorkshire.

When we arrived at the ground, the cops herded us into a street leading to the stadium. Thousands of us were now hemmed in by terraced houses and the stadium towering up at the end of the street. It was a trap. The Bradford fans looking down from the stadium pounced; bricks, bottles and other tasty projectiles rained down on us. In the chaos I lost a shoe, while my mate had a brick glance off his head – he barely noticed.

Somehow, we scrambled through the turnstiles and scurried into the stadium then marched up to the top of the standing area and took in the sights. It was packed. The atmosphere was spine tingling, and as the decibels increased we started singing our Huddersfield anthems.

'Those were the days my friend
We thought they'd never end
We won the league three times in a row
We won the FA cup and now were going up
We are the Town
Oh yes we are the Town'

(Repeat 5 times.)

Then we swung into our version of that old classic 'Seasons in the Sun'

'We had joy. We had fun.
We had (Bradford) on the run,
But the joy didn't last
'Cos the bastards ran too fast!'

Mid-chorus, I noticed that the fans around us weren't singing along, in fact, they seemed to be glaring at us. I was just about to help them with the lyrics when I noticed they were wearing yellow and black scarves. Odd. These were the Bradford colours. Shit, we'd taken the wrong turn and ended up behind enemy lines. After a quick briefing we made a strategic retreat before the impending pincer movement caught us in its deadly grip - we ran like hell back to our section.

As the match kicked off, we turned our attention back to the football. Within twenty minutes Bradford had smashed one into the back of the net, setting off mass celebrations in their end and a rampage in ours. Play stopped as the Bradford fans scrambled over the walls and onto the pitch to get away from the persuasive kicks and punches of the Town fans. The match resumed and the opposition's battle plan went into full swing.

The first salvo came when their artillery started revving us with a hail of half-bricks, rocks and ball bearings – ripping through the Town fans to soften us up. Then just as they started running out of ammo they got innovative; using hammers that they'd snuck into the stadium, they began chipping away the concrete of the terrace steps. We were soon bombarded by so much concrete shrapnel, I was amazed there was any stadium left. Thankfully, halftime arrived. We were two-nil down, but our fans were about seventeen down. There were a lot of cracked heads.

The second-half kicked off and we got a goal back and all hell broke loose. Bradford had saved dessert till last; metal kung-fu stars and darts came flying over. Then came the piece de resistance; potatoes – not as hard as bricks but when embedded with razor blades, they could sting a bit. Our section looked like a demolition site, but now we had a load of ammo. We swiftly counter-attacked but after five minutes our ammo dwindled and a ceasefire was declared. The rest of the match was just a blur. We lost three-one, I recall, but I'd stopped caring, I just wanted to survive. But first we had to escape from behind enemy lines. The stewards let the Bradford fans out first, assuming they'd pop home for their supper and bed, ready for church the next day. Twenty minutes later, they let us out into the terraced street we'd entered through. Once the adrenaline had died down, I just wanted to get home to my mummy. My mates and I ended up at the front of our mob as we headed back to our coaches. Suddenly, out of nowhere, thousands of Bradford fans swarmed into the street to block our escape route.

We turned to run back, but faced with our own hooligans we decided that Bradford were less terrifying. Grudgingly, we advanced on them; more of a gentle jog than an advance to be honest, I wanted to live for a few more seconds.

The charge of the laaitie *brigade began.*

As we got closer I could see the anger in their eyes. At twenty metres, I could smell their hatred. At ten metres, their eyes began widening as they realised we weren't stopping. At five metres they started having second thoughts and at two metres they slammed on brakes and tried to turn around: too late, we were onto them, kicking and punching.

They'd made a basic military blunder: always allow your cornered enemy an escape route, and then nail them as they retreat in disarray. They'd given us no choice but to go through them. The hunted became the hunters as we chased them down.

Our main hooligans eventually corralled us before we spread too wide and were picked off by the roving Bradford gangs. We regrouped and headed back to what remained of our coaches. After a few final skirmishes, Bradford left us alone and we fled back to Huddersfield. I'd survived the battle of Valley Parade but not my Mum's wrath. My excuse that I'd lost my shoe whilst studying at the library fell apart after the first klap.

Kroonstad, 1987

I love sport, so coming to South Africa was brilliant. South Africans are sports fanatics and alongside religion and *braai-ing* (meat burning), sports are revered and sports stars worshipped. Serial killers will be given a hearty pat on the back if they score a try or hit a six. I'd heard of troeps who were top surfers who'd never sniffed an inspection because they were too busy hitting the lip in Hawaii - A few lips would've been hit if they'd tried that at Bossies.

In the Orange Free State there was only one true sport and it wasn't football. You could hit a golf ball four hundred metres with a putter, dribble past seventy defenders and score

a goal using your cock, but if you couldn't tackle an angry tight head weighing 140 kilos, you were nothing.

Upon arriving at Pinelands High School, in 1977, I had decided to give rugby a crack. I shyly approached the coach, who, after realising that I wasn't a dwarf, made me the scrumhalf for the practice. Having never played before, I wasn't quite prepared for my first scrum. The first part was easy: take the strangely shaped ball and hurl it into a bunch of giants but it was more complicated trying to get the ball back again. Eventually, it popped out, I grabbed it, looked around triumphantly and waited for some polite applause. A split-second later it all went dark. Once the coach had prised me out of the turf and checked that I still had a pulse I wandered off in search of the hockey pitch.

Seeing as I still had no desire to have my only body smashed into small pieces by Staal, Baksteen or Boetie, I joined the army football team.

The presidents of the various rugby provinces weren't keen on seeing their top talent poached, so they were called up to bases in their home provinces. If you from the Northern Free State, you were immediately sent to Kroonstad. Eric Herbert, the stalwart Northern Free State fly half, was a year ahead of us, while Jacques Klaven and Jan van der Walt, two big forwards, joined us in India Bungalow.

Our CO had been given strict instructions to look after the rugby players, so they travelled in a luxury coach, while us footballers were stuffed into an old Bedford truck; half of us picked up injuries just getting to the matches.

I should have sued the army for ruining my chances of playing for Real Madrid; the adoring fans in the Bernabeu would never get to witness my silky ball skills and expert diving technique.

On our first sports afternoon, we set off for the main base in Kroonstad. Once assigned our sports we headed off to our various fields of dreams. I was with Sneezer, Suggsy and a couple of others from India Bungalow and were soon joined by Pete Wainwright, Ross Peterson and some other football fanatics.

Huge Bonus. Our football coach, Captain Louis Snyman, turned out to be an ex-Clyde Pinelands player and the step-uncle of one of our best mate's; we soon reminded him about the importance of club loyalty. About forty troeps had signed up for football and many had represented their provinces. For the next two years, football would be my release valve from army life.

One sports day we got to the football pitch to find a load of rugby players hanging around. Their coach was late so they'd decided to train with us. They were keen on showing us soccer wankers a thing or two. We weren't keen. We just wanted to play some footy and not get killed by some bloodthirsty trolls.

"Right, you soccer *moffies*. We're going to show you how to play this game," said a troep, who looked like the rear end of a sewage truck after a pile-up.

"*Voetsek, jou dom doos*," I said… in my head.

After a gentle jog around the pitch, some sprints and a stretch we were ready for a re-enactment of the Boer War. The rugby lads lined up twenty metres back, ready for a drop kick to start the match; this could get interesting.

The first ten minutes consisted of us passing the ball around, trying not to be maimed. The rugby lads were fit but they weren't used to non-stop running. In rugby, there are loads of built-in rest breaks: lineouts, scrums, penalty kicks and amputations.

They were soon tiring and we started knocking in a few goals.

We had some top players in our team. Lads who'd played provincially: Sneezer, Mark Butterfield, Rudi Pahl, Pete Wainwright – plus Suggsy and me who hadn't played for our provinces but ran around yelling for a pass that never came.

As the rugby players flagged, their play became a bit cynical. They started smashing into us, kicking our shins and even the referee was scythed down with a high forearm tackle – probably deserved it. They were menacing, but after weeks of basics we were *gatvol,* so we started going in just as hard. Suddenly, my eyesight began to fail me and my normally precise tackles were suddenly missing by several inches. On one occasion, I missed by a couple of feet, resulting in my studded boot connecting at great velocity with the shinbone of one rugby player who'd given me shit. There was a sharp crunching sound, followed by a scream from my victim, who began rolling around clutching his leg and screaming out the Messiah's name. As I hurried over to assist, I accidentally ground my studs into his outstretched hand, eliciting another stream of naughty words. Although sympathetic to his pain, I had to remind him that not even Diego Maradona would have got away with that prima donna bullshit. Eventually, he limped off and glared at me from the side-lines.

When their rugby coach eventually rocked up, he saw a third of his team injured on the sidelines, ice packs attached to throbbing body parts. With the cream of his beloved rugby team crippled, he immediately banned them from practicing with us. Forever.

As they walked off, some insensitive soul called out, "Fucking rugby moffies!"

To my great delight, I discovered that Kroonstad was also the headquarters of the South African Jukskei Sports Association. Jukskei is similar to bowls, but instead of aiming your bowl at a little white ball, you put a stick in the ground and threw another stick at it. Not a sophisticated game but better than underwater basketball or boomerang rugby.

In the football off-season I got roped into playing, and bugger me gently but I was a natural. Maybe all those hours throwing bricks at Bradford City fans hadn't been a complete waste of time. The players were keen on showing the Soutie how to play and I had such great fun that I was thinking of playing regularly but after some research I found out that their top players were paid in Boerewors rolls and cases of Hansa beer; I still had dreams of multi-million rand football contracts, red Ferrari's and Anneline escorting me down the red carpet of the World Footballer of the Year awards. So I sadly gave it up and returned to the football pitch.

There weren't many football teams in Kroonstad, so we ended up in a league with teams from Welkom and Virginia. Most of them were from the gold mines in the area, plus one team from the Portuguese Club in Welkom.

At this stage of 'Apartheid' most sport was strictly segregated, but the National Party had concluded that because it was mainly blacks, coloureds and deviant souties who played football, they'd turned a blind eye to it. Every week, we'd head off to play the black teams from St. Helena Gold Mine, Harmony Gold Mine and the other mines in the area.

It was great to get out of Bossies every week and we had the added bonus of a compulsory stop at the Lantern Roadhouse in Welkom. This pseudo-Hollywood diner was run by the culinary geniuses behind the biggest and best burgers in the known world. They were the size of a small couch and just the sight of them brought us trembling to our knees, bowing and prostrating ourselves in front of the bemused staff. The burger buns were so big the roadhouse had to bake their own and you needed both hands and one knee to hold it upright. Being on the brink of starvation we'd buy three at a time: one for immediate consumption, one for the trip home, and one to feed the rest of the bungalow. It was the highlight of the week.

After arriving at the football ground, we got changed and warmed up. Most times we'd have to wait for the other team, who were often finishing their shift down the mine. Probably not the best warm up for them, crawling around in forty-degree heat, a few kilometres underground. I wonder how Messi, Ronaldo and Kane would have coped with those conditions. Or us.

Finally, our opponents assembled and the match kicked off. Because we were the army side it soon became a white vs. black; oppressor vs. oppressed; European style vs. African style match. Although there weren't too many fights, the matches were fierce and uncompromising, shin pads took a beating and elbows were in regular use. The baying crowds were fanatical and desperate for us to lose and with them gambling on the match it got pretty rowdy.

The mine teams had the flair and the *shibobo* tricks but we had the stamina and the tactics. However the mine teams had one secret weapon, which caused havoc with our game plan: chemical warfare – African style. As the crowds huddled together in the freezing Highveld nights, little plumes of *dagga* (weed) smoke rose up and soon a yellowish haze covered the pitch. It wasn't long before you couldn't even see the goalposts. The sweet smell of *wacky backy* became overwhelming and after ten minutes we were so goofed that missing an open goal made us fall around laughing.

Strangely our matches often drew massive crowds, sometimes up to two or three thousand. This amazed us as it was just a small match in a minor league, but for the miners, football was one of their only forms of entertainment and allowed them to be out of their shitty compounds for a while. By the final whistle nobody had a clue who'd won, yet we all seemed to be humming Bob Marley songs and devouring packets of Nik-Naks.

After the match, the black players headed back to their squalid ghettos while we were warmly welcomed at the whites-only sports centre and bar. So no after match chitchat about the obvious penalty we should have been awarded when I tripped over my shoelaces.

Hopefully, one day, the Oppenheimers and the other billionaire mine owners will remember to share the immense wealth extracted from the South African earth with the miners who toiled, sweated and often died to make them rich beyond their dreams – maybe they could sell a couple of their racehorses.

Chapter Eighteen
Nelly the Elephant and the dropkick

Every bungalow was ordered to come up with its own rousing song for route marches, general running around and the occasional 'standing around waiting for things to happen' session. We already had a few old classic running songs such as:

I wanna be a Texas Ranger
I wanna live a life of danger.
Texas Ranger, life of danger.
etc

As is the case with all jolly singsongs, we got sick of the same song every time we ran – where was Bles Bridges when we needed him?

I realised that this was my big opportunity to shine, especially after my recent foray into the exciting world of music as the lead shouter of the tragically misunderstood and recently disbanded punk rock band The Tommy Tits (11th place, Battle of the Bands, The Mix Nightclub, Cape Town, 1981). In collaboration with Suggsy, we set out to make India Bungalow the funkiest bungalow in Bossiespruit.

Given our complete lack of musical ability, we decided to follow in the footsteps of many famous musicians – we stole someone's song.

It had to have something to do with India, have a martial beat and a nice rhythm to run to.

We chose a little ditty called 'Nelly the Elephant' by the British punk band The Toy Dolls – a song about a *gatvol* elephant that ran off to join the circus, an Indian elephant, obviously. With our creative juices supplemented with over-diluted mango juice, modified lyrics started gushing forth and soon, we had a hit on our hands; unfortunately there weren't many major music labels based in Kroonstad so we failed to make an impression on the Top Forty. Bono breathed a sigh of relief.

Nellie the Roefie

To Bossies a travelling circus came
They brought an intelligent Roefie
and Nellie was his name
One dark night he slipped his iron chain,
and off he ran to Bossiespruit
and was never seen again

Ooooooooooooooooooo...

[Chorus:]
Nellie the Roefie packed his kas
and said goodbye to civvy street
off he marched with a trumpety trump
trump trump trump
Nellie the Roefie packed his kas
and trundled off to do basics
off he rode with a trumpety trump
trump trump trump

Night by night he danced to the army band
When Nellie was marching in the big parade

he looked so proud and grand

No more tricks for Nellie to perform
They taught him how to shoot and sew
and he took the two comma four by storm

Ooooooooooooooooooo...

[Chorus x2]
 The head of the unit was calling far far away
they met one night in the silver light
on the road to Bossiespruit
Ooooooooooooooooooo...

If only Verwoerd could've seen a squad of Christian Nationalist soldiers proudly singing along to a punk classic as we ran around Bossies. He'd have been turning in his mausoleum.

The Dropkick

The day began well enough.

The regulation screaming at our daily inspection, followed by a chilly one-minute shower and finally, some delicious boiled bacon scraps accompanied by yellow collateral damage impersonating scrambled egg. But even that couldn't wipe the smile off our little faces because it was injection day. Hooray!

We had to receive multiple vaccinations for smallpox, typhoid and yellow fever just in case we were sent to some disease-ridden country to shoot its occupants. Due to the debilitating after-effects of these little doses of deadly disease we'd been given the rest of the afternoon off. Happy days.

As our emaciated bodies shuffled along in the queue outside the medics, we chatted amiably and discussed what we'd do with a whole afternoon off. Sleep was the number one choice, it was also choice number two, three and four. Somebody mentioned a game of football but was immediately re-educated with a resounding klap around the ear.

With six hundred arms to inject, the medics didn't have much time to reassure us or answer questions.

Jab, jab, jab.

Eina fok.

Off you go, *roef.*

Being a skinny bastard, the drugs whizzed through my veins, leaving me zonked within seconds.

As I marched back to the bungalow, looking forward to some extreme *balles bakking,* Corporal Scowler started screaming at me; in my drug induced haze I'd forgotten to *strek* him as I passed him – he went *befok.* And to make matters worse, with my sleeve rolled up for the injections, he spotted my usually well-hidden England tattoo. The Third Boer War kicked off. Scowler laid into me about being a lazy soutpiel who should fuck off back to England, telling me I was a useless piece of English shit who should never have been allowed into their army. He dragged out every insult he could remember, ending his tirade by telling me to *voetsek.* Half the camp witnessed it.

After all the insults and humiliations of the past month, that was the final slap in the face. Basics were tough enough without having my heritage insulted. I was the *poes-in.* I marched back to our bungalow, kicked the door open and stomped in. The red mist descended. I cursed Scowler, the army, Groot Krokodil, Manchester United and the World.

I got to my bunk, took a run-up and drop kicked my helmet towards the wall. Naas Botha would've been proud.

Naas: "Here at Bossies full time is nearly up. Province is two points behind but still in possession, they are setting up for a drop kick. Six phases now and they are on the twenty-two line. Soutie is screaming for it. Can they get it out of the maul? Here it comes. He takes it cleanly and lines it up. He kicks. It looks good, it's got the distance. Has it got the height? Yes it has, maybe too much height. It's missed the wall and shattered the window. Soutie is in big kak. And now back to the studio."

Oh my *fok*, what had I done? The troeps who had the misfortune of sitting under my window, were showered with broken glass. I looked at the damage and they stared back at me with a combination of shock, anger and sympathy. A shit-storm was about to hit India Bungalow, and I was in the eye of the storm. This meant an *opvok*, a big *opvok*. I'd seen enough already to know that this was deadly serious; a combination of fear, anger and survival instinct kicked in. Being so deep in the shit already, I went *Full Metal Jacket* crazy. Moose had always said that if you're in the kak, act crazy; "They can't deal with *mal*."

Within seconds I'd devised a cunning plan but it was a massive gamble that might see me end up in detention barracks for some time.

I psyched myself up and stormed off towards our HQ where all the CO's and Major Rabid were stationed. By the time I got there I'd built up a nice head of steam. I went screaming in, *bosbefok* style.

"Waar die fok is die Major? You fucking bastards!" I screamed to no one in particular.

Adrenaline pumped through my body. I started barging into offices, shocked faces staring back at me.

"*Waar die fok is die Major?*" I demanded, with manic eyes and my tiny fists clenched. So far, so good. They'd dreaded this moment; a crazy troep on the warpath. Doors were swiftly locked and the civvies made a quick exit.

I was half-crazy and half in control. I knew what I was doing and I'd stored up enough anger, frustration and hatred that the anger was real - red mist but with a peephole.

"You force me to come here, then insult me for being British. Fuck you. If you don't want me here, I'll fuck off home!" I shouted.

Luckily Major Rabid wasn't there because I have no idea what would have happened then. I also hadn't taken my rifle on my little tantrum or that would've been another ball game altogether – with my balls being firmly in the crosshairs. I eventually ran out of steam, and rooms to barge into. Realising that Major Rabid wasn't there and that my rant had created the desired effect, I marched off, swearing and gesticulating. Once I got back to the bungalow I was met with shocked silence and some concern from my mates.

"You okay?" asked Suggsy.

"Couldn't be better," I replied.

"You seem to be missing a window," Suggsy pointed out.

"Ah yes, it was getting in the way of my view of Kilimanjaro so it had to go."

The 'crazy' was only slowly wearing off.

I sat on my bunk and faced the imminent collapse of my blossoming military career. I was either going to receive a visit from military police, who'd march me off to detention barracks or the corporals would try and hush it up to save their own skins. I'd always been told that the one thing the officers were scared of were troeps going *mal*. It didn't look good on their CVs.

Finally, I heard the corporals arriving.

"*Kaserne, kaserne aandag*!" the Bungalow Bill yelled out.

We stood to attention and Bumfluff and Scowler walked slowly through the bungalow and up to me. Scowler looked me up and down before glancing over my shoulder at the glinting remnants of glass still clinging to the window frame. His hatred for me embedded in his face.

This is it, I thought as scenes from *Midnight Express*, *Papillon* and *The Hill* played through my mind. I was shaking with fear, my mouth as dry as a Karoo Alcoholics Anonymous meeting, my stomach twisted in knots.

He glared at me for what seemed like an hour before slowly moving on.

He's savouring my fear, toying with me. I thought. The bastard.

What's he got planned for me?

When will the kak hit the fan?

"*Tree-aan buite*!" Scowler yelled.

The next second we were all running over to the lecture tents for a couple of hours on 'holding defensive positions and the art of bridge building'- exciting subjects but my concentration was more on the art of escaping from prison.

I waited for the Military Police to arrive and the others looked at me like I was a dead man walking. The following hours were torment.

If you've seen any poor soul return from DB, you knew it was a scary place to be sent. Happy-go-lucky troeps came back like lobotomised zombies. Every spark of humanity crushed until only a fragile shell of a human remained. It was a torture camp. Not a place you wanted to end up.

Finally we were sent back to our bungalow and I fearfully shuffled to my cubicle. As I turned the corner I looked up and saw a shiny new window, miraculously, the glass had been replaced. Santa Claus had come to Crown Town and the gamble had paid off – I was off the hook. The powers that be, had decided to sweep this incident, and the broken glass, under the carpet. Troops going *bosbefok* before they were in the *bos* were a bit of an embarrassment. I'd never been so scared in all my life, but I'd survived to fight again.

Chapter Nineteen
Three Wise Men and an Astrophysicist

Hallelujah! We were finally getting out of Kroonstad – for the day.

It was the annual Engineer Corps Sports Day in the optimistically named town of Bethlehem – the base for 2 Field Engineers Regiment, whose troeps would probably end up minesweeping on the border. A day away from the dreaded routine of basic training, a real treat. I was on the football team so we'd be up against their best side. We were well up for it.

After a quick brekky, we piled onto a fleet of Bedford trucks and headed down the R76 road to the Eastern Free State. Within ten minutes, everybody was fast asleep - evidently four hours of sleep a night wasn't sufficient.

When we trundled into Bethlehem I was bitterly disappointed. The only Jesus we could find threw us out of his shop for squeezing his avo's, the innkeeper was passed out on the stoep, Marietje hadn't been a virgin for quite a while and the Three Wise Men had been mistaken for Indians and booted out of the Free State for overstaying their twenty-four hour legal limit. But at least we weren't in Bossies.

One man desperately waiting for sports day was our Regimental Sergeant Major (RSM). He was a fanatical *toutrekker* ('tug of war enthusiast').

In fact, he was so desperate to regain the *toutrek* crown off his nemesis, one of the NCOs at Bethlehem, that he held trials for the team.

I'd have happily helped him achieve his dream but my dainty British hands weren't designed for pulling a thick, frayed, dirty rope. It soon became abundantly clear that my talents lay elsewhere.

"Maybe in sewing class," our RSM bellowed as I skulked off.

Harsh but fair.

Clearly, the RSM was possessed. He eventually assembled his crack team of rope warriors and they began intense practises: lifting weights, rope pulling techniques and bulking up. I think they got some extra boiled bacon as well.

The team was anchored by the heaviest troep in the camp, Baobab, the bastard we'd been pulling, pushing and rolling around the 2,4 km route everyday for the past two months. Every mealtime I kept an eye on him to make sure the RSM wasn't fattening him up; if we had to keep pushing the bugger around, I wanted him to slim down or at least allow us a share of any *toutrek* triumph.

On arrival in Bethlehem, we decided to take in the sights; which took about ten seconds. Moments later, we found ourselves being extorted by a local 'Dankie Tannie' who ran the camp tuck shop. We were soon gorging ourselves on boerie rolls, vetkoek, hamburgers and NikNaks; the diet of champions. After wiping the vetkoek stains off my face and the yellow MSG off my fingers I changed for our match.

It was a brutal affair and one of our players got kicked before the match had even started – not very sporting, especially as it was by their referee.

Our opponents set up in a 4-4-2 formation with the intention of luring us into a false sense of security. Within seconds of the kick off it became clear their only strategy was to cripple us; half of the team were soon writhing on the pitch clutching bloody shins, bruised ankles and freshly squeezed testicles. We screamed at the ref to stop the foul play but he was so busy applauding that he didn't hear us. Luckily, we had a couple of hard nuts of our own and it soon became a bloodbath. Celtic versus Rangers looked like a pensioners' croquet match in comparison. As a devout coward, I made sure I played very wide on the left wing; so wide that the linesman thought I'd been sent to relieve him. He even handed me the flag and buggered off. After that, we started getting a few decisions, although my teammates were a bit pissed off when I flagged up one blatant offside goal – especially as I'd crossed it. Rules are rules, though.

With half the players limping or nursing cracked ribs and black eyes, the match turned into a fight for survival rather than a goal fest. It finished in a goalless draw and the walking wounded staggered off to desultory applause.

The main event of the day was the rugby match and the stands were soon filled with troeps from both camps, baying for blood. Even I was screaming my nicotine-filled lungs out. With a team stocked full of Northern Free State players, we overcame some brave resistance and triumphed over Bethlehem. "In victory, magnanimity" Winston Churchill famously said, so we magnanimously booed the losers off.

Sitting in the stands surrounded by my fellow troeps, I felt the first stirring of pride in being part of the Genieskool battalion – I'd better be careful.

The finale for the day was the tug of war. The two rival coaches gathered their teams for a quick pep talk before sending them into battle. We watched as Baobab took his position as anchor, the rope wrapped snugly around his vast waist, while the others took up their positions in the line.

The teams bent down to take up the slack and the rope went taut. Once the referee was happy with the set-up, he signalled for them to start and sixteen bodies took up the strain and started pulling. It was brilliant. Both teams heaved and swayed as if to an ancient rhythm. Their boots dug into the ground, carving wounds in the dark earth. Evenly matched in all respects, neither side was making ground. This would be a test of stamina, not strength.

The coaches went crazy; screaming at their teams, urging them to hang on. Sinews stretched, sweat poured and teeth gritted. Nobody wanted to let the coach down. Up in the stands, we shouted encouragement and threats; a bit of carrot and stick psychology, or in this case, *biltong* and *poesklap*. We were desperate. A pissed-off RSM might be detrimental to our health.

After ten tense minutes it was one-all and they started the third and final pull. Both teams were exhausted. This would be close. As the decider began, the coaches, having run out of swear words, were reduced to encouraging grunts and threatening sign language. One year of bragging rights was on the line. Five minutes in and it was a stalemate – both teams on the verge of collapse. Baobab, who'd aged five years and lost about five kilograms, was turning cross-eyed as he hung on desperately. This would probably determine his military future; victory would send him straight onto JLs but defeat would send him straight to the scrap heap.

What Baobab lacked in technique he made up for in flab. They just couldn't shift him. He was deadweight. Inch by inch, we pulled Bethlehem towards the finish line. Their coach was going *befok*, spluttering incoherently as he promised them all kinds of rewards and punishments.

The promise of his Theresa magazine collection spurred them on for a moment, but it wasn't enough. With Baobab unmoveable, the opposition ran out of steam and with one final pull, Bethlehem collapsed into the dirt and the win was ours.

Cue joyous celebrations and massive relief.

A couple of fanatics attempted to lift Baobab on their shoulders. It didn't end well. Our medics were soon busy treating a few hernias.

We loaded up the trucks, and, guided by the light of a strange celestial star, we headed home.

Gert was the oldest troep in the bungalow at twenty-eight years of age. He was a nuclear astrophysicist; you could tell by the size of his spectacle lenses. They were so thick the frames needed steel reinforcing to support them. Sometimes he'd let us look through them so we could find new moons around Saturn. He could've filleted an amoeba with those things. Unsurprisingly, he wasn't a great athlete.

One day, he received a letter from his old varsity, Potchefstroom, requesting that he deliver a speech at the World Conference of Nuclear Astrophysics being held in Moscow.

For three years prior to the army he'd been leading an international team on a massive project and they'd requested him as their spokesman.

It would be the highlight of his career, his shining moment, and a time to bask in the glow of the world's intelligentsia. All he had to do was request leave – in the middle of basics – to give a speech in Moscow – the capital of heathen Commie Russia – our mortal enemy.

This could get interesting.

Headquarters:

Major Rabid (*Face getting red*) and Gert (*Face going pale*)

"So you want to go on leave?"

"Ja, Major."

"In the middle of basic training?" (The *moer-in*).

"Ja, Major."

"To Russia?" (The *poes-in*).

"Ja, Major."

"To discuss nuclear kak?" (*Blood pressure up to 180/120 mm Hg. Heart attack zone*).

"Ja, Major."

"Do you know who we is fighting against in this fokken war we is training you for?" (*Dizziness; eyes bulging; chest pain*)

"Nee, Major."

"Dis die fokken Commie Russian bastards and you want to go and tell them all about our nuclear kak. I should be hanging you for treason, you fokken bliksem."

"Jammer, Major."

"Why should I let you sell our volk out and destroy our nation?"

"Because I have a personally-signed letter from the Minister of Defence ordering you to let me go."

"Right, where do I sign?"

A week after Gert came back from the conference I found him throwing buckets of rotting vegetables to the camp's massive pig (no, not Major Rabid) and asked him how the conference had gone. He nervously plucked out some photos and showed me. There he was, at the podium in the historic, gigantic and ornate Lenin Hall, in the footsteps of some of the greatest scientists history has ever witnessed. In the audience, ten thousand ears attached to some very clever heads listened to his every word. Gert looked at the photo sadly. For a moment wishing he was still there, before hurling some more stinking slops into the trough. Well, at least the pigs were happy he was back.

During basics, we got our first taste of guard duty. It was a novelty. We were enthusiastic. It soon wore off.

After a blood and gore speech about what the terrorists would do if they caught us, the corporals put us into pairs to guard the camp. Suggsy and I were paired up. Well, at least now we'd get our itchy militaristic fingers on the trigger of a gun, I thought.

"What gun will we be given, Corporal?" I enquired.

"It's not a fokken gun! This is a gun!" Corporal Scowler screamed as he grabbed his crotch and squeezed his genitals.

Brilliant, we'd be defending our base armed with a pair of hairy Afrikaans testicles. Scowler stomped off, unlocked a metal rifle locker and slowly turned around holding two gleaming metallic...whistles.

"What the fuck are those? Miniature hand grenades?" Suggsy chirped.

"*Fok jou, soutie*. These is high-powered whistles, designed to scare off terrorists and alert the rest of the camp in case of an attack," Scowler tuned

"So if we whistle really hard, will the piercing sound waves rip the limbs off the terrorists and save us from being shot to death?" Suggsy continued.

"One more word from you, soutie..."
We took the whistles and marched off sarcastically.

South Africa is known as one of the best stargazing spots in the world. Bossiespruit was no exception.

"No clouds, no lights, flat terrain and a high altitude, " Suggsy explained to me as he wandered off into the veld.

"It's also fucking dark and there could be some angry people out there trying to kill us," I mentioned to his rapidly departing back.

Compared to Suggsy, I was Captain Paraat. This was our first experience defending the 'civilised world'.

We moved away from the camp to our designated patrol route and it got even darker. I couldn't even see my trembling hand in front of my face. We then stumbled around for the next two hours, hoping not to disturb anyone.

It is amazing how your hearing improves when you can't see anything. A gust of wind became a battalion of orcs, the scurrying of a disturbed lizard was an attacker and one of Suggsy's long farts was like automatic fire – I hit the ground hard, Suggsy laughed and a jittery lizard fled the scene.

"This isn't funny," I whispered sharply.

Two hours later, we finished our patrol, and I went to change my underwear.

A week later I ended up doing a shift in the tiny guardhouse at the main entrance to Bossies. It was late at night and the only light to be seen on the veld came from my little sanctuary. I was ordered not to leave my hovel unless a vehicle approached. There weren't many social visitors at that time of night so I was stuck in there.

Having the only light in the area meant every local beetle, bug and flying ant headed over for a party. It was a miniature Jurassic Park featuring the most evil-looking insects you could imagine.

Millions of them were soon bouncing off the walls and trying to access the VIP space around the solitary light. They were going *mal*, either trying to *pomp*, eat or commit suicide – it was like payday in Welkom.

The only way to escape the incessant attacks of the bugs was to constantly blow tobacco smoke at them. After years of sticking to a pack a day I became a twenty-an-hour smoker. In my noble efforts to save the world from the evils of Communism I probably knocked ten years off my life. I still reach for a smoke when a flying bug invades my space.

Bugs 1 - Humans 0

Across the road from Bossies was *Die Magasyn*. It took me a while to realise that this wasn't the headquarters of *Scope* or *Huisgenoot* magazines but a high security compound where our explosives were stored. (A pity, because I'd have willingly given up my life to defend those high-quality publications.)

Realising that a few tons of high explosives blowing up might be detrimental to our health, they were stored in an underground bunker. To defend this strategically important site, they sent in Bossies' bravest soldiers then once their shift finished, Slab and I shuffled over.

We'd already done enough guard duty to become *slaapgat* (lazy), so our *paraatness* was down to level two (level three, was not giving a fuck). As I extinguished my cigarette on the 'Explosives: Strictly No Smoking' sign, I heard a sharp crack overhead. I told Slab to stop fucking around and tried to get back to sleep. A few minutes later, another sharp crack interrupted my erotic dream of Anneline dancing for me in a skin-tight Voortrekker dress.

Now I was really annoyed but Slab vehemently denied any involvement. Mid-argument, another crack ripped through the air.

Shocked, we looked at each other; surely not. Fuck! We were being attacked. This was it – our first contact; with the exception of the ripe guava incident on the train up here, of course.

What to do?

This time we'd been issued with rifles but no bullets. Admittedly, this was an improvement on the whistles but try producing a shrill whistle sound by blowing down the barrel of an R4, not easy. Our radio communications was twenty metres away in the guard hut but that stood directly in the line of fire. I suggested that Slab, being a short shit, should be the one to crawl over and radio the base – he suggested that I should get fucked. After a few minutes of self-preservation, we both leopard-crawled over to the hut. Once safely inside, we called the guardroom. No answer – *Dallas* must be on TV.

"Try again!" I screamed.

Nothing.

We were in the middle of World War Three and the arsehole corporal was asleep.

We continued calling frantically until, after what seemed like a lifetime, somebody picked up.

"Ja?"

"We are being attacked," I screamed.

"Afrikaans, asseblief," he replied nonchalantly.

"Ons word aangeval!" Slab repeated.

The line went silent, except for what sounded like sniggering in the background.

"We need some backup!" I demanded.

We were in the middle of nowhere with bullets zipping over our heads. I was extremely *gevaared*.

"*Ja, wag 'n bietjie*," said our only lifeline to survival.

We *wagged* for more than a *bietjie*.

The shots stopped. About an hour later, two corporals dropped off the next guard shift and drove us back to the safety of Bossies. The driver sniggered all the way back. It dawned on me that the shots might have been fired from our own camp, by our own corporals. The *naaiers*.

Was I the only one taking this war seriously?

For the rest of basics we stood guard at least once a week. We also had to stand guard at one of the old training camps called Vegkop. This was an old nunnery that had been converted into a training centre for basics and the officer's course. It had been closed down a few years before I'd arrived. It was a spooky Victorian building with spires, towers, hidden rooms and dusty basements. Because it was still army property we had to guard it. During the day it was a cool gig, we'd be away from Bossies and the mayhem but at night it was a different story – the ghosts of Vegkop came out to play or at least that was the rumour. The corporals had mentioned that for years the spirits of dead nuns wandered the halls and corridors. I had no intention of making their acquaintance but my fellow guard Suggsy decided he wanted to explore.

It was dark and the wind had picked up just enough that anything that could creak, creaked. We'd been expressly forbidden to go into the building so in we went. We'd been issued with a torch to look for terrorists but Suggsy was using it to find hidden treasure. He'd heard a rumour that the nuns had hidden some valuable artefacts in the convent.

"What kind of treasure would a bunch of frugal, poverty-seeking nuns hide?" I enquired.

"Gold" he replied, lifting a mouldy mattress off the floor and shining the torch under it.

"Don't you think all the troeps who've been here would have found it by now," I mentioned as I looked in some cupboards. I might be cynical but I'd look pretty stupid if I missed a pile of gold bullion hidden under a pillow.

"Ja, but maybe they hid it as well," Suggsy tuned me.

"Why the fuck would everybody hide the gold again instead of cashing it in? I shouted.

He wasn't listening anymore in fact he wasn't there anymore. The idiot had suddenly disappeared, pitching me into the dark. Immediately my senses, including my sixth, went into overdrive; had he been killed by a nun ghost; spirited away by malignant spirits from another world; teleported to another dimension? I couldn't see a thing. I panicked and ran towards where I thought the door was. My shin met an iron bed, my scream caused a storm of bats to panic and my foot slammed through a rotten floorboard. I was stuck, waiting to feel the bony death grip of a ghostly Mother Superior's hands around my throat. Just as my heart was ready to explode the Suggsy strolled back in and told me to stop messing about, as I'd wake the dead. I tried to throw the bed at him but it was too heavy.

We never found that gold but if you're ever up near Vegkop go and have a look. Just don't do it at night.

Chapter Twenty
Marching to a Different Beat

Marching has always been a big part of military training and history. Who could ever forget those death-defying marches at the Somme, Delville Wood and Gallipoli, where generals thought that marching their troeps into a hail of bullets would somehow win the battle? Unfortunately a speeding bullet doesn't appreciate or even understand heroism. It only understands Newton's first law of motion.

Every object will remain at rest or in uniform motion in a straight line unless compelled to change its state by the action of an external force.

The external force being an oncoming soldier; who'd been too busy to read the terms and conditions regarding 'Dying for King and Country'.

Marching into bullets was not a great tactic; it meant death, injury and almost certain defeat. Regrettably, the upper class generals had thousands of innocent, patriotic kids to sacrifice and so kept repeating the strategy until they finally realised it wasn't working. By that time, the muddy fields of Europe were full of bloody corpses including my great uncle. The generals were shocked and saddened; some even spilled their red wine and had trouble finishing their *foie gras*. Fortunately by the time I joined the army, marching had progressed from a ritual sacrifice to a system of instilling discipline and synchronisation.

My first attempt at this ancient military art got off to a poor start. I was keen to strut my stuff but I couldn't understand the Afrikaans orders that the corporal screamed at us. I asked the Dutchie next to me to translate, but he just stared back at me in fear, he also couldn't understand a *bleddy* word – the army had invented a whole new army language; *Weermag Taal.* JRR Tolkien would've been pretty impressed because it sounded like something Sauron would've yelled at his Orcish armies.

Weermag Taal was a combination of grunts, expletives, shrieks and barks. Its main ingredient was Afrikaans with a sprinkling of single-syllable English words; none of which resembled anything you'd heard before in normal conversation. The corporals grunted out the orders. I think they'd practiced by placing golf balls in their mouths and speaking Swahili. If the Dutchies couldn't understand the orders, what chance did a linguistic barbarian like me have?

Since I couldn't rely on my fellow troeps and YouTube hadn't been invented, I knitted my brow and tried the old concentration trick. Though it took a while to grasp what the hell they were saying, I started getting the hang of it.

"Unk" was *links; which* means left.

"Ex" was *regs;* which means right.

"Furry Ass" was *Voorwarts mars* which means "forward march". At first I thought the corporal was insulting one of our hairier troeps, but it wasn't the case.

Hut normally meant something like a shed, but in the army it just meant run or stand to attention.

Omkeer meant we were going the wrong way and had to turn around by doing some fancy footwork that would've impressed Michael Jackson.

I also added in a few of my own touches, such as an occasional sexy swing of the hips, but it didn't catch on.

It was absolute chaos on the parade ground. Some troeps marched left, others went right, and some of us just stood still and whimpered. All over the parade ground, troeps marched into each other. Some even went off in their own direction and began merging with troeps from other units. Even the corporals were struggling with the format; this was their first time trying to march a bunch of non-co-ords around.

Once the units got going, it was difficult to stop them or turn them around. The parade ground was large but with ten out-of-control units each marching to its own beat, disaster wasn't far off. It was like super-tanker dodgems.

After a few near misses, our unit ended up marching straight through another unit. Next thing I knew, Suggsy, who'd been on my right, had been replaced by a troep I'd never seen before. We exchanged confused glances before I noticed that, instead of Bumfluff screaming at us, it was Corporal Psycho from Golf Bungalow – I'd ended up in his unit. Shit, he was even worse than Bumfluff. I needed to get back to the more refined brutality of Bumfluff; easier said than done. By now, my newly adopted unit had marched off across the parade ground and was practising the slow march – typically performed at funerals. Was Psycho trying to tell me something?

As another unit stuttered past, I jumped ship and joined them. They were in such disarray that nobody even noticed their new stowaway. Just as I was losing hope of ever seeing my *maatjies* again, I spotted the unmistakable swagger of Suggsy in the distance; stiff arms swinging, eyes forward, a proud smile on his cherubic face and completely out of step. As they got to within thirty metres of me, I swiftly calculated the trajectory and speed required, then peeled off from my temporary unit. There's nothing quite so conspicuous and vulnerable as a solitary troep marching on his own on a massive parade ground. I'd never moved so quickly in my life; I looked like Benny Hill on ecstasy, being chased by one of the buxom blondes he'd regularly get into trouble with. Fortunately, Bumfluff was on the other side of the unit and didn't see my undignified docking back into India unit. I aimed straight for Suggsy, who quickly made space for me to re-join.

"Where the fuck have you been?" He whispered sharply.

"I was mingling." I explained.

After another half-hour of the worst marching ever seen at Bossies, they called it a day. Corporals wept softly as they realised how much time they'd have to spend getting us idiots into shape. Their dreams of going home for weekends had been dashed. They'd take it out on us later.

If the Big Crocodile had been watching, he'd have quickly raised the white flag, surrendered to the nearest newspaper vendor and fled to Paraguay.

Baby steps. Our early attempt at marching. Not an inspiring sight.

Marching became a daily routine and using a combination of threats, incentives and the occasional English words, the corporals made sure we started getting the hang of it. We were still kak, of course, but our kakness tended to go in the right direction...most of the time.

A well-drilled, synchronised marching unit is a wonderful sight to behold. Legs and arms swinging in perfect unison, turns and U-turns delivered with finesse, and the solid *thud* of sixty-four boots hitting the ground at the same time when we halted – or in our case, sixty-three – I hadn't quite gotten the hang of it. Somehow, I would lose my rhythm halfway and never get it back. A lot of our unit did, to be quite honest, but I made it my signature move. After some intricate manoeuvres the corporal would finally order us to halt.

This was akin to the final sentence at the end of a great novel, the dismount on the high bar, the timing of a Joe Parker punch line; it had to be perfect. As the corporal bellowed the command, we clenched our buttocks in unison, breathed in deeply, and with a focus usually reserved for potting the black ball, counted down before slamming our right boots into the ground with a satisfying crunch. Half a second later, my boot would come down, creating a little echo. The corporals went befok. They thought I was doing it on purpose and took it personally. We had to act quickly. There was talk of transferring me to another unit but nobody would have me. Eventually, with a combination of me getting a bit quicker on my stamp and the rest adding a small delay to theirs, we got it right. I bet the Duke of York never had these problems.

Once all the units were up to a decent standard, they decided it was time for the top brass to watch us perform. This meant full-dress parade and no fuck ups, or Major Rabid and the rest of the rank would have some explaining to do.

The night before the big parade we made sure all our step-out kit was in perfect condition. Our posh belt, with its Engineer colours and fancy buckle featuring our insignia, was brought out for the show, and the white putties that wrapped around the top of the boots were scrubbed clean. We even had cravats – just in case we spilled our Moët & Chandon as we performed an about-turn.

India Bungalow had always been pretty crap at marching, but on the big stage, there'd be no place to hide. Each bungalow had to show off its marching skills for about seven minutes, while the top brass did the judging.

The corporals and Looty Beetge were kakking bricks: a bunch of invalids, asthmatics and arrogant rugby players didn't make for a great marching combo – we were odds-on favourites to finish last.

The competition began, and we sat on the side, watching the others units strut their stuff. After a month of practice, most had improved dramatically. This time, there was no chance of units crashing into one another as it was one unit at a time – leaving only the sound of clear commands, boots slamming in unison, and a few 'oohs' when somebody went out of sync, dropped a rifle or screwed up a command. When our turn came, we *tree-aaned* and marched to the centre of the parade ground. No hiding now. Every wrong move, every misstep would be clear for all to see. Our mouths were dry, our crotches weren't.

"Voorwarts mars!" sent us off in a blur of sharp turns, marching on the spot, slow marches and presenting of arms. I was amazed; we'd become a synchronised, well-oiled machine. After what seemed like hours, we came to the finale. I was in the zone, my movements in sync, and my steps on the mark. The final command to 'halt' saw us

thudding to an immaculate stop. The unit waited for my little echo to crash the party – but it never came. We turned as one and saluted the massed ranks. I'd nailed it. We'd nailed it. How the hell did that happen? Fear turned into jubilation. Our hearts that had been firmly in our mouths, slowly descended back to their normal positions, and we caught our breath again. Hotel was last to perform and put in an average display. Then they announced the winners: India Bungalow. Bloody hell – I wish I'd put twenty rands on us.

With all the G3K3s being in India Bungalow we'd always been the butt of the jokes. According to the local wits, we should've been passing out from the heat, having heart attacks and violent bouts of asthma. Instead, our clinical performance earned us a lot of respect that day, which, of course, we basked in.

Due to all the marching and keeping my back ramrod straight, my posture radically changed – my natural Northern English slouch disappeared, and I now stood about four inches taller than before; I felt as if I was in somebody else's body. When I got back home on my first long pass I found myself looking down on mates who'd always been taller than me. I didn't even recognise some of them as they all seemed to have shrunk. They were a bit pissed-off but at least it got me out of buying a few rounds.

Loose Forwards

About two months into basics our rugby team headed off to a big tournament in Welkom – the hometown of Jan and Jacques, India Bungalows two rugby stars. Afterwards, they snuck off and spent the night at home, but got caught sneaking back into Bossies early the next morning.

The golden boys of our bungalow, the best rugby *ouens* in the Northern Free State, were hauled before Major Rabid. We expected them to get a mild kakking out, but no such luck – this was Bossies – they'd be getting *opvokked*. Already fit from rugby and army training they were in peak condition and not too concerned about a little extra bullshit. The next evening, they began their ordeal.

The *opvok* started with the normal exercises: carrying poles, carrying each other, leopard-crawling through mud, etc. Then they had ten minutes to get cleaned up, iron their kit, and *tree-aan* again. It soon became obvious that they wouldn't make it without our help, so as they collapsed onto their beds covered in dirt and sweat, the rest of the bungalow got to work. Some cleaned and polished their boots, others ironed their uniforms or smuggled food out for them to gobble down before being dragged out again. This carried on all night for three nights and each time they crawled back in there'd be a team of us to clean and feed them. India Bungalow stood together. It was heartening to witness such solidarity.

By the end of their punishment, our blue-eyed boys were like anorexic zombies on heroin; their once-mischievous eyes glazed over.

Jo'burg jolling

After two long months of basics we received our first weekend pass; a sweet taste of freedom. Of course, the corporals used it to blackmail us into all kinds of outrageous humiliations. We didn't care.

Cape Town was too far away, so Suggsy invited me to stay with him and his family in Jo'burg.

On the Friday afternoon they let us out. It felt weird. Two months of constantly being ordered around meant that we'd lost our ability to make decisions. We'd become institutionalised.

We piled into the back of a bakkie that belonged to a laaitie we had bummed a lift off. He took us as far as Heidelberg and then we hitched the rest of the way to Jo'burg. Suggsy lived in the deep south with his dad, Paul Ditchfield; an actor and TV presenter as well as the lead singer of The Bats, a famous band from the sixties and seventies. It was eye-opening to stay at Suggsy's place; his dad's friends were all actors, musicians and writers. That weekend, the house was full of visitors; laughter and raucous conversations rang out into the small hours. It was a relief to be surrounded by decent, fun-loving, normal folks. Nobody shouted at me. I loved it.

Even though we'd only been in the army for two months, it already felt like a lifetime. Small talk was difficult, as we had little conversation to offer other than our recent army experience; which nobody wanted to hear about. We were the new outcasts.

After a relaxing weekend, we began our journey back to Bossies. We were first dropped off at Doornkop Army Base on the outskirts of Soweto. It was early evening, and the haze of burning fires drifted over us. It was my first sight of the famous township, the beating heart of the ANC and home to the Freedom Charter. This was where, on June 16, 1976, the Soweto Uprising erupted; twenty-one people were shot by the police that day, an event that served as the catalyst for the ANC's launch of the armed struggle. It was nerve-racking being there, and there were no cheery goodbyes from the good folks of Soweto as the Bedford trucks carried us down the N1, back to Bossies.

Telling my Easter joke at Suggsy's place. I think this might have been on our only pass during basics.

On another pass up to Jo'burg, Suggsy and I attended the wedding of his dad and Judy. We wore our step-out uniform and looked fit, tanned and, dare I say it, almost handsome. We received many admiring glances from the ladies, and even some of the men – it was a theatre crowd, after all.

This brief performance as normal human beings was soon swept away once we arrived back at Bossies, where we were soon reminded of our grim lot in life. Civilisation seemed far away, especially when nature called deep in the bush and there wasn't a clean porcelain loo to park our dainty bottoms on. We didn't even have the dignity of kakking in the mielies.

The Fifteen Steps of Kakking in die Bos.

Step 1
Eat army food.

Step 2

Go out into the bush for a rondvok or a gentle 14 km route march with full kit.

Step 3

Feel the bubbling in your bowels.

(Some guys didn't go to the toilet for days. Some could hold it in until their next pass; my bowels weren't so disciplined.)

Step 4

Scrounge some toilet paper from the only troep who realised that it might be needed; this might require some persuasion, usually in the form of money or repeated begging.

Step 5

Ask the corporal if you can have a kak.

Step 6

Wipe his spittle off your face and beg the corporal to go for a kak.

Step 7

Ask the other corporal.

Step 8

Realise there are no 'mielies to gaan kak in.' Sneak off.

Step 9

Find a tree, big bush or large rock (no, not a Northern Free State prop forward) to lean against.

Step 10
Scout the surrounding area for snakes, tarantulas, scorpions, and corporals.

Step 11
Gently disrobe from your overall; place doibie nearby, lean up against tree, bush or rock. Bend your knees, forming your body into an h-shape. Allow your bum to float in such a way that you don't kak in your overalls, as that was frowned upon and destroyed the morale of nearby troeps.

Step 12
Breathe deeply. Appreciate the beauty of your surroundings, listen to the music of the veld as the cicadas sing and the wind whistles between your butt cheeks.
Squeeze your eyes, puff out your cheeks and push.

Step 13
Have a kak.

Step 14
Hope you have enough toilet paper for a happy ending.

From early on, the Legend of One Sheet ran through the camp. After a kak you take one sheet of toilet paper, fold it twice, and tear one corner off – creating a hole in the middle. Put your finger through the hole and stuck it up your bum. Wriggle it around to collect your poo, extract and clean your finger with the sheet. Then use the torn-off corner piece to clean under your fingernail.

The final step was to sneak back into your unit and remember not to high-five anyone.

With a few weeks left of basics, Pete and the rest of Golf Bungalow mutinied. Corporal Psycho and their Looty, had given them so many *opvoks* and injuries that they were already on edge. The final straw came after a raft race carrying bridge parts down the Vals River went horribly wrong and they were punished with a 2,4km run by the Looty who was trying out his new stopwatch. They hurtled around the course only to discover that the stopwatch hadn't worked, so they were sent off again. When they were sent off the third time, they refused. Major Rabid was summoned and threatened all kinds of retribution – but they'd heard it all before and refused to budge. Standing together meant they couldn't beat you. Major Rabid admitted defeat and Psycho and the Looty had their wings clipped. Bossies celebrated.

Thanks to Golf's heroics, our corporals were put on notice to curb their excesses. They backed off a couple of millimetres.

Camouflage training session was up next; hide-and-seek with guns – sorry, rifles. It's an ancient samurai discipline the Japanese called 'bushido no movee', or 'the bush that doesn't move'. Perfected by Bruce Lee who once sat looking like a thorn bush for two hours in 40-degree heat with a fly up his nose and a meerkat down his jocks. I was looking forward to a bit of a lie down but the preparations seemed over the top: it was bad enough having to cover ourselves in shrubs, cacti and dirt, but the last straw was the order to go 'blackface'. Thank God social media didn't exist in those days, or we'd have been social outcasts. And it wasn't just the face – we also had to cover our arms and necks, with a thick black paste that was a nightmare to get off.

Not sure if it was made by L'Oreal or Dulux, but 'Black is beautiful' certainly worked as a camouflage weapon. You'd apply it to your maatjie and he'd return the favour.

Camouflage lesson No. 7: Don't smile.

Once satisfied, the corporals ran us down to the riverbank and instructed us to hide in the veld. We scattered like a taxi boss spotting the taxman, scrambling to find the best hiding place. This was difficult because the veld was dry and flat with only a few tufts of tall grass to sneak behind. I spotted a dent in the baking earth with a few grassy tufts high enough to let me blend in. I crawled into position, panting and sweating. My visions of grabbing a quick nap were soon destroyed by the curious nature of the insect kingdom, which was trying to work out why a sweaty Michael Jackson impersonator was in their backyard. The crawling ones crawled all over me, while the mozzies performed their normal buzz-in-the-ear trick. We soon heard another buzz as a Ratel's powerful engine came around a bend. Corporals on board, tried to spot us behind the shrubs and boulders.

When they did they'd throw a stone to show that we'd been discovered. Baobab, having decided to impersonate a termite mound, couldn't get settled in time and ended up resembling a blancmange during an earthquake; he soon felt the ping of gravel hitting his doibie. I didn't last much longer. Not realising the bastards would be on top of a Ratel I'd positioned myself too close to the road – easy to spot. I bade a sad farewell to my new crawling friends and joined the rest of the walking shrubbery. It hadn't been a great success, and it took us hours to scrape off our make-up and prune our uniforms.

One evening, just before tucking ourselves into bed, our corporals gleefully ordered us back into uniform. Now what? We ran for a few kilometres to a small clearing on top of a hill, where we were met by South Africa's own version of Harvey Weinstein; he had more craters on his face than the moon, which was prophetic, as he was going to teach us all about the stars above.

Realising this was his one shot at transforming us into defenders of the vulnerable Caucasian tribe our resident astronomer took full advantage of his captive audience by giving us a bizarre lecture on white supremacy, he might've taken the Milky Way a bit too literally.

Eventually he got on with explaining about the stars and how we could navigate by them – we started listening again.

I can't recall much but I remember he taught us how to find due south by using the Southern Cross constellation: With your pinky and index finger, measure the gap between the top and bottom star of the Cross – using that gap as a template and starting at the foot of the Cross, extend it four

times in a straight line. From the end point, imagine a straight line stretching down to the horizon and that is due south, or, at least, fairly close.

Handy when you need to find your way home from Foxy's pub after you've crashed into a pavement that shouldn't have been there.

'Genie 'n Fok Nie'

With basics coming to an end, they decided to ease off on the infantry training and give us some engineering drills; bridge building time.

Because the mobile bridges were made in Britain they'd have to hand us over to some soutie instructors – Fairey Engineering had come to Bossies. (Not exactly the best name for an engineering company, but at least they didn't have pointy ears.) I was hoping that upon seeing our pitiful condition, they'd send a complaint to the RSPCA or the Queen; then I remembered the concentration camps, and threw away my extradition request.

We trooped off to the dams that had been set up to simulate Angolan rivers; not a bad replica, but lacking in starving and bewildered locals – although, we did a fairly decent impersonation. There we stood to attention, as a Birmingham accent rang out over the Free State veld – the sweetest sound I'd heard for a long time. It gave me renewed hope that I'd survive.

After two months of infantry training, it felt good to be doing some engineering. The bridges looked like a combination of LEGO and Meccano sets with huge metal parts that required four troeps to lift and slot into place.

The pieces all interlocked, and when fitted together created a bridge that could span a small river – ingenious, but make sure your fingers are out of the way. Hundred-kilo metallic parts slamming into your hand can leave a mark.

The Faireys gave us a demonstration and then it was our turn. Of course, the army had to make it a competition: a weekend's pass for the winning bungalow. Great, except the first thing the Faireys had mentioned was the chance that someone would lose a finger if we rushed things.

Each unit was timed. We were second last to go, allowing us to spot the mistakes from the other units while we waited in the blazing sun. The Faireys, who didn't understand Afrikaans, hadn't realized that a full-blooded competition was underway. When Alpha unit sped out of their blocks and started racing with their bridge parts, the Fairey sales and marketing team went pale; broken limbs and missing fingers didn't make for a good sales pitch. I saw them remonstrating with some of the lieutenants, which did little good, a Birmingham accent doesn't work in a Looty's ear.

As the first ones to go, Alpha Unit struggled and as they staggered back, counting their fingers, we gave them a warm round of boos. Bravo weren't much better, and by the time Echo was up, the Fairey's were attempting to slow things down. They'd realized that the corporals were more interested in having a weekend off than explaining to parents about their sons' missing fingers – the competition continued.

Spurred on by threats of mutilation and disembowelment, Golf put in a strong showing and leapt into first place. We were next up. By this stage, we'd been fried to a crisp by the unrelenting heat. The corporals had somehow forgotten to

bring the gazebos, electric fans and cucumber sandwiches. We trundled off to our starting positions.

Each troep got a metal bar with a flat hook on the end. This was inserted into a slot on each side of the bridge part. Four slots per part, thus four troeps to each bridge part. We had to lift each one, carry it about fifty metres then slot it into place. We gave it our best, but pairing up huge rugby players with asthmatic midgets resulted in mayhem. Not our finest moment, as Bumfluff implied, we soon hit the dirt for push-ups.

Miraculously, no fingers were lost, although a few fingernails were bludgeoned and the Fairey boys nearly had a collective heart attack. I hope they got their danger pay.

Postcards from the Edge

I wasn't always the best at corresponding with friends and family during my two years. It meant having to discuss the past and I was more concerned with the future. My Dad didn't give a shit, but Mum seemed to be going through a late-blooming maternal phase, and regularly demanded news from her little boy.

The army forced us to send a letter home every week. I sat on my bunk for ages, trying to wring out some interesting details about army life but it was all repetitive and boring. Or at least it was to me. While I struggled to fill half a page, other troeps were writing novels to their people back home. After the first few weeks of writing about the food, the corporals, my kak pillow and everything associated with Bossies, I couldn't be bothered anymore. I stopped posting letters. Mum wasn't too happy about my lack of social media

so in desperation, she sent me a pile of stamped and addressed postcards with *'Yes, I'm well'* already written on them. All I had to do was post one every once in a while. I still forgot.

Twenty years later I had some fun at Mum's expense. The restaurant Panama Jack's, in a marketing blitz, had handed out free stamped postcards featuring scenes of their place. I grabbed one, dated it '1987', wrote a load of kak about how my day at the army shooting range had gone and mailed it over to my Mum, who was living back in England.

When she got it she called me up, amazed:

"So you weren't lying about the ANC stealing all the mail."

"See, I told you," I said.

"Hold on a second. I was living in South Africa in 1987, not England. You little bast..."

"Cheers Mum, got to go.

About a week before the end of basics I was called up for a *Keurraad* (Selection Board) to see if I would be sent on to the Junior Leaders course. I knew my theory marks were good enough, I was super fit, my shooting was passable and I'd always been a team player.

My Looty was confident I'd get through, I wasn't so sure. I was marched into a dimly lit room where a row of the Engineer Corps' top brass sat. I stood to attention, gave my name and was ordered to stand at ease – easier said than done. The highest rank I'd dealt with was Major Rabid but these guys had so many castles and swords on their shoulders that I was temporarily blinded from the glare. They soon put me at ease by telling me, in English, that my marks were good. Then they started with some basic questions, mainly of a technical or military nature. No problem, I sailed through.

Then, just as I was deliberating whether I'd prefer the Pinotage or the Shiraz in the officers' bar, I was hit by a curveball. They moved onto politics and religion. The board asked me what I thought about my Archbishop. What Archbishop? I thought – I assumed it was a test to see whether I was a real Anglican. All I knew about the Anglican Church was that they served cold beer on Tuesday nights and their version of the Pope, was some posh English bloke whose name I couldn't remember. I made one up.

"Do you mean Archbishop Smyth-Ramsbottom?" I guessed.

They shook their heads and kept probing until, getting frustrated, one of them said, "We're talking about the black guy. The South African Archbishop"

"Ah, why didn't you say so?" I thought.

I realised it was 'The Arch' they were talking about. Archbishop Tutu, the man the Nats hated more than Mandela. He was a thorn in their side, but, being a man of God, they'd struggled to shut him down. I was entering a political minefield, so I acted a bit *dom* and said I'd never met him so I wouldn't know. They didn't look convinced.

The next question was regarding any contact I'd had with the End Conscription Campaign. It had been one of the questions we'd been asked when we'd klaared in and I'd answered truthfully by admitting that I had been to one of their concerts – I'd been to quite a few actually: they always had the best, most radical bands playing but I didn't want to brag. (The ECC was an anti-Apartheid organisation created by conscientious objectors in the early 1980s to oppose conscription. Although it was illegal to persuade someone not to do military service, it wasn't illegal to call for an end to conscription. In 1985, Parliament announced that 7 589 conscripts had failed to report for the January call-up of that

year, a huge leap from only 1596 AWOL troeps in 1984. Several thousand fled to Europe, but many remained in the country evading the police, or becoming perpetual students I wish somebody had told me. Evidently, Riaan Cruywagen had kept that one quiet. Thanks a lot, Riaan.)

Despite those minor hiccups I thought I'd left a good impression with the selection board. Their demeanour was positive and I marched out with my head held high and my *poephol* slowly relaxed.

After finishing basics I was informed that I hadn't been selected for Junior Leaders. No reason given. Of course, all the lazy bastards I'd pushed through the obstacle courses, 2,4's and route marches got onto JLs, including Baobab.

No wonder we drew.

Rifles and Revelations

The final days of basics were upon us and the Major had transformed the parade ground into a mini-Nuremberg for our passing out parade. It was resplendent with flaming torches and South African flags.

But first we had to complete a mammoth route march, set up a defensive perimeter in the bush and then fight off a night attack by our corporals. They issued us with a full magazine of blanks.

The march was tough but after three months of basics, our feet had toughened the fuck up, our bodies were lean and muscular and our stamina levels were through the roof. Our exhausted bodies ultimately staggered into the bush camp for the night.

Basic training was all about pushing your physical and mental limits, and then smashing through them. Just when you thought you couldn't go another step, you realised that you were stronger and more resilient than you'd imagined.

We set up a defensive perimeter and split the unit into three guard duty shifts. Darkness soon crept over us. We got stuck into our rat packs, while those not on duty fell into a deep sleep.

A couple of hours later the fireworks began. Muzzle flashes and the crackle of gunfire woke me from my slumber. I sat up, bleary-eyed, to see a few heroes acting like soldiers, getting into proper firing positions and making it look like a valiant defence. Most of us were so tired, we just rolled over in our sleeping bags and fired straight into the night sky; noisy and fun, but rather ineffective. Our corporal's kakked us out but it was futile; they couldn't even get us out of our sleeping bags, so they gave up and went and got drunk.

The next morning, the corporals allowed us back into our bungalows to prepare for our passing out parade. It was a fancy affair with family and friends invited to attend. I told my folks not to bother. I didn't want my Dad driving all the way up as he'd been ill lately, and Mum was up in Ellisras in the far north of South Africa, too far a journey to make in a beat-up old Fiat. I don't really want too much attention, anyway.

Later that afternoon, as the blood-orange sun slipped below the horizon, we marched down to the parade ground. All ten units – six-hundred-and-forty troeps minus the few dropouts and rejects – gathered in the fading light. A podium decorated in the traditional Guardsmen red and Oxford blue colours of the Engineer Corps held chairs for the top officers.

Behind them sat rows and rows of proud families, horny girlfriends and maybe a few boyfriends. They had good reason to be proud. Their kin and lovers had just survived the toughest three months of their young lives. Army basics are one of the most exhausting physical and mental ordeals any human can endure. It took us to places we didn't want to go. It gutted and galvanised us, stretched our limits and laughed at our tears before spitting us out. Nobody was the same after those three months, for good or bad.

All around us, the flames of the embedded torches cast their flickering light across the grounds. The first strains of military music started humming through the speakers and we stiffened our spines.

The dominee was first up. He'd mellowed a bit since our first encounter. After a few prayers and an Old Testament sermon about different-coloured sheep, human sacrifices and the perils of coveting your neighbour's donkey, he showed mercy and quickly wrapped up his sermon.

Speeches of varying boredom levels from the top brass followed – we just wanted it to end so we could fuck off and celebrate.

As the gas in the torches began running low, they hurried up the proceedings. With great fanfare, each troep marched up to some general who solemnly handed them a rifle and a Bible – just to remind us who we'd be killing and dying for.

The best part was receiving our *baltjie (Corps badge)* that we'd pin to our berets to show that we'd passed basics. As we marched back to our bungalows we clung onto those tiny badges more tightly than our rifle. That night, bursting with pride, we solemnly attached them to our berets.

I was now a Sapper.

One of the traditions at the end of basics was for the corporals to receive an *opvok* from the troeps. And when I say an *opvok*, I mean a beating. I don't remember it too clearly, but I think it was only Bumfluff who pitched up. He received a few kicks, punches and whacks from a balsak with some irons in it, but our thirst for revenge had already dissipated. He'd gone too far, too often, but then again, he was just another *doos* that one encounters on life's journey. We were better than him.

Because we were a leadership camp, most of the troeps hoped to progress to the Junior Leadership course (JLs) to train as corporals or lieutenants. If you didn't get onto JLs, you'd be transferred to Bethlehem for border training (mine sweeping, bridge building etc.) or to the main base in Kroonstad to do fuck-all. We nervously waited to find out what our futures would hold.

Chapter Twenty-one
Snor and the PF Factory

Basics were finished and finally I was a fully certified Sapper. We weren't lower than dog shit anymore, we were one notch up; we now hovered just above the poo. Sapper Bardsley, along with all the other JL rejects, cripples, poor marksmen, professional coughers and one or two heathens was transferred to the headquarters of the School of Engineers at Kroonstad Main Base. I was disappointed not to have made JL's but maybe now I'd get a chance to further my civil engineering education. I might as well hone my skills in constructing bridges, roads and buildings or blowing them up.

My concrete-tinged dreams were soon dashed when they informed us that the only available vacancies were: admin clerks, chefs, the RSM's bitch, coffee-makers, store men, tinkers, tailors, soldiers, spies or drivers.

I'd been allowed an extra day on my 'end of basics' pass to attend my graduation from the Cape Technikon, so I'd arrived back a day later than most. After nervously reporting to the HQ, I was soon klaared in and marched off to my newly assigned bungalow. It was an upgrade from India Bungalow: instead of sharing it with sixty-four pairs of smelly feet, it was now only ten pairs of mouldy paws.

No more double bunks; we now had our own fancy single beds. The ablution block was within staggering distance and a couple of taps even dispensed a few dribbles of lukewarm water. There were about fifty of us HQ troeps housed in five bungalows. It was like moving into the Hilton.

Gramps (topless), Jacques (middle) and Peppie (broom) outside a HQ bungalow; our little Sun City.

The best part was having a few maatjies from Bossies – Slab, Peppie, Gramps, Neil, Suggsy and others. I settled in quickly, while we awaited our assignments. Suttie had advised me to try for the stores as it was a cushy job and might further my criminal career. My hopes were soon dashed when I was assigned to the Construction Vehicle driver's course.

Although the School of Engineers was predominantly a training base, it had other functions like construction work and hosting the 35 Engineer Support Unit, which maintained the construction vehicles and equipment. They needed some new drivers, so, rather than handing me a cushy job pouring ink into the Xerox machine or making coffee they sent me on

a driver's course. Sounded okay, except I had a slight problem – I couldn't drive.

Unlike most South African boys who'd learnt to drive at the age of about eleven when a slightly inebriated dad handed them the wheel for a few kays as they trundled along the sand road to Infanta, this soutie had never been near the driver's seat. Now they expected me to drive a ten-ton front loader without so much as a learner's licence. I couldn't really complain though, it was way better than having to disarm landmines on the border.

Day one of the driving course started off well. Breakfast was decent; the HQ chefs had learnt how to switch the grill on, so crispy bacon was now on the menu and the scrambled eggs even contained traces of egg. Most notably, the chefs had introduced the greatest culinary invention the world has ever witnessed: baked beans. A solitary tear rolled down my cheek as I dished some up. Kids in the north of England had for years survived the harsh Arctic winters on a diet of baked beans on toast. The British Empire had run on baked beans. It was the fuel that kept on giving. However an unfortunate side effect of the heavy bean consumption was a marked rise in CO_2 emissions in our bungalow – cost me a fortune in rose-scented Glade air freshener.

After breakfast we toddled off to our first parade at our new home. Because the parade ground was directly in front of the HQ, there'd be lots of prying, critical eyes, so the PFs had to make sure it was well attended and *paraat*. Little did we know how much of a pain in the ass parades would become. Most camps had the occasional parade for 'the sake of appearance', but because Genieskool was an officer training camp, we needed to have a full parade every day.

For the remainder of the two years, we had to get up early to prepare for it. Sometimes I hid under my bed, but my repeated excuse of searching for a lost contact lens, when caught, soon wore thin.

Winter mornings were the worst. We'd begin with some frostbitten marching, pretend to listen to some religious shouting and then endure some amateur propaganda. If it was a long sermon, most of us had hypothermia by the time we marched off.

After the parade, we headed off for lectures about the construction vehicles we were expected to drive. There, we were met by an angry whirling dervish otherwise known as Staff Sergeant Snor. He had a face like a hooker's ear and the soul of an Aussie referee. Though this was our first meeting, Snor had already decided that he hated us – and he let us know it. He just glared at us for the first minute; steam pouring from his hairy ears, his whole body taut and the veins in his neck popping out – before going on a rant about the evils of communism. We'd heard it all before, but this loony was more than just brainwashed – he was living the fantasy.

He saw Commie danger around every corner, under any bridge, and especially in our liberal minds; it was our solemn duty to pass the course, to deliver the Volk from evil, and maybe, while we were at it, drop off some sand and gravel at our building sites. And if we failed, Mandela and his evil ANC *maatjies* would rule over us. No pressure, then.

Like many PFs, he was a nutter. There must've been a top-secret factory, hidden behind tall barbed wire-topped walls somewhere near Boksburg with an assembly line that churned out these PF Staff Sergeant psycho clones.

Staff Sergeant Mark 1
Step-by-step assembly instructions:

1. Start with the chassis: Cannot exceed 1.72m in height (*guaranteed short man syndrome*). The lower rank models should weigh about 80kg, but with extra storage space for beer, brandewyn and boerie rolls.
   (*Many of the older models ballooned to well over the 120kg safety level, and were either scrapped or promoted to RSM*)
2. Attach mounds of coarse black hair to chest, feet, ears, nose, asshole and back.
3. Use only a small penis or none at all. (*No point in wasting them, as they'll be too ugly to find a mate*)
4. Insert beady little eyes. No window to the soul required, as soul is not an option in the entry-level model and will only be introduced later. Deluxe model to be fitted with X-Ray vision; to spot troeps hiding under their beds at parade time.

5. Weave obligatory bristling moustache onto the face. (*Due to sanctions shortages may occur in which case pubes can also be utilised*)
6. Add bad-breath dispenser to the throat. (Comes in garlic or rotting polony flavour.)
7. Fit the brain into the thick skull: Consists of a 4KB second-hand RAM drive and 1KB memory. Programme with a vocabulary of 100 words, mainly made up of swear words, insults and orders.
8. Switch the mode button to 'Always Angry'. Programme default volume to loud screeching level.
9. Unit powered by nuclear-strength Duracell batteries. (*Those PFs never seemed to stop running around trying to make our lives hell.*)

Once our hearts had resumed beating after Staff Sergeant Snor's welcoming attack, he taught us about the vehicles. The fleet stretched from simple trucks for carting building materials, to water trucks, front-end loaders and trench diggers.

We learnt all about the engines, their specifications, their uses, and what they weren't to be used for: joyrides and taking a chickie out to the bioscope.

After a few days of lectures, they took us over to the obstacle course; a stretch of land next to 35 Regiment peppered with dongas, small tracks and hills where they'd teach us to drive the beasts.

We lined up next to a load of ten-ton trucks, expecting a driving lesson. Next second, Snor ordered us to get in and start driving. What the fuck? What happened to learning first? The others happily jumped in and started revving their engines, but all I was revving were my bowels. I couldn't even drive a normal car, and now they expected me to get into this metal monster and whizz around the circuit.

I was rooted to the spot. Fortunately, Snor hadn't seen my predicament and his assistant, a sergeant who'd somehow broken the mould and was a nice guy, came over to ask what the problem was. I explained my dilemma, and after a quick lesson he had me driving around in a bakkie out of harm's way.

For the next week, they used me to deliver food and tea to the real drivers. Naturally I failed the course, and a few years later the ANC got into power. Staff Snor hadn't been joking.

Looking back, I wish I'd passed the Drivers course. Peppie and the other drivers had a great two years driving around the Free State picking up building material, gouging trenches and taking chicks on joyrides to the bioscope.

I ended up at the HQ construction office.

Chapter Twenty-two
Operation Steel Injection

After failing the Construction Drivers course, a few of us with diplomas or degrees were thrown into the construction offices. Supposedly, we'd be involved in any construction projects on the main base or out at Bossies. In reality, they had no idea what to do with us.

School of Engineers, Kroonstad. Construction office. The drawing desks were great for sleeping behind.

One fateful day, the CO ordered Slab and I to attend a meeting with him. This was a big deal. He was hard-core, and any summons to his office was met with fear.

(Once he'd had great fun demanding that I request my leave in Afrikaans. I stumbled over the words, leave was denied and I stayed in base while my mates left for the weekend. I wasn't a fan.)

We marched in, stamped our feet in a poor impersonation of a proper troep and stood at attention. It was a nice room; lots of polished wood panelling, Old Testament quotes and military certificates. I think it even had a carpet.

"We've chosen you to manage the building of the new sports centre, " the Colonel announced

"Yes, Colonel. Certainly, Colonel," we spluttered.

Brilliant. Finally some building work to do, and we'd be the main men – they'd already started on the sports centre so we just had to finish it off. He'd obviously recognised our building talent and technical know-how and we felt honoured to have the —

"We do have a slight problem, though." he cut in. "Somebody forgot to put the steel reinforcing in the base foundations." He mentioned nonchalantly.

We looked at him, bemused. After a minute spent processing this information, Slab eventually piped up: "Do you mean the base foundations that support all the steel posts, that support the slabs, that support the roof that holds the whole structure together?"

"Correct," said the Colonel.

Right. Erm - this was a slight hiccup. In layman's terms, structural concrete needs steel reinforcing like Klippies needs coke. Without the steel, the building has no structural strength, and will eventually collapse, bringing pain, anguish and two convenient soutie scapegoats. Without steel reinforcement the World Trade Centre would've keeled over on day one; thousands would have perished as Loftus Versfeld Stadium collapsed as the crowd went crazy when Naas finally tackled someone, and your newly built house would've become rubble after your first high-powered shag on the dining room table.

Clearly, they'd decided to pin the imminent collapse of the sports centre onto a pair of dumb troepies so they wouldn't have to take the fall. But after months learning how to gyppo in basics, they'd messed with the wrong ones. We tentatively agreed to be in charge, as long as we could fix up their mistakes at any cost; we might require a few bits and pieces of steel, we implied.

"No problem. Order what you want, just make sure the bleddy thing doesn't fall over," the Colonel said, slamming the door behind us.

And with that, he put out the order that Slab and I were now in charge, and had free rein to buy whatever we wanted.

Within a week South Africa's sluggish economy, weighed down by sanctions, strikes and lack of investment, perked up as massive steel orders poured in. Trains transporting the ore were extended and the iron ore mines went into overdrive. Coalmines had to work 24 hours a day just to provide the fuel for the smelters. The JSE rose by 3.2%.

The press were confused; had the Big Crocodile decided to build our own Statue of Liberty in the shape of a Voortrekker maiden holding up a *stukkie biltong*? Was the Navy getting a fleet of aircraft carriers? Had Staff Sergeant Snor ordered extra burglar bars to fend off the *swart gevaars*? There was no way that sports centre was going to collapse on our watch. We'd put in enough steel reinforcing that it would survive a nuclear bomb.

For the first week, Slab and I worked feverishly to come up with an all-encompassing plan for Operation Patriotic Steel Injection. Realising that we couldn't undo their cock-up, we decided to add more reinforced concrete around the base foundations, as well as make sure all the other foundations and ground beams were strong enough to take any slack if the non-reinforced parts started buckling.

At least that's what I think Slab meant – I had no clue, and just nodded, dropping in the occasional *erm* and a round of polite applause at the end.

When we presented the plan to the CO, he told us to proceed but to leave him out of it. Now we just had to convince the sergeant who was running the site. He'd ended up looking like a complete *doos* for not raising the alarm when the previous project manager had failed to use steel in the foundations, and now he had to take orders from a couple of *roefs* fresh out of college and basics.

The Looty brought us down to meet him and introduced us as the new management team. It was difficult to gauge the Sarge's reaction; he communicated mostly with grunts, 'foks' and minimal eye contact.

The Looty seemed terrified of him and soon fled, leaving us to deal with Sarge on our own; he soon made sure we knew who was the boss. Our attempts to rectify the steel problem was met with Sarge sternly reminding us that he was the sergeant and we were the troeps, and we had to listen to him and not the other way around. Slab and I were caught between a rock and, well, another rock; a psycho, soutie-hating Colonel demanding we run the show and another psycho, grunting, soutie-hating Sergeant who demanded that we didn't run the show.

We were fokked.

As with millions of angry dickheads around the world, life had disappointed Sarge. He was a good builder but couldn't communicate with other human beings. He'd realised that it was easier to throw in his lot with the army so he could boss the troeps around and not have to deal with any backchat.

When an armada of trucks started delivering tons of steel to the site, Sarge was stunned. It wasn't long before he realised that he'd be the one installing it and, as this was all our doing, Sarge set his sights on destroying us. He was a worthy adversary, but we had a cunning plan.

The next day, with some apprehension, we made an appointment to see the Colonel.

We were marched in by the sergeant-at-arms, saluted and then stood at unease.

"*Wat nou? Ek is besig*," roared our friendly Colonel as he put down his Louis L'Amour book.

Slab explained our predicament, making sure to emphasise the futility of mere sappers trying to tell a sergeant what to do.

"What does he say when you ask him to do something?" the colonel asked.

"'*Voetsek, jou fokken sapper*," Slab replied.

"Right," he said, "So what do you suggest?"

"Well, maybe you could come and give the orders every time we need something done," Slab said, trying to be diplomatic. "It would only mean five or six visits to the site every day."

The Colonel's eyes grew wide and his survival instinct kicked in. This might mean he'd actually have to do some work.

"Or we would need to have rank that was higher than the sergeant. Maybe staff sergeant or something," suggested Slab helpfully.

"Impossible," Colonel grunted. "They are permanent force or campers so you'd have to join up for longer."

"Or maybe we could be one pip lieutenants?" Slab was pushing our collective luck.

"That would be highly irregular." Colonel countered.

"Certainly, Colonel, probably best if you come down to give the orders – five or six times a day. Probably have to start off at about seven thirty in the morning." Slab was pushing all the right buttons.

"Luckily, we usually finish before dark unless we're pouring concrete – which is most days now." I added.

You could see the panic in his eyes as he realised his well-ordered life of coffee, buttermilk rusks and afternoon naps might be interrupted by tedious trips down to the worksite.

"*Moenie so hastig weesie.* Let me see what I can do," he mumbled. "Come back tomorrow morning."

As we were marched out, a little glimmer of hope swept across our happy little troepie faces.

This could be our big chance. Our lives would be transformed. We'd be officers. Eating steaks the size of dustbin lids, swilling wine that hadn't been decanted out of five-litre boxes and bossing the Sarge around.

Giddy with excitement, we headed back to our office. At first we agreed to keep our plan secret from our fellow troeps as we didn't want to hurt their feelings – and to make sure the bastards didn't rat us out. Of course, as we skipped into our offices, we couldn't help but spill the beans. The others were naturally sceptical but our upbeat mood dissolved any doubts and soon they were devising ways of sharing in our unexpected bonus. For the rest of the day, piping hot cups of tea and previously hidden rusks were graciously served to us.

Ahhhhh, the life of an officer. I pulled out my copy of Platters wine reviews and surveyed the choices – I just hoped the officers' bar served a decent Kanonkop Pinotage.

The next day we merrily trooped back down to the CO's office, giving the sergeant-at-arms a knowing wink as we strutted inside.

"*Wat is dit nou?*" the colonel yelled as his buttermilk rusk broke off and sank into his mug of *Ricoffy*.

"*Fok*! Now look what you made me do," he yelled as he tried to rescue his rusk from the depths of his cup. Taking his feet off the desk and sliding his *Scope* magazine into his top drawer, he eyed us up and down. Even though he was a short shit, Slab had managed to maintain a bit of decorum and could just about pass for a soldier. I probably wasn't at my military peak; scrawny, with a cowpat beret and broken glasses held together with gaffer tape (never head a football while wearing glasses). I wasn't quite the image of the brave warrior soldiers of the Valkyrie.

"Erm, it's about the building site situation, Colonel. The one we discussed yesterday," said Slab.

The Colonel eventually recognised us and sadly shook his head.

"*Nee, fok*, I can't make you two losers into lieutenants. It would demoralise the whole army and the Commies will know we're scraping the barrel and start a new onslaught. Just tell the Sergeant that whatever you say is an order from me."

"But Colonel, he won't listen," Slab pleaded.

"I've had a chat with the Sergeant and I'm sure he will fully understand the strategic importance of this project and follow your orders."

"But Colonel—" Slab's desperate plea faded as the Sergeant-at-Arms escorted us out, making sure to give us a long slow wink as we slunk away to the site.

This was a massive blow. As we got closer to the site we realised that our dreams of getting rank had gone up in smoke. Slab was devastated and I knew I had to cheer him up. We got onto site to find Sarge struggling to fit yet another ten tons of steel reinforcing into the foundations.

"Don't worry mate," I said. "I'm sure that if the Colonel has ordered Sergeant to start taking our orders he'll start listening to us..."

"Morning, Sergeant, is there any chance of......."

"*Voetsak, jou fokking sapper.*"

....or maybe not.

We were back to square one or almost square one – we soon found out that the foundations were already skew. "Bollocks to it" we said and pissed off back to the office.

Our fragile state of mind wasn't helped by our comrades saluting us every five minutes and asking us if we'd prefer the 'specially-made-for-lieutenants' buttermilk rusks or just the 'basic shitty sapper rusks'?

There was a certain lack of sympathy in the office.

We soon realised that if we were going to throw most of South Africa's steel reserves into the foundations, we'd better make sure we didn't skimp on the concrete. We upped the ratio of cement into the mix; nothing but the highest strength concrete for our little Taj Mahal.

For the next few months, our main job was testing the strength of the concrete. Every time Sarge and his crew poured, we came along with our little moulds, took a sample, and then pissed off back to the site office. We then patriotically snoozed until the concrete moulds set, and then used a compression machine to test their strength – an important measurement to ensure that the structure would be safe and strong.

Occasionally we'd have to show our graphs and stats to prove how robust the concrete was. Amazing how a few complicated calculations and technical words could bullshit the PFs – and me.

Scene 17
Day: Site Office:

Sarge barges into the site office, awakening two handsome young troeps mid-snooze.

"Wat die fok? Is you sleeping, troep?"

"Nie Serseant, just trying to work out a really complicated calculation in my head. Ahhh, got it now." I quickly replied, hiding my pillow and pulling out my earplugs.

" Just finished that concrete test report for you,"

"So kan ons carry on?" Sarge demanded.

"Ja Serseant, dit is vyftig MegaPascals to the Newton metres per millimetre cubic-squared to the perpendicular axis," Slab nonchalantly announced.

I nodded to confirm his findings and Sarge grunted in confusion and left. Slab should have done his Masters in bullshitting.

Watching concrete set makes watching paint dry look like a fiesta. At least you could try and sniff paint fumes. In a moment of utter desperate boredom and hoping to get a buzz, I tried sniffing some cement powder. Not recommended, unless you want to reinforce your sinuses and empty your tear ducts.

We'd sit in our little site office for hours on end. It was like a Wendy hut: just a thin cladding of wood that couldn't keep out the winter cold or expel the summer heat. It was a miserable existence for nine hours a day. Basically, we were in hiding, but even we couldn't hide from the dreaded guard duty.

6 May 1987
The ruling National Party wins the general election and the right-wing Conservative Party replaces the PFP as the official opposition. Anglican Archbishop and Nobel peace prizewinner Desmond Tutu noted after the election, "We have entered the dark ages of the history of our country."

Because we were HQ staff, we were given the honour of standing guard, at least twice a week, every bleddy week. We had to guard the entire HQ plus the 35 Mechanised Battalion areas that were full of construction vehicles, workshops and building material. After our day's work we'd head back to our bungalows, have a shower, iron our uniform; polish our boots and then head up to the guardroom. There we had a little parade to make sure we were neat and tidy then we made ourselves at home in the pigsty they called a guardroom.

Kroonstad was also home to the 35 Engineer Support Regiment. Their job was to maintain the engineering equipment and vehicles and few were also working as labourers and artisans at the sports centre. Many were Code 7's – troeps with learning disabilities. Nowadays they'd be diagnosed as ADHD – in those days we medically diagnosed them as 'fucking crazy'.

Legally, they shouldn't have been issued with a sharp stick, never mind a rifle but the HQ desperately needed guards, so the corporals happily handed them "the sticks that blow fire". As soon as they got hold of the rifles, they started playing 'cowboys and Indians' in the guardroom.

Eventually it dawned on the staff sergeant that the first self-inflicted massacre in SADF history might look bad on his resume – so he only armed them as they went out to their posts. I was more nervous of getting killed by the Code 7's than by the ANC – I still am.

The guardroom was like Sodom and Gomorrah on a Friday night; stinking of testosterone, sweat, grubby mattresses, and occupied by the hyperactive 35 loony's who never stopped shouting or play fighting.

When they finally passed out they'd often sleep entwined. It was like a homo-erotica nightmare. Brokeback Mountain had nothing on our guardroom.

We were all assigned a number of two-hour shifts throughout the night. I always aimed for the series of shifts that meant I'd miss parade in the morning. Once our shift came up we lined up with our rifles and marched around the inner perimeter until we got to our assigned *hokkies* (guard posts). There, we climbed up the ladder to relieve the guard, who then marched back to the sanctuary of the guardhouse.

The *hokkies* were little huts on tall stilts, strategically placed at the corners of the perimeter fence or in between. They were approximately two metres by two metres, made of timber and clad with steel sheets on the sides and roof. Inside there was nothing, except for a plank-seat on one side – cunningly devised to provide the illusion of comfort but slanted in such a way that you couldn't sit on it for more than ten minutes without either sliding off or getting piles from the strain of holding on. There was a telephone line to the guardroom in case any bad guys attacked and we needed some assistance. It also had a spotlight for seeing terrorists and illuminating the sumptuous curves of Miss November in the Scope.

Some of us had favourite *hokkies*; mine was close to the corner of Nic Diedricks and Klasie Havenga Streets. From my hut in the sky, I could see into the nearby homes and feel the warmth of human contact. I watched the rising smoke of the braais from miles around and salivated as the aroma of burning cow wafted past. It made me feel less lonely and isolated, but also angry and bloody hungry.

We sat there for two long hours; watching for terrs, rereading *War and Peace* and sleeping. It was difficult to stay awake during the early morning shifts, with 04h00 to 06h00 being the worst and with Staff Sergeant Snor sneaking around and throwing bricks into our *hokkies*, we were more on the lookout for him than any attackers.

There's a common misconception that South Africa is a hot country but if you are inland during winter it's bloody freezing. I'd been brought up in the north of England, an area not renowned for sunburn and massive Ray-Ban sales. Many winters saw us shovelling snow away just to get out of the house. When the 'Beast from the East' blew in from Russia, you soon realised why the Russians wear furry hats and can't smile. As four-year-olds we staggered through icy blasts from the North Sea just to get to school, after which we still played football in shorts and a threadbare shirt. Yet, I've never experienced cold like I did one night standing guard in the middle of a Kroonstad winter.

It was mid-August, and bloody freezing. I was wearing every piece of clothing I owned: four pairs of socks, three pairs of underwear, jacket, big jacket, even bigger jacket, football shirt, two pairs of pants, tracksuit bottoms. Then I cocooned myself in my sleeping bag. I might as well have been naked for all the good it did: the icy wind simply swept through my clothing buffer zone, chilling me to the core.

I'd never heard of wind chill factor before that night but now I understood why Eskimos club baby seals. Minus-two degrees centigrade was just about survivable if you moved slowly, but when the wind blew, the layer of warm air on your skin got blasted away, driving down your body temperature. The faster the wind blew, the faster the heat was carried away. Hypothermia was a real threat.

You could even calculate it:

```
Wind-chill = (12.1452 + 11.6222 × 1.16222
Wind √ Windsfc - × sfc) × (33 - T)
```

Or, translated into South African:

Windchill = (Poes cold) × (Fucking Windy) × (Extremely Gatvol) = Fuck This Shit.

Two hours in the freezing cold shuffling around a tiny hokkie is not pleasant. I smoked non-stop so I had something warm to hold onto as my teeth chattered. You couldn't touch the metal on the rifle or it would freeze onto your skin and you'd need hot water to prise your fingers off. I didn't see my penis for weeks afterwards. It's never fully recovered.

Out of loyalty, I'd always stuck to fantasising about my dearly beloved Anneline, but I might've strayed a couple of times. One stormy night in the hokkie, I might have fooled around with Anneline Wucherfening, the famous show jumper. I'd obviously confused them because of the same first names, and the thought of jodhpurs and horsewhips was pretty tempting, but my love for my beloved Suikerbossie was still paramount. I reared up and showed my hooves to the transgressor. She dismounted and trotted off.

Trying to defend the Motherland while satisfying two sensual women wasn't as easy it looked. Ask FW de Klerk.

If only our glorious ex-president JZ had been a bit more innovative in his days as head of MK intelligence. Dropping off the latest copy of *Scope* close to the *hokkies* on the roadside next to our camp would've immediately sent the guards into furious masturbation sessions, enabling the thousands of brave, eager Umkhonto we Sizwe troeps hiding in the koi pools of the oppressor to leap out, towel themselves off and then manhandle the colonial oppressors. A strategic blunder if I've ever seen one.

ANC Headquarters. Angola

Chief of intelligence, Jacob Zuma, is sat with Commissar Schaik looking over a map of Kroonstad.

Zuma: Hee, hee, hee. Our latest intelligence reports show that Sapper Soutpiel will be standing guard tonight, a perfect opportunity to launch Operation Naughty Centrefold and finally capture the Kroonstad.

Commissar Schaik: It's a bit of a shithole, boss.

Zuma: But he's bound to be fiddling and then we can sneak in and conquer the crown of all towns.

Schaik: A common misunderstanding boss, but Crown was actually the name of a dead soggy horse.

Zuma: But I thought there would be jewels and gold there.

Schaik: You're thinking of Saxonwold, boss.

Zuma: Bliksem! But we need a victory. The Boers keep fucking us up.

Schaik: Patience boss. Sapper Soutpiel has cornered the world market for steel to build the greatest sports centre in the Free State. The government will be bankrupt by Christmas and that's when we will strike and claim the glory.
Zuma: And the gold and jewels?
Schaik: Maybe, boss, maybe.

The SADF launched Operation Moduler, aimed at halting the Angolan advance on Mavinga to prevent a rout of UNITA.
4 August 1987

Being in the army was similar to being in jail. Mealtime was practically all we thought about. If the food was shit or if it didn't arrive on time, the anger was righteous. If anybody knows the whereabouts of the twisted soul who decided that vegetables taste better when they've been boiled for an hour and then sweetened with a bucket of sugar, please let me know; we need to talk.

After a month in main base, I was already *gatvol* of the army. Every day was shit. There was no chance of a lie-in, our uniforms always had to be in tip-top condition, and we were forever under the microscope. In a big base like Bloemfontein you could gyppo easily, but there were only about fifty HQ troeps in Kroonstad and plenty of nosy, ass-licking, promotion-seeking PFs sniffing around – ready to pounce if we stepped out of line. We were cornered. But just as depression was hitting, the army gave us a glimmer of hope by dangling the prospect of leave in front of us.

I needed to get back home; my Dad had been diagnosed with some weird disease that normally only affected Eastern European Jewish folks. He'd always been healthy and his Sunday hikes up Table Mountain combined with eighteen holes every Saturday morning had kept him lean and strong.

But now he was getting tired quickly and "didn't feel so good", as he put it. He tried to downplay the problem, but a month later they had to amputate one of his fingertips – this was getting serious. There was no one to look after him at home and I knew he didn't like any fuss to be made.

Somebody mentioned that I could request a transfer to a base closer to home on compassionate grounds. I filled in the form and sent it off to someone in Pretoria. A couple of weeks later it was rejected. I wasn't surprised. I'm sure they received thousands of transfer requests and most would've been more deserving than mine. I shelved my dreams of getting home permanently and waited until my next pass.

Chapter Twenty-three
Booze at Magoos

After completing basics we were allowed regular passes home; a weekend pass every two weeks or four days every month or eight days every two months. For troeps who were a long way from home, like yours truly, it made sense to take the eight-day option. But two months stuck in Kroonstad felt like a life sentence so I 'made a plan'.

After my Looty (who was a top bloke) had signed my first pass, I saw that he had a fairly simple signature – one that might be easy to replicate if only I could find a dodgy forger. The next morning I found one – looking back at me in the mirror. Admittedly, I was more of a piss-artist than a real artist, but after painting loads of punk emblems on my leather jacket I realised that I was decent at copying stuff. I had to get the lines and angle right, plus it had to be done swiftly and smoothly to lose any tell-tale jitters. I practiced for a few hours until I got it right. I was a natural. Getting a pass became a lot easier.

My artistic fame soon grew, and before long I had a thriving new trade. It was strictly illegal to have more than one passbook so most of us had two or three. Obviously I used my new skill to help the poor and disadvantaged – myself. I started forging signatures for beer or in exchange for doing my guard duty. HQ was a bit slack on checking up on our passes since there was no established rule on who could issue them, so we naturally took full advantage.

Soon I was sneaking off to Jo'burg or Pretoria every second weekend using my forged passes, and then I'd use my legitimate passbook for my regular eight-day passes.

Getting a pass had become easier, but neither Suggsy nor me had a car, so we had to bum lifts or hitchhike home. Luckily, *Genieskool* was right next to the N1 highway; which took you north to Jo'burg, or south to Cape Town. We just had to sneak over the security fence and we were soon hitching on the highway to heaven.

We'd pray that a serial killer or some sad sack drowning his sorrows in booze wouldn't pick us up. It was a lottery but the army came up with a solution to our commuting woes: *Ride Safe*.

Ride Safe was a scheme devised by the military brass to make sure troepies could get home safely, and more importantly – didn't cost the SADF any money (fillet steaks and Shiraz in the officers' mess had to be paid for somehow). They put up Ride Safe road signs near all the SADF bases and in the big cities. Then they issued us with a luminous sash to wear; so we wouldn't get knocked over by eleven-year-old laaities who'd taken the wheel from their Klippies-infused dad. We were ordered to stand by these road signs when we were hitching, and were strictly forbidden from sticking our thumbs out. This might have made sense if the signs had been posted in every town but that would've cost money. Saving lives or bigger steaks for the officers? "Make that a 400 gramme fillet please waiter."

If you were offered a lift to a place that didn't have a Ride Safe sign you were then legally obliged to walk to the next sign so you could humbly stand there, head bowed, awaiting your next lift. In my case, being dropped off somewhere on the road between Beaufort West and Laingsburg would've meant a three-hundred-kilometre stroll through the bone-dry Karoo. Brilliant thinking. Like most army rules, we ignored it and made our own plans; which often meant kneeling in the road begging for a lift nowhere near any Ride Safe sign.

Standing on the steaming roadside for hours on end could result in strange thoughts and delusions. On long stretches of road, I often glared at oncoming cars that were just a speck in the distance, imagining myself as 'Ridesafeman' with powers of autosuggestion beaming telepathic waves that would persuade the driver to give me a lift. My superpowers worked – once every hundred cars or so.

Once a year, the Big Crocodile grudgingly bought us train tickets for our annual leave. If they'd actually given a shit about us, we'd have had automatic passes for all public transport and at least one flight home a year. Hundreds of troeps needlessly died in car accidents as they tried to make it home or back to base. Strangely enough, I never saw the Big Crocodile or Magnus sticking their big thumbs out on the side of the road.

The worst feeling in the world was hitching from the sanctity of home back to a place I hated. Facing a 1200 km trek, I had to set off at a sparrow's fart to get back before parade the next day. I'd get dropped off on the N1 near Goodwood and start staring down drivers as they passed me by – I was saving their pathetic lives from the hordes of Communist heathens amassed on our borders, but most didn't give a shit.

The Yanks might be bat-shit crazy but at least they get their troeps safely home; admittedly, hitchhiking from Iraq to Kentucky for a weekend pass would require some decent lifts.

251

> State of emergency declared. Regulations governed security, media and black education. Initial period of detention extended from fourteen to thirty days.
>
> 11 June 1987

Weekend in Durban

My mate Speedy and his girlfriend were heading up to Durban for a week, so I decided to pull in for the weekend. He'd just finished his national service and was ready to celebrate. Like me he'd never expected to do his time but his tale was a bit different.

Speedy had dodged national service by joining Safmarine – part of the South African merchant navy. They had a massive fleet transporting South African wine, fruits and nuclear bomb-grade uranium around the world.

He'd signed up for five years and had studied at the Louis Botha Naval Training School in Green Point; a dodgy area full of sweaty joggers, sliced golf balls and over-friendly dolphins.

For years he'd sailed the high seas, sampling the illicit wares of Hong Kong, New York and Sydney and experiencing some local culture. These cultural exchanges mainly occurred in the red light districts and his generous offer to teach the ancient African dance of jiggy-jig usually ended in mass brawls and a night in a local police cell. At least he made an effort.

After bidding *bon voyage* to Safmarine he ended up on the oilrigs that had mysteriously sprung up around Mossel Bay. International sanctions were biting hard and South Africa was relying on him and his mates to find oil.

Speedy sporting his expensive new sunglasses, which I customised, to make sure he didn't look too cool.

We were in deep trouble. Even with the future of the country in his trembling hands he never seemed to show any signs of strain. Luckily, his Zen-like philosophy of 'not giving a fuck' helped him deal with the stress.

Speedy was meant to have done five years service in the merchant navy which would have exempted him from National Service but he'd left after three and a half years for the lure of the oil rigs. Good bucks but as the navy was in desperate need of some fresh blood especially with a seafaring experience he got called up for six months' National Service. So after years of swanning around on the rigs, he now had to do three months' basics at Saldanha and another three months in Wingfield. This was a shock to his system and would put his skills of deception and manipulation to the test, fortunately he'd gone to Pinelands High and within a week he was out on leave.

Using a combination of lies, threats and financial incentives he'd swung the balance of power into his favour. The leading seamen in charge of training were putty in his hands, although I nearly screwed it up by attempting to punch one of them at the Pig one night – not my brightest idea, as the leading seaman's dad, owned the Pig and a lot of the other pubs I frequented. And I'd have been *moered stukkend*.

After finishing his basics, Speedy somehow became a law officer at Wingfield. This was mildly surprising as his only knowledge of the law was gained from breaking it...repeatedly. The next three months consisted of him breaking all the rules, putting himself on charge, marching into his own office, berating himself for his various misdemeanours and then handing himself a lenient suspended sentence; a bit like the ANC nowadays.

I couldn't wait for Friday to arrive; I even snuck off a bit early, utilising my new leopard crawling skills to reach the security fence, scrambling over, and with a bit of *loop-en-val* action got far enough away that I couldn't be seen hitching.

I got a quick lift to Bethlehem and then another all the way to Durbs.

It was my lucky day. Speedy was only landing a bit later, so I headed to Magoos bar near the beachfront. It was infamous, as it had recently been bombed by the ANC, which had resulted in multiple deaths and injuries. Despite the humidity, I was wearing my big jacket. Security was tight, and a huge bouncer sized me up as I approached.

"We need to search you for weapons," he said

"No problem, can't be too safe, hey?" I replied.

I was knackered after the combination of a long journey and having drunk my traditional two-litre Klippies-infused

Coke. As he patted me down, he felt a metal object in my pocket.

"What's that?"

"Ah, hold on, just my penknife, wanted to be safe on the road."

I pulled out the offending object and put it on the table.

The security guard was now a bit rougher.

"Anything else?"

"Nope, that should be it."

As he felt in my pockets he pulled out an eight-inch hunting knife.

"Sorry, forgot about that one"

"Can't be too careful hey?" replied the increasingly wary bouncer. "I suppose I'll find an R4 next?"

I nervously laughed as I tried to remember where I'd left it. Then he pulled out a bayonet from another pocket. I expected to be kicked out immediately, but instead, shaking his head, the bouncer simply took them away for safekeeping and let me in. He'd been a troep as well.

Speedy finally rocked up and we had a great night at Magoos. Eventually I staggered out into the steamy Durban night with my little arsenal of weapons back in my pockets. We spent the rest of the weekend, carefully avoiding the beach by sticking to the many pubs that lined the beachfront. On Sunday afternoon, I hitched back to base, my luminous Ride Safe strap complimenting my badly sunburnt face. I looked like the Mouille Point lighthouse by the side of the road. By midnight, I was back in base.

1983. Corner of Liesbeek Parkway and Durban Road, Mowbray, Cape Town.

My boet was killed when he got knocked off his motorbike, slid along the road and broke his neck on the pavement. The next day we had to identify him at the morgue. Our family would never be the same again.

My boet Andy; a gentle soul forced to become tough. Sadly missed.

We lost many troeps on the border but many more were killed in car crashes during their service; troeps who'd jol on the weekend, have no sleep then try and race back from their distant homes at the last second. All over the country exhausted troeps would attempt the dangerous journey back to base. Many fell asleep at the wheel with deadly consequences for them and their passengers.

We lost many at the School of Engineers during my time there. I can recall a carload of corporals crashing on the way to Bossies. Many of them died.

Chapter Twenty-four
Broken Promises and Broken Windows

This is a tale that has little relevance to this story but I'm hoping to bribe the Looty who caused all the kak, so please bear with me. Hopefully, he is now a pillar of society with a large bank balance and a wife who'll *moer* him *stukkend* if she ever hears the truth.

It was a messy evening. Lightning was splintering the stars and rapid-fire raindrops were scaring the cockroaches. Slab and me had been requisitioned for a vital mission to save the civilised world. At least that's what they told us. With a sweetener of a hundred bucks we were happy to risk our lives, limbs and souls. The dirty truth was that our Looty had scored a private land-surveying job in the quaint Northern Free State town of Heilbron – about a hundred clicks from Kroonstad. He'd already pulled in another Looty who was a qualified surveyor (the blackmail candidate). Now they needed a couple of troeps to assist. Slab and I had some amateur surveying knowledge and being broke, we were obvious candidates.

It was a Friday night when we headed off and for once I didn't need to forge my Looty's signature. He did however look a bit perplexed when he saw seven pages of his forged signatures in my passbook, but before he could ask any awkward questions I ripped it out of his hand, made a joke and scuttled out to the car.

For years, the provincial government had been sending the Heilbron Municipality millions of rands for them to improve conditions in the local township. But instead of putting it into desperately needed basic infrastructure projects like a sewage system, roads and electricity, a town clerk had always returned the money. Not sure why; maybe he couldn't be bothered with the paperwork, maybe he thought the township folks preferred candlelit meals, bucket toilets and broken car axles – maybe he was just a *doos*. Eventually he resigned and a new town clerk decided to spend the money on what it was intended for and called in a land-surveying firm. Luckily it was the firm my Looty used to work for before he went to the army. A week later, we entered Heilbron.

By this stage my initial ecstasy of earning some illicit bucks had been tempered by the first four letters of the unknown hamlet that I was entering. Heil-Bron. Who the hell was Bron and why was he being Heiled? Maybe we'd stumbled into the final hiding place of the SS.

We booked into the local guesthouse and excitedly headed out to hit the local hot spots. Ten minutes later we were back, clutching toasted sandwiches, a case of Castles and the distinct impression that the good folks of Heilbron didn't enjoy outsiders invading their only pub. Even though I was the only real soutie in our group, the patrons of the *kroeg* had decided that we weren't to be trusted and after one *dop* the barman started ignoring our plaintive requests for liquid sustenance. It was an insult but we were so tired we headed back to the inviting luxury of our four-inch foam mattresses and pine beds. The locals had won. Or so they thought.

The following morning we wolfed down our breakfast of creamy scrambled eggs, baked beans and extra crispy bacon. Then the town clerk escorted us as we nervously headed to the township.

In those days, there were no tourist-friendly tours – showcasing arts, crafts and traditional dancing; townships were supposedly dangerous.

We drove down the main road full of green lawns and then klapped a quick right into the township, where we entered another country. It was like landing on Mars during a bad drought. No green grass or vegetation, just desolation and red rock.

It was pretty obvious why the local black folks were pissed off. Although their township was only metres away from a well-maintained town centre, it was clear that no money had been spent on their needs. First-world tar roads dissolved into third-world dust as soon as they hit their area. Electricity cables came to an abrupt halt as soon as they came within half a kilometre of a shack. There were no tarred roads just dirt tracks with speed bumps in the form of dongas, hills and rocks strewn across the roads – 4x4 enthusiasts would've loved it.

Somehow the locals, using their innate ingenuity and perseverance, had constructed strong homes and further up the hills there were some brick houses with gardens and commanding views of the rest of the township.

We weren't quite sure how to start so we just parked our car and began surveying. The job was to survey the valley so the builders could install sewage pipes and electrical cables and maybe turn the dirt tracks into tarred roads. We slowly moved in, metre by metre. We soon passed the first house where inquisitive eyes peered out from behind the curtains.

Heilbron was not Soweto. It was a quiet place but the locals were still wary of us and followed our every move. When they saw that we looked like confused idiots they calmed down.

However, by day two we realised that one local resident was following us a bit too closely. He was a young man, about twenty, and he didn't like us. Wherever we went, he was one step ahead, warning people that we were coming. We couldn't understand it. We were trying to make life better for the residents. What was the problem?

One resident told us that he was the local ANC representative. This was our first confrontation with the enemy. Eventually, we got so close that we asked him to come chat with us. He declined and moved off.

The next day he started asking questions.

"Who are you? What do you want?" he shouted from a suitable distance.

As proud members of the SADF we were confused and angry about his questions.

"Fuck you. We are here to make your lives better," the Looty shouted back.

"Ja?"

"Ja, we are going to build roads and put in electricity."

"Where have you been for the last fifty years?" he demanded.

"Not sure, I'll ask my superiors and get back to you," our Looty replied as we carried on.

He kept following us and then interrogating the locals about what strategic questions we'd been asking. He must have been disappointed; we were on a strategic hunt for cheap Castle quarts.

It was hot and dusty work, but by Sunday afternoon we'd finished the survey. Parched and starving, we headed to the local pub, where they treated us like shit again so we returned to our guesthouse to have a few beers in the Looty's room. All military hierarchy went out of the window as we slowly got pissed together.

Hours later I staggered off to bed and passed out, only to be woken mid-slumber by our Looty barging into the room and informing us that we had to leave immediately. He made it clear that this was an order and not up for discussion. We grabbed our shit and headed to the car where the other Looty was already waiting in the front seat, looking worse for wear. We were barely out of Heilbron when our Looty burst out laughing. In my dazed state, I had no idea what was going on, but then it all came out.

The other Looty, now slumped in the passenger seat, had decided to show his displeasure at our treatment at the local pub. Unfortunately, this was at about four in the morning and nobody was there to accept his verbal complaint, so he spent a few minutes throwing bricks and stones through the pubs windows. Upon completion of his complaint, he staggered back to the guesthouse and mentioned that we might need to leave a bit earlier than expected.

For the next few weeks, we waited for an order to report to the CO's office, but when nothing came, we knew we'd gotten away with it. The local ANC guy probably got the blame.

Hopefully the other Looty has since repented and seen the error of his ways and if he'd like my bank details, he can contact me on: blackmail1@goldmansachs.com.

R100 000 should ensure I don't release his name.

Chapter Twenty-five
Cough

Not sure how he pulled it off but Slab got a transfer to Pretoria. This was a sudden and unexpected development. It shook me to the core and although I was happy that Slab was escaping, I was the *moer-in* that I wasn't getting out. Now I was on my own against the Sarge, the Colonel and what felt like the whole army. Our little site hut became an even more lonely and depressing place. Even in our most desperate times Slab and I could somehow conjure up some humour, usually aimed at our oppressors. Now I had nobody to chat to or plan the building work with.

I was now in charge of the project, which was a slight problem since I knew fuck-all. Slab was a proper civil engineer, university educated – so at least he had a bit of a clue. He knew the big words that could confuse the Colonel and Sarge, but I had just played along, nodding wisely.

My days were kak. It was either freezing cold or stinking hot. If I ventured out of my little refuge I'd be stopped by Sarge and asked what I was doing. *"Fokol"* would have been the honest answer but that would've meant even more questions and maybe some work. The days dragged on.

I had no other goals except finishing my two years and getting my life back on track. My only respite from army life was having a beer or two in the canteen after work.

Fortunately Castle beer was super cheap in the army.

Thank you, Charles Glass. I'd shake your hand, but it would probably fall off and my grave-digging days are over.

The canteen was great for getting shit off your chest, and we had a lot of shit to deal with. Maybe it would've been better for my sanity to pitch in more with the Sarge; spending more time bricklaying and trying out some carpentry, but he despised me. I did help out a few times and when you're left alone, bricklaying can be quite relaxing. Monotonous but you drifted off into peaceful oblivion as you trowelled the mortar, added brick onto brick, squared them up and tapped them into perfect alignment. Standing back, I'd admire my masterpiece until Sarge came along and kicked it down – just because I'd gone fifteen degrees out of line and blocked the entrance to the toilets. Fucking perfectionist. I skulked off to have a cigarette break for a couple of hours.

Huddersfield, 1976

For centuries, the tobacco industry had pulled off one of the greatest marketing frauds the world has ever witnessed. They had claimed that not only were cigarettes cool and trendy, they were actually good for your health. They even had thousands of doctors recommending them. However, by the mid-seventies, smokers were increasingly keeling over from strokes, heart attacks or lung cancer. The cat was out of the bag: sucking in the burnt ash of the tobacco plant might not be good for the lungs – the anti-tobacco campaign began in the UK.

As my folks were both heavy smokers, most British adults were, I decided to do my bit. Not wishing to become an orphan I put Operation Cigarette Capture into practice. Ably assisted by my boet, we went about stealing our folks' and their mates' packets of Rothmans, Senior Service, Woodbines

and other glamour ciggie brands, and hid them around the house.

A month into the operation, we were running out of places to hide the contraband. Our dog, Jingles, was getting grumpy from having his sleep disturbed by the uncomfortable layer of a hundred cigarette packets we'd hidden under his blanket. Drastic action was required, so I started selling the cigarettes we'd confiscated. I soon had a thriving business with all the juvenile delinquents and teens stressed out by school. Unfortunately, running an illicit business and surviving school is also stressful and after going through a crash-course on tobacco sucking, I was soon smoking a packet a day myself. I'd cut this down to about fifteen a day by the time I arrived at Bossies.

Similar to prisons, cigarettes were a currency in the army – an early form of crypto-currency, but without all the overheating computers. Cigarettes were the opium of the armed forces. Whenever we got bored, we smoked, we were always bored. I was bored before I was even awake. It got so bad that before I opened my eyes in the morning, I found myself shoving a cigarette in between my lips. Everybody was so stressed that even the top athletes were smoking twenty a day, and when you ran out, you became desperate and vulnerable enough to do someone's guard duty shift for a packet of ten Cavalla Kings.

You could often work out the background of a troep from his cigarette brand:

Chesterfield: The mainstay of army smokers; toasty and flavourful, a trusted and proudly American brand. The majority of troeps were Chesterfield loyal, which posed a major problem because everybody bummed off you.

Gauloise: A French newcomer to the lung cancer market, but for those who could take the powerful hit, a trusted companion. Mainly for romantics, who visualised themselves blowing smoke into Ingrid Bergman's angelic face during their exile in Casablanca. A bit more expensive, but gave you a good dizzy buzz.

Cavella Kings: For the poverty-stricken; popular in Thornton and other suburbs on the Cape Flats. Not a bad smoke if you could only scrape together enough small change for a packet of ten. Popular in the week before you got paid.

Texan Plain: For prop forwards, bricklayers and PFs. A macho cigarette for those who wanted to cough like a cowboy. The downside was spending hours picking tobacco strands out of your teeth.

Peter Stuyvesant: For movie buffs, alpine skiers, super yacht owners and army admin clerks.

Rothmans: For the mentally deranged, trainee smokers and army chefs.

Benson and Hedges: For juvenile girls and troeps with superiority complexes.

Senior Service: Designed for sailors, marines and masochists. Tasted like dog shit mixed with straw. Nobody bummed them. I smoked them throughout my two years.

Gunston : For surfers, car mechanics and army barbers.

Most mornings in our barracks weren't heralded by the soaring trumpet notes of the Reveille, but rather a coughing symphony of tar-filled lungs, desperately trying to ingest some air.

Most troeps had a signature cough:

The Coronary
Cough, cough, ccccccccough, ker, ker, ker, cough, oh shit, arrgggh, cooooooooofffffffffffffffffff. Clutches chest, leans against wall, sweating and hallucinating.

The 'Can I join this conversation?' cough.

Ugh, ughm, ughm, Uuuuuuuuuughm.
(Repeat until somebody notices you.)

The Elevator
Cough cough gurgle clang grrrr hack hack Hack HACK POP. Repeat.

The Beethoven's Fifth.
The first cough of the day, otherwise known as 'Morning Has Broken'

A subtle rhythm of hacking coughs that built to a crescendo, followed by a cannonball of phlegm exploding from the mouth, which shot up a metre and went back into the mouth of the sleeping troep to continue the cycle, until it was finally swallowed, causing choking, tears and a terrified awakening.

There were also a lot of dagga rookers in HQ. In fact, the leader of the Dagga Party, Jeremy Acton, who spearheaded the partial decriminalisation of dagga in South Africa, was in

our HQ media section, or the goofball squad as we called them.

Many evenings saw some of us taking surreptitious strolls into the veld to smoke a joint. I wasn't a big *rooker* but I'd tag along for the laugh. It reminded me of my early days living in Pinelands when I met a *femme fatale* who turned both my head and my five-speed bicycle.

She was called Wendy Oldfield, but most folks knew her simply as Wendy Ohhhhhh. The face of a cherub and the habits of a sinner. A flamboyant wild spirit, with a heart of nine-carat gold. The singing queen of Garden City.

1977. Pinelands, South Africa

I first met Wendy at school. She was in my boet's class. A sassy, classy girl with the voice of a fallen angel who'd swallowed Maria Callas. For some reason she'd fallen for Andy's bewildered innocence. Unfortunately, he was too bewildered and innocent to realise his golden opportunity for love in the first degree. Wendy was throwing so many signs that Andy got dizzy, so I tried to assist and ended up jolling with Wendy and her best mate, Cathy Turnbull; two stunners with characters to match. They took us under their luminescent wings and, lo and behold, we felt safe and protected from evil.

Later, Wendy would teach us all about the wonderful fauna and flora of our new country including a lovely plant used by the indigenous people to ease childbirth pains. Fascinating, and even though Wendy wouldn't be pregnant for many years to come she would regularly smoke its leaves just in case.

Every day, fellow journalist/newspaper boy Suttie and I would congregate just behind the Central News Agency

(CNA) in Howard Centre and wait for the newspapers to arrive. Wendy Oh would sometimes pop over to buy a banky of 'Easy Childbirth medicine' off the paper deliverymen. Sometimes I'd join Wendy as she headed down to the canals to expertly roll a joint and we'd sit on the canal bank, watching the litter float past and natter about music. We were both fanatical music lovers who devoured copies of the New Musical Express and Melody Maker. As we got more medicated we'd discuss The Sex Pistols, The Police, U2 and her all-time favourite, David Bowie. We sat there until I'd hear the distant sound of drums (that might've been the dagga working) or Suttie yelling for me to pick up my load of newspapers.

Doing the paper round also meant that I made my first proper contact with the local Xhosa folks. Back in England, many of my friends and football teammates were multi-cultured – from Pakistan, India, and the West Indies and other exotic countries that have always fascinated me. I'd never been programmed to hate other races, as my folks were too busy to be racist. I was fortunate to have that kind of upbringing; it's allowed me to meet and become mates with great people of all shades, from around the world.

Most of the deliverymen came from Langa, a township next door to Pinelands. They were great characters and made a mockery of the 'swart gevaar' tactics used by the Nats.

Like us they would cycle around our quaint little suburb chucking the Argus or Cape Times onto the pristine lawns and some would make extra bucks selling some of the best agricultural crops Transkei could produce. They always seemed happy. They might have been doing some quality control testing.

Moor End Comprehensive School first-team football.
Black, white, brown and ginger.

Pinelands was way ahead of the curve when it came to the decriminalisation of marijuana. Even in the seventies, most people in the Garden City turned a blind eye to it. Possibly because nobody knew what it was, what it looked like and what it smelt like.

It was all going so well until one fateful day at the Howard Centre shopping centre. The loading area for the CNA was where we congregated to wait for our bundles of highly anticipated (and heavily censored) newspapers to arrive. Sometimes, the delivery was slightly delayed and so swayed by boredom and pangs of hunger we'd huddle in a corner and spark up a few joints.

One day, upon finding our regular corner blocked by a stack of building material, we ended up smoking in a different corner.

In the midst of discussing the post-modern relevance of Andy Warhol's retrospective portrayal of Marilyn Monroe, we were cut short by the arrival of the CNA manageress, Mrs Schmidt, who stumbled around the corner and started screaming at us. We tried to work out what she was saying, but it was plain to see that she was gerook. 'Not setting a great example to the youth of Pinelands', I remarked. Then a procession of grannies staggered out of the CNA clutching their copies of Fair Lady and laughing their blue-rinsed heads off as they headed to Pick 'n Pay to buy munchies and condoms. Suttie, who had only smoked half a joint as he was busy training for the army, soon pointed out the cause of the mayhem; an air conditioner directly above us was greedily sucking in the dagga fumes and pumping it straight into the CNA shop. We never smoked under the aircon again, but at least the deliverymen got a few more dagga orders from the local retirement home.

Kroonstad 1987

Romance in Genieskool was sadly lacking. The women in base were either already married to some creep in the army or preferred a soldier who actually had some gold kak on his shoulders.

The lowly sapper wasn't going to be getting any tender loving in Kroonstad, unless you were Doopy and Swanny, our resident gigolos. These two legends of 35 Regiment had met up with a couple of local girls desperate for some military manoeuvres. So every time Doopy and Swanny were on guard duty, they made a plan to meet up with the girls at the main gate. The main gate was shit to guard because you had to stand at attention the whole time, ready to leap into action as cars drove in and out. Nobody wanted to do it, except Doopy and Swanny.

After taking up their posts, they'd contact their chickies, who'd sneak into the little main gate guardroom with bags of food and an insatiable desire for a *bietjie vry* (bit of fun). One would be escorted to the toilets where the defender of the free world would perform his gentlemanly duties while the other stood guard. If anyone asked where the other guard was, they explained that he had gyppo guts and was occupying the toilet. Doopy and Swanny were the most sexually satisfied troeps on the base – and the fattest.

---

9 July - 12 July 1987

Sixty-one white South Africans, mainly from the Afrikaans community, meet the ANC in Dakar, in search of a democratic alternative for South Africa. Eric Mntonga, an IDASA official, who organized the meeting, is found stabbed to death shortly afterwards.

Chapter Twenty-six
No room at the inn

In the army every second felt like a minute, every minute like an hour and every hour like a day. My first year felt like a lifetime, or at least two years and a bit. It makes you go *mal*. You think you'll never get out.

I'd literally stare at the clock on the wall and that bastard second hand would just linger, laughing at me, then slowly tick over and snigger. I eventually snapped it off.

Just before I completely lost it my Looty decided I deserved a stripe. He'd obviously mistaken my hiding from work and forging his signature for signs of a dedicated sapper. I loved him.

Getting a stripe was a big thing. 'Lance Corporal' was the first rung on the long ladder to earning respect in the army. It also allowed you to stroll out of the base, go into the NCO's bar, get a pay raise and steer clear of guard duty.

By this time we were on guard duty three nights a week; three nights freezing my sensitive soutie balls off and getting no beauty sleep. I was turning into an ugly eunuch.

Practically everybody in the army had a bloody stripe by the time my Looty proposed me for a promotion. I was being ordered around by assholes that could barely tie their own bleddy bootlaces; I thought I'd be a shoe in. A week later, the Looty stuck his head in and told me I'd been rejected. I thanked him profusely then forged his signature for a well-deserved weekend away to get over my disappointment.

After a few rants in the pub about the unfairness of my lack of promotion, one of the admin clerks slipped me my army file for a quick read. Written in big red-ink letters across the front was the reason for all my hassles: *Geen Godsdiens Nie* – Not Religious. Bliksem! Evidently you had to be a Christian to get rank. Had they never heard of famous genocidal atheist killers like Adolf Hitler, Pol Pot or Stalin? Unfortunately, various bloodthirsty Christians like George W. Bush, Tony Blair and other Crusaders had trumped them.

5 October 1987

President P.W. Botha decides against scrapping the Separate Amenities Act, but agrees that some residential areas can be opened to all races.

Just as I was losing all faith in humanity the end of our first year came up and that meant a nice juicy pass. We could choose to take our first end-of-year leave either over Christmas or New Year's Eve.

The thought of sitting with my Dad in our dingy flat with a sad plastic Christmas tree and a couple of paper bells nailed to the wall as we *suiped* half a bottle of medium-cream sherry wasn't too enticing. (We never took our Christmas decorations down, not much point when you have to put them up again in ten months, so they got a bit tatty).

My vacation plan was to head down to the coastal resort of Plettenberg Bay where I'd meet friends, party and chill out.

This had been a tradition since a rowdy bunch of Pinelands High skollies headed up there in 1979 after finishing matric and established what is now known as the Plett Rage (we might've had a shit rugby team, poor academic marks and a dodgy reputation, but I'm claiming this one for us. I don't remember any other schools being proudly represented by marauding drunken packs like PHS). I'd been up to Plett every New Years since then, and I didn't intend missing out just because of a war.

By the middle of December we were short of guards due to a scarcity of JLs, who'd just finished their training, meaning guard duty every alternate night. Then, with half the HQ troeps on Christmas leave, those remaining had to stand guard all day and night. This was going to be brutal in the mid-summer heat. Once I stood guard at the main gate where there was no shade and my lips turned dark blue due to my soutie blood trying to get to the surface to cool down – or so I was told when I finally regained consciousness in the medics' room.

After seven days of being pan-fried and surviving on less sleep than an insomniac dung beetle on Tik, we were all cracking. As soon as my last shift finished, I staggered out of the guardhouse, grabbed my balsak, climbed over the fence and headed down the N1. Now I just had to hitch from Kroonstad to Bloem, then to Colesberg, klap a left in Beaufort-West, straight down to Oudtshoorn, through George and Wilderness and into the welcoming bosom of Plettenberg Bay or at least somebody's welcoming bosom.

I headed off with my standard issue re-hydrating two-litre Klippies and Coke to keep me company. What could go wrong?

I quickly got to Bloem and by two that afternoon I was already in Colesberg. Things slowed down after that and by ten that evening I'd only made it to Wilderness.

By now it was so dark motorists couldn't see my gentle, non-threatening hazel-brown eyes. All they saw was an exhausted, drunk and fucked-off loony gesticulating wildly on the roadside. They would have been crazy to stop for me.

Finally, it dawned on me that our noble leader, PW Botha (Big Croc) had a home in Wilderness. Surely the man we were fighting for would be honoured to host one of his loyal and brave troeps for the night? After a few bemused looks from the locals at the pub, I was directed to a house by the lake.

It was a dark night and after stumbling through ditches and bushes, I was covered in mud, grass and branches; add in some Black is Beautiful and I was ready for an ambush. A couple of lights were still blinking in the distance and I aimed for them. It was a house called Die Anker. Original. I approached and pressed the buzzer.

"*Ja?*" came a distant sleepy voice.

"*Hoegaan dit President? Dis Sappeur* Bardsley reporting for a bed *vir die aand asseblief.*"

"*Wat?*" replied our glorious president.

"*Ek is op pass en ek need a plekkie to slaap.*"

"*Dis die fokken President se plek,*" said the person on the other end who probably wasn't the president.

"*Ja, ek weet?*" I mumbled.

"*En jy het gedink dat hy 'n fokken gastehuis het?*"

"I'm not sure what that means but I promise to be quiet and not leave a mess," I pleaded.

"*Voetsek!*" shouted the person who definitely wasn't the president.

"Is that a no?" I inquired.

I heard the distinctive click of the phone being slammed down.

Bastards. What kind of leader leaves his troeps in danger and despair? This one.

"*Dankie for fokol*! FREE MANDELA!" I screamed back.

I saluted smartly, about-turned and marched straight into a bush. Which idiot had put that there? God, it was dark.

My faith in humanity destroyed, I spent the next hour trying to get back to the N2 highway, which was clearly visible in the near distance – unfortunately there was a great big bloody lake in the way. My shortcuts kept ending in wet feet and more swear words. When I finally staggered back onto the highway, I found a truck driver at a garage and after a short monetary negotiation I was on my way to Plett.

The next morning I woke up in some bemused stranger's tent. Apparently I'd barged in during the night, requisitioned his tent in the name of the SADF and told him to stand guard outside. I apologised profusely, handed back his girlfriend and blamed it on PW. Then I went looking for my mates and that welcoming Plett bosom I'd been promised. After a week of intense *ballas-bakking* and sucking on a lot of Castles, I dragged myself back to the N2 and headed up to Kroonstad for my final year.

About a month later I took my bungalow buddy Gramps down to Cape Town. He was from the sleepy Eastern Cape dorp of Dordrecht and I promised him a weekend of debauchery in Cape Town. After working out what debauchery meant, he happily signed on.

We set off early one Friday morning and were just outside Bloem when a red VW Golf came screaming past at approximately Mach 2. Incredibly, he slammed on brakes, came screeching to a halt a kilometre passed us and reversed as we jogged towards him.

I dived into the front seat and Gramps took the back.

I thanked our driver for stopping and he told us he was headed for Cape Town and was in a bit of a hurry. We'd scored a fat luck.

Our chauffeur was about thirty-five years old, fair hair, skinny but muscular. He didn't say a lot – the quiet broody type. He wore leather driving gloves, had a thin moustache and reflective sunglasses. Not always good signs.

Within seconds of setting off, the G-forces kicked in. I glanced over to the speedometer, which was already up to about 180km/h. My left hand slowly crept up to grasp the grab handle above the passenger window. It stayed there, held tightly, until we got to Cape Town. Our speed hovered around 220, occasionally coming down to 180 when negotiating short curves. We swiftly swept past any cars and trucks that got in our way and within seconds, they were mere dots in the side mirror. There was little chatter. Gramps and I stared ahead in terror of what was coming up on the horizon. We were convinced we were going to die a fiery death in the Karoo, and by his constant reciting of the Lord's Prayer I sensed that Gramps was regretting his decision to visit the Mother City.

Somewhere close to Colesberg, we thought our time was finally up. In the distance, I saw movement in the road. As we screamed towards it, I saw the silhouette of a man forming. He stood, arms folded, in the middle of the road. Our eyes widened, silent screams forming in our throats. He must be on a suicide mission. With five hundred metres to go, the figure raised an arm to stop us. Fuck! It was a traffic cop – whose eyes were also widening. We were going too fast to stop. The cop dived to his left as we flew past him. We nearly splattered him. Shaking like a leaf, I swung around to see him staggering up off the roadside.

I expected Mad Max to try and escape. No chance.

He slammed on brakes and headed back to the shaken traffic cop who was dusting himself off. Just as I was expecting a dramatic arrest, Mad Max wound his window down and started *kakking* the cop out.

A brilliant strategy as the cop was now confused and flustered; he'd nearly been despatched to the afterlife by a small German automobile, and now he was being insulted by its insane driver. Mad Max claimed to be a captain in the Secret Service and on an important mission. Not sure why he couldn't have taken the plane like most self-respecting secret agents, but I'm sure he had his reasons. The cop fought back valiantly, showing us the speed trap data. We'd been doing 202. At that speed, he told us, he couldn't even fine us. We were supposed to go straight to jail, where we'd remain until we were hauled into court. Mad Max scoffed at the cop, showed him a bunch of official-looking papers and told him to phone some general in Pretoria. We sped off again, leaving the cop scratching his head and readjusting his tattered uniform and ego.

Thanks to the delay, Mad Max had become Furious Freddie. He slammed his foot down again. I tried to close my eyes but that was even scarier. Gramps whimpered in the back.

We powered past Colesberg and through the Karoo until the traffic lights of Beaufort West slowed us down to about 100. Touws River and Three Sisters were a blur, and in a flash we'd cannonballed into the Hex River Valley – one of the most beautiful valleys in South Africa; a rich tapestry of golden vineyards and colourful fruit farms. A head spinning collage of rustic gold's and bright reds framed by towering granite mountains reaching up to a bright, innocent blue sky or so I've been told; we were too busy clenching our teeth and hanging onto the grab handles to notice.

The previously straight N1 highway had transformed into a series of sharp bends, that, on one side, featured an unyielding mountainside, and on the other, nothing but a poephol-opening drop that plunged hundreds of metres into a rocky ravine. The speed limit was down to sixty, but Furious Freddie wasn't going to be deterred. He kept his foot down, and we hit the bends at about 120. The tyres locked into long skids, then resumed their normal cycles into the next straight until we screeched around another bend. I don't know how we got through, maybe he was Jody Scheckter in disguise, or maybe he was just lucky.

Once through the Valley, we flew past Worcester and entered the newly opened Huguenot Tunnel. Furious Freddie even attempted to overtake a truck in there, until another truck in the opposite lane nearly took us out. When Gramps finally dared to open his eyes at the other end of the Tunnel, he got his first glimpse of Cape Town and Table Mountain; he thought he'd gone to heaven.

Five hours and fifty minutes after leaving Bloem, we were dropped off near Goodwood. Furious Freddie didn't say much as we stumbled out of his Golf; he simply waved us goodbye with a leather-gloved hand and roared off. I couldn't believe it. We'd covered nearly a thousand kilometres in less than six hours. It was still light – I'd always arrived back home in the dark of night. I was also amazed at how this particular little Golf had handled the road and how fast it was. I'd ridden in other Golfs before, but nothing like this one. It was their souped-up model, a serious sports car. The signage at the back read 'Golf Oettinger' – it should've been called a 'Golf OooohIthinkweareallgoingtofokkingdie'.

After gripping onto the grab handle for almost six hours, I couldn't bring my arm down. It remained stuck in that position for the next few hours, making me look like Hitler at a Nuremberg rally – I received some strange looks from the locals and a couple of Sieg Heils from some AWB fans as we strolled towards Thornton.

After facing death on the highway Gramps now had to survive a weekend jolling with my mates. Out of the *potjiekos* and into the fire.

> Fierce fighting erupts between Angolan and South African forces for control of the strategic town of Cuito Cuanavale in Angola.
>
> 29 February 1988

Chapter Twenty-seven
The Viking

The Viking was a Swedish-born Capetonian who'd pitched up out of the blue in Kroonstad. Tall, blonde, heavy Nordic accent and still in his blue navy uniform – didn't stand out a bit.

He'd just finished his civil engineering degree so had been posted to the School of Engineers. However, he hadn't fancied the idea of a fun-filled two-year stint in sunny Kroonstad so on his call-up day, he pitched up at Saldanha Navy Base and claimed he'd been called up to the Navy. They had no record of him, but seeing as he'd had the decency to pitch up, they klaared him in and he completed his basics there.

Although the wheels of the SADF bureaucracy turned rather slowly, even those dimwits realised Viking wasn't meant to be there and eventually they despatched him from his cushy posting in Simonstown to his original call-up in not so cushy Kroonstad.

Viking was allocated to our bungalow and ended up in our construction office. Within 24 hours he'd had enough and requested a transfer back to the Navy in Simonstown. He was so desperate that he even refused to change his Navy blues for our army browns. We all laughed at his naivety but he was dead serious.

There wasn't a lot required of me at the sports centre, other than popping in once a week to do a report, so I was put in

charge of building a security fence around the storage area for the mobile bridge parts at Bossiespruit. Viking joined me and we got chatting. Although both his folks were Swedish, he'd also been caught up in the SADF's sweep for young, foreign cannon fodder. For a race of people notorious for raping and pillaging Northern Europe, he was remarkably calm and collected; admittedly, there wasn't a lot to pillage in Kroonstad.

The basic plan for the security fence was to sink metal posts into concrete bases, attach wire mesh, tighten, and *hey presto!* – a secure park for the valuable bridge parts. We were joined on our venture by David; a local Sotho worker on the base. David, Viking and I would be dropped off at Bossies every day after breakfast.

Chatting to David was enlightening. Though initially hesitant, he soon opened up about his life, culture and hopes for the future. Like most black people, he wasn't a commie radical but a hard-working family man who simply wanted the best for himself and his family. Together, we got stuck into the heavy physical work. It was stinking hot, so by mid-morning we were all bare-chested and drenched in sweat. I was in peak condition, my well-defined torso glistening and sexy little smudges of red dirt handily disguising my acne. If Anneline had got a flat tyre on her way to the Thaba Nchu Sun, and wandered past looking for a garage, she would've lost her shit. I'd have needed to hold her off while the concrete set, but would've definitely been up for a ravishing afterwards – so long as we had a shower first, obviously. Luckily for Sol, her re-treads must have lasted.

One day, while riding on the sports truck back to base, a roef told David that he should sit at the back because "k****r's don't sit with whiteys."

To my eternal shame, we put up little resistance. We were exhausted from work and outnumbered by his fellow rugby players, but we should've done more.

It certainly confirmed that this war wasn't about preserving the 'love thy neighbour' ethos of Christianity, but about us whiteys being the *baas*. David took it in his stride. He'd experienced it too many times. Classy bloke.

Maybe it was a combination of the solitude, being our own bosses plus the satisfying hard work but we enjoyed ourselves and took our time finishing our assignment. Then, Viking got his wish and ended up being transferred back home – still in his blues. What the actual fuck? How did that happen? What about me? I should have worn a clowns costume and been sent back to the circus. I realised that I was in for the duration.

Chapter Twenty-eight
Operation Hot Dog

With eight months left before freedom, most of us were running short on money. The pay in the army was pitiful: R200 a month, or R220 if you had a degree or diploma – they hadn't mentioned that at the career guidance seminar. Although we were fed, clothed and housed, we still needed to buy toiletries, snacks, smokes, booze, group therapy sessions and the latest *Scope*. Any pass also involved expensive rounds of drinks as we attempted to impress unimpressed girls at the bars we frequented. We were skint.

One evening, while arguing about whose turn it was to lick the condensation off our communal beer bottle, we decided that we needed to make some extra bucks. Maybe we could hire ourselves out as mercenaries or male strippers. Once we'd stopped laughing I recalled a conversation I'd had with Sneezer's younger brother, who was doing the CO's course at our base. He'd mentioned that they were starving and would pay anything for a hot dog. I looked at the others, realising we could help him achieve his dream and make some bucks at the same time. It wasn't exactly Ocean's Eleven; more like Bossies Four, but I was sure we could pull it off. And so Operation Hot Dog began.

I'd be the brains and financier, because I had just about enough money to buy the rolls and Vienna's. Glen would do the cooking; surely even an army chef couldn't screw up a hot dog.

Mike, the lance corporal, was our logistics expert as he could get out of base without a pass and make the hazardous trip to the Seven-Eleven for the ingredients. Peppy would be the lookout – he was so tall he could look over walls.

It would be a task fraught with danger. We would have to sneak past the PF houses, cross no-man's land, pierce the inner defences by climbing over a perimeter fence, and finally locate Junior Sneezer and his salivating comrades. If caught smuggling hundreds of illicit hot dogs we'd be in deep kak so it needed to be attempted on a dark night. We worked out the date of next new moon and synchronised our watches with Junior Sneezer. The countdown began.

The Bossies Four soon met to discuss pricing. It had to be a decent 'Return On Investment'; no point risking an *opvok* for a few extra bucks. We decided on two bucks each – five times the going rate on the street but since we were defending Capitalism we might as well exploit the desperate.

Two days before D-Day (Dog-Day), Mike bought two hundred Vienna's and rolls. The shop assistant was naturally suspicious but Mike's claim that they were for the upcoming World Jukskei Championships allayed her fears.

Dog-Day finally arrived and as darkness crept over the camp we gathered in Mike's room, ready to spring into action.

Although Glen had keys to the kitchen, we only had a small window of opportunity to complete our mission: the greedy officers often demanded food up to midnight and we had to be out before 4 a.m. when the chefs arrived to prepare breakfast. Glen headed off to the kitchens to give us the all clear and we silently exchanged glances, wondering how The Big Crocodile's noble warriors had descended to the level of selling boiled pig entrails just to survive.

A rap on the door sent us scurrying under the bed before Glen whispered the password: "Letmeinyoufuckingidiots" – we sheepishly opened the door. The kitchen had been liberated.

Glen carefully unlocked the kitchen door and we snuck inside. Phase One of Operation Hot Dog had passed without a hitch; no Vienna's were lost and the rolls suffered zero collateral damage. We kept the lights off just in case Staff Sergeant Snor was sniffing around and soon large pots of water were boiling under gas flames. We got to work, buttering the rolls and slipping glorious pink Vienna's into the churning water. Before long, our first pork martyr popped its head up above the water and was immediately engulfed in the warm embrace of a Sasko roll.

Phase Two; After slapping tomato sauce on the first fifty hot dog rolls we headed off with our stock, leaving Glen to boil some more pig sludge. It was well past midnight and pitch dark, the only sound was the buzz of cicadas conducting their prehistoric symphony. I wasn't fooled though; that nocturnal nightmare Staff Snor specialised in ambushing unsuspecting troeps. I kept my eyes peeled and my ears open for any suspect movement. We skirted the edge of the PF suburb, praying that the aroma wouldn't wake the greedy bastards and cause a food riot.

Once past suburbia, we leopard-crawled through no-mans land where I was suddenly struck by a premonition that the troeps would be asleep and wouldn't want our culinary delights. I'd be down fifty bucks and lose all the respect of my maatjies, or whatever was left of it. I shook away the thought and kept crawling until we reached the vibracrete wall that marked the perimeter of the junior COs' barracks.

Phase Three: Peppy hauled himself up the wall and confirmed that the coast was clear. Now, we could put our wall-vaulting training into practice. He and Mike got into position next to the wall and I clambered over them, vaulted the wall, executed a sweet Parabat roll and waited for the applause that never came. Peppy lobbed the hot dogs over and Mike joined me and we sidled along the side of the bungalow to the front door. Luckily there were still signs of activity as the troeps were still finishing their inspection preparations. We snuck in, silenced the Bungalow Bill and soon found Sneezer Junior.

As soon as we lifted the lid, the porky aroma filled the room and a feeding frenzy erupted. Troeps crammed as many dogs down their throats as possible. They were practically throwing money at us and I thought I was going to lose my fingers in the chaos.

A few weren't happy about our extortionate prices but after hearing our explanation about the free market system and its inherently exploitative nature, they abandoned their Marxist doctrine and were soon six rands poorer but a bit fatter. We soon ran out, so Peppy and Mike headed back for more supplies while I continued taking orders. Other bungalows heard the commotion and came to investigate; the orders shot through the roof. We'd stumbled on a gold mine – a starving gold mine.

After three more trips we ran out of Vienna's. Even the ones we'd strategically requisitioned from the kitchen store had been scoffed. To appease the troeps still begging for more, we slapped tomato sauce on some old rolls, and charged them fifty cents.

With a fistful of dollars we bade farewell to our satisfied customers and asked Sneezer Junior to help us over the wall.

"Why don't you just use the gate?" he tuned.
"What?"
Five metres from where I'd left some shin skin climbing over the wall was an unlocked gate.
Bloody hell. Who'd put that there? Red faced, we scarpered back to our barracks. Luckily Staff Snor wasn't around; probably busy throwing bricks at the guard huts.

As we sat on my sagging bed dividing up the profits, my chest filled with pride. The Bossies Four had joined the illustrious company of the Berlin Blockade heroes, the Siege of Kimberley saviours and Frank Sinatra, who'd defied international sanctions and bravely sung at Sun City for Anneline and some money.
Capitalism had triumphed and Communism had suffered a bloody nose.

Chapter Twenty-nine
Flower Fountain

For some odd reason, just as winter peaked, I was asked to go to Bloemfontein to assist them on a building; another bloody sports centre. Had they forgotten the concrete this time? Hadn't they learnt that I didn't have a clue about construction? Army logic.

Bloem was only two hundred clicks away, but it was a bustling metropolis compared to Drowned Horse Town. The Bloem army base, called Tempe, was the largest in the country. Within its massive perimeter lived The Panzers, 1 Special Services Battalion, School of Armour, Parabats and 1 South African Infantry; so there was plenty of pent-up aggression, fear and rivalry – like a Sandton gym after a delivery of steroids.

Fortunately, the Big Crocodile had found a surplus thirty rand in the defence budget for train fare, so I didn't need to walk there. When I got off the train at Bloemfontein Station, I was so busy strekking and saluting all the officers hanging around that they thought I was having an epileptic fit. Luckily, they didn't pin me down and ram a wooden stick between my teeth – Kroonstad had really fucked me up.

Far from the madding crowd, I heard a faint voice calling my name. A corporal had been assigned to escort me back to base and *klaar* me in. After I'd stopped kissing his boots, he ceremoniously hurled my kit into the bakkie and we headed off.

It was my first time in Bloemfontein and my eager soutie

eyes tried to take it all in. It wasn't quite as bad as all the comedians had joked; I didn't spot many combs secreted down socks and only a few women were carrying oxen on their shoulders. Surely Joe Parker hadn't lied to me?

As the judicial capital of South Africa, Bloem had some magnificent buildings, including a university, which meant there might be people willing to converse in English. I brightened up.

We eventually drove into Tempe and without a snarl or an insult I klaared in. One PF even smiled at me; must be a trap, I thought. Then I was taken to my new barracks. I was nervous about who I'd be sharing with as it was always a bit of a lottery; a mixture of the Good, Bad and the Befok.

On our way there, we drove past the expansive parachute training facility of the Bats, the massed ranks of the Panzers' Olifant tanks, and the sprawling obstacle courses specially designed to sprain the ankles of the troeps at 1 SA Infantry. A quick left and a sharp right, and we stopped outside a smart block of flats. The corporal got out I stayed put; they'd obviously mistaken me for a corporal or a lieutenant or a civvy.

The corporal looked at me like I was an idiot.

"This is it."

"Are you sure, Corporal?" I asked, checking to see if I'd grown stripes or pips on my short journey.

I eventually got out, and together we carried my heavy kit inside. Though it was a nice block, the idea of sharing a tiny flat with guys I didn't know wasn't very appealing. The corporal led me through some corridors and up a flight of steps until he unlocked a door. Not daring to walk in, I hung back and peered around the corner. What the hell? It was a bachelor flat; one bedroom with a single bed, a tiny lounge and a bathroom. I looked like a stray dog that had finally

been adopted. It was luxury. Lassie had come home.

"But Corporal, I don't have any rank."

"Lucky you," he smiled as he strolled away. "Breakfast starts at six, be on site for seven."

His voice trailed off and I tried to work out if this was my guardian corporal back to rescue me. Possibly but he'd grown a moustache and put on some weight, probably all the good food up in heaven.

The next morning, I woke up in my own bed, in my own room, with my own bathroom and last but not least, NO PARADE. I merrily skipped down the stairs to the dining room; crispy bacon and fluffy scrambled eggs for breakfast. Nobody screamed at me. I was in seventh heaven, okay, I was in Bloemfontein but it felt like seventh heaven.

In Kroonstad, your stomach was always tight as it waited for the next bit of kak to hit the *windpomp* so this was unbelievable. I almost felt like a normal human again. I finished brekky, asked directions to the new sports centre and trundled out into the stark, barren landscape of a Free State winter. It was ball achingly cold and the lifeless, frozen grass crunched under my boots. I was soon lost but that allowed me to see how big Tempe was. I walked past the training grounds of 1 SAI, spotted parabats carrying their rocks, saw some tanks revving up at the Panzers, before I eventually found the sports area.

Having experienced months of kak with the sarge back in Kroonstad, I was expecting the same in Bloem. I found the building site and marched over to the two sergeants who were standing around a glowing brazier, drinking coffee. I slammed to a halt, stamped my feet and came to attention.

"Sappeur Bardsley reporting for duty, Sergeant," I bellowed.

They nearly dropped their coffee.

"*More, Sappeur Bardsley*," one said, wiping Ricoffy off his chin. "We need to ask you something."

Oh dear, that didn't sound good.

"How many sugars do you want in your coffee?" I thought I heard him say.

"Pardon, Serseant," I replied.

"I have three but I'm trying to cut down," said the other one smiling at me.

Bloody hell, what was going on here? Where were the cameras?

They were serious.

Soon, I was sipping on a big steamy mug of boerkoffie, with three heaped sugars in. My Guardian Corporal had also thrown in the most chilled sergeants in the whole army. They were *ou toppies* (old guys), who'd spent all their army time doing building work, and it showed; they weren't interested in pulling rank, and cared only about getting the work done. They'd been there for ages, and, having reached the rank of sergeant, weren't bothered going any higher. They could've been back in Civvy Street, but the army took better care of them.

For the next two months, I helped the sergeants lay bricks, install doors and windows, and drink lots of coffee. I was also responsible for drawing up the plans for the interior cupboards and storage space; they'd obviously confused me with someone else – I'd never designed a cupboard in my life. I did my best, hoping nobody would actually use them because they'd probably fall apart in minutes.

My sergeants never stopped smiling and saying what a lovely day it was, even when we were getting soaked in one of Bloem's occasional freezing cold storms.

They were 'Born Agains', who, not long after I'd admitted to being a three-spoons-of-sugar-in-my-coffee person, asked me whether I'd 'seen the light'.

I started scratching around in the storeroom in search of some sixty-watt bulbs until they gently insisted that they meant "Had I found Jesus?". Before I could even ask when he'd gone missing, they launched into the story of their own salvation. Seems like the two of them had been a bit naughty in their youth, but had seen the errors of their ways and become born-again Christians. Now they wanted to know about my relationship with the Son of God. I ummed and aahed for a while, but they had the patience of saints. I finally confessed that my relationship wasn't great; in fact, it was non-existent – I was agnostic – I wasn't sure if there was a Son of God, or a God. They were taken aback, but instead of giving me shit, they insisted on praying for me – which was even worse. For the next two months, they gently attempted to guide me back into the light – while I gently hid in the dark.

Now that I was in the culturally adequate environment of Bloem, I figured that I ought to bring Anneline down for a visit to my new home. I naturally needed to spruce the place up a bit as she'd become accustomed to the opulent, kitsch architecture of The Lost City.

To make Anneline feel more at home I scoured the shops looking for an exact replica of the ten ton, six metre high sculpture of a magnificent bull elephant that graced the entrance of the Lost Palace. Unfortunately the Seven-Eleven had just sold the last one so I had to make another plan.

I immediately consulted the Yellow Pages for interior designers in Bloem. Unfortunately, Koekemoer Butchery and Hardware had recently closed down, forcing me to use my own fertile imagination. Maybe some doilies and a nice chandelier would add the finishing touches to my new home (I'd been a chandelier cleaner in London in 1981 so at least I could do the maintenance). Anneline always had a thing for chandeliers; she'd swung on one in a highly respectable video shoot, and it had made an impression. I needed one badly, but sanctions were biting deep and the Venetian Glass Chandelier Company wasn't returning my calls. It was no use, I'd have to use African improvisation. The next day I clambered over the security fence, leopard-crawled down to the Seven-Eleven and bought forty-six copies of Die Volksblad. I stuffed them into my balsak and after remembering that I wasn't in Kroonstad and didn't need a pass I boldly strolled back through the main gate.

After two days of masticating 921 Volksblad pages, I made the world's biggest papier-mâché chandelier. I then spent the next two days suffering from ink poisoning and lockjaw. I retreated to my cold, single bed, joyous in the knowledge that it wouldn't be long before I felt the sweet gentle touch of Anneline's well manicured hands wiping my fevered, and slightly inky, brow.

After a few sessions talking to the porcelain telephone I'd recovered enough to call Anneline on our private line. After spending forty minutes listening to the recorded message of my nemesis (Sol), and giving them my Dad's credit card details I was finally put through to Sun City.

"Hi."

"Hi."

"How are you?"

"I'm fine."

"I'm fine too."

"Please, could I speak to Anneline, please?"

"Which one?"

"The blonde one."

"Ja."

"Thanks."

Twenty minutes later.

"Hello sir, can I help you?'

I'd recognise that slightly nasal Welkom accent anywhere. I could barely contain my emotions.

"Is that you, Suikerbossie?" (My nickname for her)

"Would you like the amazing two-week high-season special Sun City offer, or the one-week pathetic losers package?" her sad voice replied.

What the hell was she on about? Her voice sound strained, almost Brakpan-ish. My sensors pricked up at the danger signals. I had to think quickly. With my highly sensitive sound receivers (ears), I'd noted a distinctive click sound in the background; a Beretta .45 being cocked. Sol must've heard of my recently acquired, compact yet classy residence. He'd also realised that his captive lovebird (Anneline) was desperate to admire my handcrafted but still soggy papier-mâché chandelier. That multi-millionaire bastard was holding a gun to her head. She was his hostage! My chirpy songbird was in mortal danger. What could I do? I hedged for time but it was no use; I could hear Sol's heavy breathing bearing down on her. I did what any honourable man would do: with an anguished sob I bought a weeks timeshare at the Cabanas in Sun City – off-season, obviously.

For years afterwards my Dad tried to fathom out why he was paying seven hundred rands on his credit card for a timeshare he'd never bought. But my 'Suikerbossie' was safe for the moment, and that's all that mattered.

It was weird staying in the flats. I was one of the few troepies there without rank, but nobody gave a shit. Once you took your beret off, there was no saluting, so it came off as soon as you entered. It was amazing at first, but without a pub or braai area, everyone stayed in their own flat so there was very little social mixing. This was great, if you wanted to be a hermit but I was eager to mix with the general population so I started going into the city centre looking for some entertainment.

I found a couple of hotel pubs where I'd grab a beer and try to start a conversation, but it wasn't easy. Like most locals, the people of Bloem didn't trust outsiders, even those from the army – especially those from the army. As national servicemen, we were like a red flag to a bull, or a cheetah, in Bloem's case. They thought we were there to steal their girlfriends, we were but that's not the point.

On weekends, I'd often watch the rugby at the Free State Stadium, which kept me entertained for at least one afternoon but apart from that Bloem was no Las Vegas. The other downside to Bloem was its weather; it was winter, and even colder than Kroonstad. I was outside most of the time and had to wear loads of warm clothing and thick leather biker gloves just to avoid getting frostbite. It was a bugger trying to lay bricks with them on, but at least I still have all my fingers.

I'd just taken my annual leave and like most troeps, I'd had the foresight to steal another passbook, so once I got to Bloem, I reapplied for my annual leave using my dodgy second passbook. They had no idea who I was, and within a few weeks I was back on the train to Cape Town for my second annual leave.

When I got my relaxed bronzed body back to Bloem my Sergeants informed me that they were going to be transferred up to the border to build a top-secret structure – probably another bleddy sports centre, I thought. Their destination was a base called Mpatcha on the Zambezi River bordering South-West Africa and Angola.

They were looking forward to a change of scenery and weather and asked me to join them. My guess was that they fancied another crack at converting me. I've often wondered how many points God awards per conversion.

<u>Conversion points</u>
Lapsed Christians: 10 points
Agnostics: 15 points
Buddhists: 20 points
Muslims, Hindus and Jews: 25 points
Atheists: 30 points
Ozzy Osbourne: 7000 points

I soon heard from Pete Wainwright, who was now a Looty on the border, that Mpatcha was a decent base – as long as nobody was trying to kill you. I was so desperate to flee freezing Bloem, they could've sent me to hell and I'd have been first on the Bedford – so I put in a transfer request. About a week later, it was denied. Bliksem! Now what? Apparently they couldn't transfer somebody who was already on an inter-unit transfer. What kind of army was this? I was willing to sacrifice myself, yet some bureaucrat couldn't be arsed to fill in some forms. No wonder we drew.

Not long after my PFs left, the sports centre project came to a grinding halt. I was gutted. Eventually, I was spotted wandering aimlessly around Tempe with my spirit level and trowel, and was sent back to Kroonstad.

I was actually happy to return, as I'd be reuniting with my mates back there. Although life in Drowned Horse Town was shit, at least you had maatjies to share your pain, cigarettes and Scope (they'd run out of the June 1988 edition).

There was a silver lining to the dark clouds enveloping me as I returned to my home base. As soon as I got back to Kroonstad I pulled out my third passbook and promptly applied for my third annual leave. A week later, I was back on the Trans Karoo train headed for Cape Town. By this stage, the train conductor and I were on first-name terms.

In my second year I *skelmed* so much leave I was thinking of getting a part-time job back in Cape Town. My mates couldn't believe it and I heard dark rumblings from some of my more *paraat* chommies.

"Are you actually in the fucking army?" Moose chirped.

"*Voetsek, jou naai*," I replied haughtily as I swept my fringe out of my eyes, closed the till, handed him his change and gave him his KFC family bucket.

Chapter Thirty
Barbra Streisand and the Groot Meneer

Somebody had screwed up; I'd been given a day pass. This was unheard-of in our base. The last thing the good folks of Kroonstad needed was random sex-starved troeps wandering their neat streets and chatting up their lusty daughters. Maybe it was a test.

By now, I'd become so institutionalised that simply walking down the driveway to the main camp gate, even with a pass, felt like a subversive act. At any moment I expected to be rugby-tackled by stern-faced military police and dragged off to jail. I kept an eye out for cameras and spies but it seemed I was in the clear. I carried on walking.

(There's not a lot to see in Kroonstad. I've just Googled 'Things to do in Kroonstad', one result – have a cappuccino. At least things have improved in the last thirty years. If we had asked for a cappuccino at the local *kafee* in 1988 we'd have been arrested for blasphemy)

After some research on the delights of Drowned Horse Town I headed straight to the closest pub. I don't like pubs – I love pubs. They're pretty much my first home, my own home being my second home.

I spend a lot of 'awake' time in pubs, unlike my real home where I just sleep, if passing out can be considered sleeping. I love the heady conflict of danger and cosiness, alcohol and televised rugby. It's always a volatile mix, especially inland, where loudmouth drunk souties screaming for Western Province are seriously frowned upon.

I aimed for the main street in town. The choice of bars in most *dorpies* during the eighties was usually limited to the Royal Hotel, the Main Hotel, and the Voortrekker Hotel. They all looked like they'd been designed by the same manic-depressive architect – bland and uninspiring. I soon sniffed out a suitable drinking hole. It wasn't quite Neo-Gothic architecture, and not really Art Deco – more along the lines of Neo-Ugly. I wasn't too fussy.

The place had a big Castle Lager sign on the outside and that was enough to bring a tear to my eye and heartburn to my chest. I strolled in through a pair of swing doors, like those in Western saloons; that should've been an immediate warning sign. As I made my dramatic John Wayne entrance, I paused for applause and the inevitable looks of admiration. Unfortunately, I'd forgotten Newton's seventh law of physics: swing doors will *moer* you hard in the back if you don't move *fokking skerpish* – I got off the floor and made my way to the bar counter. There wasn't a lot of chatter going on, these were serious *suipers*, no amateurs here – my type of crowd.

They'd clearly invested on the interior décor. Faded Castle, Lion and Hansa beer signs were nailed to the bare, filthy concrete walls. A forlorn set of kudu horns decorated one wall, complementing the 1984 Currie Cup rugby fixture list that was still prestiked onto the pine wooden cladding.

A fly-splattered fluorescent light cast a dim glow onto the row of blubbery, khaki-clad ass cracks that greeted my entry. This was the main bar, men only, and through another door was the Ladies' lounge, which was empty.

In those days, women weren't allowed in the main bar —
because we'd have to stop swearing and telling dirty jokes —
they'd obviously never spent a Friday night at the *sokkie*
(dance) in Kimberley. Personally, I think it had more to do
with not wanting the hassle of wearing underwear and using
deodorant.

Most of the men were probably shy and would have
struggled to strike up a conversation with the fairer sex. I like
women. My Mum was one and my granny as well and over
the years most of my girlfriends have been women, but the
chances of Sapper Soutpiel receiving some tender loving in
this pub were minimal, I'd have had more chance of a
Springbok call-up.

I found a spare stool at the far end of the bar and climbed
up. After adjusting to the altitude sickness I looked around
for the barman. There he was, perfectly poised, like a tightly
coiled spring, ready to launch into action. My thirst was
about to be quenched in epic proportions. I tentatively pulled
two rands out of my pocket and surveyed the multitude of
choices on the bar shelves: four bottles of Klippies, two
bottles of Three Ships whisky, a bottle of Mainstay cane, Old
Brown Sherry, Russian Bear and Smirnoff vodka for the
larneys and the Mayor. It was like being in Valhalla (Viking
heaven, not that shithole in Pretoria).

As I started salivating I thought I'd better pace myself. I'd
start proceedings with a beer. Due to the ironclad monopoly
of SA Breweries, the choice was limited to Castle, Black
Label, Lion and Hansa. My unswerving loyalty had been
swerving between Castle and Lion for many years, and on
the occasional full moon I'd even sneak in a Hansa. This was
way before the heady days of craft beers; even Windhoek
was regarded as exotic in those days and a request for an
Indian Pale Ale would've led to a swift phone call to the

police station and an escort out of the province.

After mopping up my dribble from the bar counter, I decided to go for a Castle; years of repeat marketing campaigns had done their job. The barman was still tightly coiled so I gave him the age-old signal that I was ready for some booze: a raise of the eyebrows, a slight smile and that knowing look between two compadres that doesn't need any translation.

He ignored me.

Shit. I'd found the only halaal barman in the Free State. Apart from the vastly superior Parisians, South African bar staff have always prided themselves on some of the best customer evasion tactics in the world. I, on the other hand, had always prided myself on being successful in my pursuit of booze and the thought of some twat keeping me away from my liquor stirred my loins and bowels. I settled in for the battle. Calling on many years of 'barman begging' experience I realised I'd need to bring out my A-game.

My adversary had a few obvious advantages; he knew the field of combat better, was familiar with the local conditions, had the support of the local alkies, possessed the bottle opener, and was backed up by an evil sign over the front door that said something about reserving the rights to kick me out if he felt like it. But I still held the edge – this was my Blood River, my El Alamein, my Vietnam. I was desperate and I was going nowhere without a *dop*. There was tension in the air, although that might have been my body odour. I realised that I would have to employ some of my classic moves:

The Alligator

A slow lean-over-the-counter-and-make-yourself-look-big-while-glaring-at-the-barman move. Usually assisted by standing on that little metal pole designed to help jockeys and short sappers get some attention.

The Outrageous Yawn

Designed to embarrass the barman as fellow drinkers looked around and wondered why he's allowed a fellow suipgat to fall asleep instead of serving the elixir he craved.

Can be enhanced by laying the head on the bar counter and emitting snoring noises. This was my go-to method if I'd been waiting more than two minutes at the Pig.

The Stockbroker

The money-wave-combined-with-a-subtle-drop-of-coins move (visual and sound effects to hit the senses, possible use of farting to hit all three senses, but only in emergencies).

The Hack

Like Japanese water torture, but more annoying.
Persistent coughing to get the attention of the barman. Caution: can end up in coughing spasms and possible asphyxiation. Only to be used by experts.

The Barbra Streisand

Negative psychology. Act as if you don't need a dop, totally ignore the barman and get him to beg you to buy a drink. Finally relent and make your comeback. Flick your hair and coo occasionally as you sip on your Mainstay and bitter lemon.

The Switch

Stand up and walk around so the barman sees you, then exit dramatically. Two minutes later, limp back in wearing reflective sunglasses, a gaudy Hawaiian shirt and a false beard. Never fails. It failed.

And then, as a desperate last resort:

The Oscar Winner
Walk directly up to the bar, look around wild-eyed and start blubbering about parents, God, small children, the amazing crew and the academy members. Then burst into tears and hope the barman will hand you a dop to soothe your nerves.

I tried all my methods but nothing worked. My nemesis behind the bar looked at me like I was a madman then walked off with his broom. Shit, he was the bloody cleaner. Two minutes later the barman sauntered back in, zipped up his fly, hid his copy of Scope, washed his hands in the ice bucket and shuffled over.
"Ja, wat wil jy kry?" he demanded.
Realising that I might never get another dop, I went for bust.
"Two Castles, a Lion, and a Hansa. Quadruple Klippies and Coke…."
"I'm only allowed to serve doubles," he replied.
"No problem, give me two doubles and a pint glass and Four Russian Bear vodkas and Fanta Orange," I ordered.
"What?"
"It's a cocktail, trust me. And a double Coco Rico, crushed ice and milk."
"Full cream or low fat?" he enquired.
"It's 1988," I reminded him.
"Sorry, my mistake.
"And two packets of your finest Chesterfield cigarettes, please."

Five minutes later as I relaxed in the afterglow of alcoholic bliss, the swing doors were flung open and a *groot meneer* of a *groot meneer* strode in. He was sporting the latest Kroonstad fashion, ordered from *Boere Weekly*. An enchanting ensemble of polyester, khaki cotton and sweat. His xxxxxxxl shorts, barely containing his ever-expanding legs, were stretched to breaking point, every stitch screaming in agony. His classically tailored two-tone shirt was making a valiant effort to stay intact as muscles and fat jostled for position. He had a beard that made Paul Kruger look like a model for Veet and in an amazing feat of nature, his beard and chest hair had clashed on the border and were now firmly entangled. He must have been at least fifteen.

He strolled around the bar, slapping backs and crushing hands before coming across me. He checked me out and walked over menacingly, I was obviously the target for the day.

"Hey, troepie, moenie fokken mess with our girls, okay? Groot Meneer advised.

"Ja, meneer," I quickly replied.

To be honest, most of the Kroonstad *meisies* looked like they'd been messed with quite a bit already but the fear of being *moered* by *Groot Meneer* made me stare straight ahead working out whether it was mildew on the wall or retro wallpaper. All I wanted to do was to consume a lot of alcohol and be left alone for ten minutes without hearing any kak but of course, *Groot Meneer* had to prove himself to the rest of the tribe. The bar lady from the Ladies lounge came in for some change and the bar went quiet. She walked behind the counter, ripped apart a slab of biltong with her bare hands and popped open a Black Label quart with her eye socket. Impressive. I caught her looking at me and gave her a nervous smile as she stomped out, leaving faint indentations on the concrete floor.

Groot Meneer had seen the flirtatious exchange and saw his gap.

"Is you interested in my girl troepie?"

"Nee meneer. Not interested in your girl," I replied, not daring to look at him.

"Is you saying she's not good enough for you?"

"Nee, meneer, ek sê dat sy is lelik."

As I went flying through the swing doors, I cursed my Afrikaans teacher. Lesson learnt; I dusted myself off and fled back to the safety of my barracks.

The Afrikaans language, with its deep guttural sounds, is perfect for a good rant. Imagine a Beijing road sweeper with tuberculosis crossed with a misfiring Harley Davidson and you get a clearer idea. It's not well suited for reciting early eighteenth-century romantic poetry, but it's *die fokking beste* for *vloeking dom troepies uit*. I love Afrikaans nowadays. It's a wild language, unhinged, untameable and incredibly expressive. You can't beat the lyrics of Jack Parow, Brasse van die Kaap, and the sadly departed James Phillips AKA Bernoldus Niemand of 'Hou My Vas Korporaal' fame.

Nowadays, when I'm working somewhere in the world with a fellow Saffer and need a good skinner, I quickly switch to Afrikaans and enjoy the bemused looks on all the other faces.

Meanwhile back at base Suggsy had realised that army life hadn't quite met his expectations. He decided it would be best for both parties to have a trial separation. He went AWOL.

After a couple of months hiding on the beaches and in the pubs of Durban he ran out of money and options and returned to face the music.

They warmly welcomed him back by throwing him into the jail.

Suggsy sent me a message via one of the guards that he was back in town. It was all very cloak and dagger and I had to wait until the dead of night to sneak over and drop off some supplies: cigarettes, chocolate and the latest *New Musical Express*. They were going to keep him there for a couple of weeks until his upcoming appearance at the military court in Bloemfontein. Suggsy was scared but philosophical. He didn't know what to expect, and though it wouldn't be good, he just hoped that he wouldn't have to spend too much time at the military detention barracks. That was the stuff of nightmares.

Because the jail finally had a prisoner, Suggsy got the honour of being guarded twenty-four hours a day. I volunteered for a load of shifts. If the Count of Mondeor had to be guarded, I was the man for the job. The jail had about three cells, which were all quite big and equipped with a decent bed and toilet but after a week, Suggsy was getting restless so I decided to bring my portable TV down so he could also observe the doings and screwing's of the Ewings, like the rest of South Africa.

The cells were separated from the guard area by a barred corridor, which meant that I couldn't actually see Suggsy unless I went to his cell. There was also a corporal there, so I had to be careful. After some geometric calculations, I worked out an ingenious way of letting Suggsy watch JR, Bobby, Pamela and Sue-Ellen shouting at each other. I placed my TV on top of a cupboard in such a way that the picture reflected onto a window and then by strategically angling other windows in the corridor Suggsy could see the TV and also try to work out who shot JR.

A week later he went down to Bloem for his court case.

Luckily, he didn't get any time in army prison; unluckily he would have to restart his two years and that meant back to basics. We let Suggsy out of the jail with a sigh of relief; I'd had a tiny taste of life behind bars after an excursion to The Strand with Speedy and Whitey got out of control. I was relieved to be away from our own little Alcatraz.

My Dad meanwhile, was still struggling with his weird disease and his doctor had advised him to change his diet. Salads were now on the menu. Being from the north of England, a salad meant chips, baked beans and maybe some mushy peas but Dad had gone hard-core; lettuce leaves, tomatoes, cucumber, spinach, broccoli etc. Arriving back home during one pass I thought I'd entered the wrong house after opening the fridge and finding weird vegetables piled up where the beers and rump steak were usually stacked. This was getting scary.

A joint declaration released on talks held in Geneva by Angola, Cuba, South Africa and the United States announcing a formal cessation of hostilities in the Namibian border conflict.

14 August 1988

Our barracks were bordered on one side by the PFs' houses, most of them were married and had their own little suburb on base consisting of little red brick houses, surrounded by brittle yellow grass and dirt.

Whenever I ventured close, I'd hear the soundtrack to *Jaws* playing in my mind and the hair on my back would stand up. I kept well away.

Most of the PFs had signed up for an initial three or five years but when they slowly realised they'd never get a civvy job and that abusing teenagers was quite good fun, they kept signing on. As much as they knew they were the outcasts, they also had a bit of power, and boy-oh-boy, were they going to enjoy it. And what better victims than a bunch of fresh, terrified troeps.

One day I had to deliver some reports to a PF who was sick at home. Before entering their lair, I snuck through our barracks on a recce mission to observe any enemy movements. Peering over a wall, it was all clear but after I'd jumped into the road I spotted one of the PF's wives creeping into another house. She kept glancing around nervously, clearly she was also on a mission: Operation Love Cheat. Rumour had it that she'd been servicing half the PFs and her poor hubby couldn't stop her. This seemed to confirm it: she was a double agent.

Once the coast was clear I ran over the road and strode up to the PF's house to deliver the reports. I knocked and a grunted reply invited me in. As I entered, I went into slow motion, my boots sticking to years of congealed filth, half-chewed food and bad career choices left on the carpet.

The wife, firmly anchored to the gaudy couch with a screaming baby attached to her bosom, was trying to klap some sense into their brood of wild-eyed laaities buzzing on Coca-Cola and jelly tots.

312

The place stank. The PF motioned me over, took the reports and dismissed me with another grunt. I slowly backed out, desperate to escape without being eaten. These Bible-clutching fanatics had obviously forgotten that little bit about cleanliness and Godliness.

The next day the PFs would be ripping our rooms apart to find a speck of dust so they could kak us out. Bloody hypocrites.

Barend Hendrik Strydom, a former right-wing member, massacres six black people in a Pretoria street. He appears in court on six charges of murder and of attempted murder.

18 November 1988

Virginaai

Stompie an Afrikaans laaitie from Virginia, a nearby mining town, was always practising his English on me. He didn't fancy the idea of going down the gold mines, like most of his relatives, and hoped that a good command of the Queen's English might help him get a job above ground.

He often invited me to join him on a weekend pass at his place and enjoy the delights of Virginia. I would politely lie through my teeth that I had something else on, but after claiming that I had to babysit my grandchildren I realised that my excuses were getting too outrageous, even for me.

I succumbed. The next weekend, we headed over to his hometown.

I knew he was a rough diamond, but when we got to his family's house I was in for a nasty surprise. It was a bit of a shithole, surrounded by other shitholes situated in a town that was a shithole. The rich mine owners evidently didn't think that much of their white mining workforce, either.

As we dragged our tog bags into the house, I noticed a certain similarity to the PFs' homes back in base; it looked like an elephant's graveyard. Plates of bones lay scattered around the lounge and their pets were gnawing on a few more on what was left of the carpet. I was introduced to the Stompie's mum, who was seated on the couch, gnawing on a rack of ribs. She gave me a wink and offered me some – I decided to skip the vegan diet for the weekend. More bones ended upon the floor.

They generously gave me pride of place at the braai that evening and introduced me to half the street. Very few of their neighbours spoke English, and my Yorkshire accent had them in tears of laughter; my attempts at saying "*Jy's 'n klomp kak*" brought the house down. I was like a visiting alien.

Stompie's cute sister was particularly intrigued by *'die Engelsman'* and stayed by my side most of the night. As the beers and brandy flowed I relaxed into the evening.

The evening was a jol, and I eventually passed out on the sofa, surrounded by more bones and the happiest dog in the Free State. Some time in the wee hours of the morning, I felt some fiddling around my crotch area, probably the dog looking for another bone, I thought, and drifted off again.

After a few moments, I remembered that dogs' paws don't usually have such a strong grip. It seemed that Stompie's sister was up for a bit of Yorkshire pudding. By now she was putting some real effort in and not wishing to embarrass the poor love-struck creature I kept my eyes tightly closed. After a couple of minutes, she paused to spark up a cigarette. After launching into a long hacking cough, she resumed her noble endeavours, but just as I was going to heaven and back, I realised something wasn't quite right. Earlier that evening, the Stompie's sister had told me that she absolutely hated smoking. I shot bolt upright, and came face-to-face with the mum. She gave me a wink – I screamed – Stompie and his *sissie* flew into the room – the dog fled – and the mum just shrugged and went to the kitchen for more meat. As she and the sister swapped some pretty nasty insults, I went back to sleep but this time with my jeans on.

The next morning, things were a bit frosty around the kitchen table. The sister was angry, thinking that I fancied her mum more than her, and Stompie was pissed off with his mum for ruining the weekend. The *pap, sous* and ribs for breakfast was good, though.

A local rugby match that afternoon meant I could escape for a while so I hung around the rugby club bar until they threw me out. Then I slowly walked back to the house of horrors. Early the next morning, Stompie and I drove back to Kroonstad in silence. I thought he was pissed off with me, but he was just nervous about asking me to translate something his sister had said to his mum. I didn't have the heart to tell him what "decrepit drunken slut" meant, but I did mention that his sister shouldn't learn her English from watching *Dallas*.

Chapter Thirty-one
Kiss My Ass

1988 had been another long year; standing guard, abusing concrete moulds and gyppo-ing passes. Though I'd almost finished my two-year sentence I tried to tone down my excitement whenever I saw Suggsy. Due to his extended vacation, or AWOL as the army insisted on calling it, he'd only get out sixteen months later. Having to leave Suggsy was tough. I remembered my despair and loneliness when Slab had left and I knew that Suggsy would also suffer. Within months of me finishing he'd had enough and escaped to Europe. Years later, even with the ANC in power, he found out that he was still listed as AWOL and struggled to get permission to come home to South Africa for a visit. He had to change his surname to get in to the land of his birth.

With the excitement of our last few days building, we started the clearing out procedure. We had to be signed out by all the departments before being allowed to go home. The PFs, once again, held our fate in their hairy hands, and they knew it. We were terrified that some shit would happen and we'd be held back for some stupid reason. A few years earlier, a whole intake of troeps had been forced into doing another year; there had been some big attacks in SWA and the top brass had realized they needed them for a bit longer. We were worried that we'd also have to stay on; the thought of another year was too horrific to contemplate.

As we grovelled before the PFs at the stores, armoury, and in the admin offices, my dislike for them intensified. Even after two years of service they gave us kak for no reason. All I could do was take my signed slip of paper and tell them to 'kiss my ass' (in Gaelic, of course). I looked them in the eye and boldly said, "Póg mo thóin, sergeant". Most of them could barely speak English, never mind Gaelic so I was fairly safe.

During the final few weeks, one of the sergeants came around and asked if we'd like to do another year.

"No more camps, better pay, just one more year," he explained.

Once I'd dried the tears of laughter off the floor and put my contact lenses back in, I asked him if they'd finally give me a stripe if I stayed on. He said he'd get back to me. Still waiting.

A lot of veterans say they had a great time doing national service. I believe everybody had a different experience, and many have profound recollections of camaraderie and a sense of purpose. There wasn't much of that in Drowned Horse Town. I never saw any troep strolling around with a beaming smile, jumping into the air and clicking his heels together while humming 'Oh, What a Wonderful World' – except Doopy and Swannie when they were heading down to the main gate for their 'guard duties'. We marched around, grim-faced, with our eyes glazed over. But then, as we hit forty days before klaaring out, our usual sombreness changed. Our grim little faces relaxed a bit and we started to hum a Cliff Richard song:

I'm gonna give you, forty days to get back

I'm not sure why Forty Days was such a big milestone – why not thirty days? Maybe Cliff had also been a troepie, or maybe it was more Biblical: forty more days in the desert, resisting temptation from the Devil. Either way, we rejoiced as our time drew to an end; of course the final forty days seemed to stretch forever.

Our little band of HQ warriors made sure everybody knew we were getting out by flashing the *min dae* (few days) sign. You'd form a fist with your right hand, extend your little and index fingers to form horns, then try to get your fingertips to touch. The closer we got to klaaring out the closer the fingertips got. We strutted around the camp singing 'Forty Days' and showing the roefs our *min dae* signs. They weren't happy at our childish antics, but soon they'd become the annoying assholes for a year.

Our last day.

On our final day we merrily skipped down for our last breakfast; similar to the Last Supper but a bit earlier in the day – and with burnt baked beans on the menu rather than betrayal.

After licking our lips and patting our engorged stomachs we hit the parade ground for our emotionally charged passing out parade. All the top brass were there. For two excruciating years we'd waited for this sacred moment.

The CO gave an adequate speech about us having saved the civilised world, etc. We nodded enthusiastically, not giving a shit.

He mumbled some words to the RSM who in turn mumbled some more words before marching off. We all looked at each other. What the fuck was that? Are we finished? Where was the 'Ich bin ein Kroonstader' speech, or the 'I Have a Dream' or at least a Blood River analogy? It all fizzled out and we just stood around, looking at each other, waiting for the final command to klaar out. We were fifty *gatvol* troeps primed to throw our berets up in the air, cheer heartily, and hug each other manfully then *fok* off in a blaze of glory. Seven hundred shitty days waiting for this moment and it was a complete anti-climax; the fucking PF idiots couldn't even get that right. *Poephols.*

Eventually, we just rolled our eyes and slunk off to the cars to say goodbye to our *maatjies*. Under an incessant barrage of abuse and humiliations we'd looked out for each other and been moulded into a band of brothers. My fellow troeps had endured, survived and served. They hadn't asked to be put in HQ or Construction or Stores or the kitchen or some other kak position, but unlike the PFs, they hadn't taken their frustrations out on others; decent human beings, one and all. I salute you.

We'd already piled our meagre belongings into Glen's car, just in case the bastards wanted to fuck us around and we needed a strategic withdrawal.

We had become institutionalised. Freedom was a long-term concept. Even then, standing at the end of those gruelling two years we knew we still had another two years of army camps to come. They still had their claws in us, but for now, we were free.

We slowly drove out of the gate for the last time. There was no ticker tape parade, no tearful waves from the civilised world we'd just saved. Fokol. I do recollect a working gang of prisoners waving us goodbye. What a misunderstood bunch of people. Even though most of them had been badly maimed and only possessed their middle finger, they had the decency to enthusiastically wave us goodbye.

Anneline couldn't make it as she was still painting the ceilings at the Lost City. I wasn't too disappointed because we'd have plenty of time together in the future. Now that I was klaaring out, I'd be free to give her my unconditional love and attention. After two years I'd scraped together enough to buy her a sterling silver bracelet from Foschini, which was guaranteed to seal our love for each other. I was hoping she might reciprocate with a Rolex Oyster. Must have got lost in the post.

During my time away, Anneline had become a famous pop star and her debut single 'Don't Touch my Romeos' had created a tsunami in the music world. The lyrics were clearly a heartfelt plea for me to rescue her from her ordeal at the hands of the so-called Sun King.

In my opinion, it was a classic up there with 'Owner of a Lonely Heart', 'Love Me Do' and 'Sarie Marais,' but the fake news media in the form of the *Cape Times*, *SABC* and *Huisgenoot* in their liberal, elitist fashion declared it a

monumental flop. Fools. It was definitely monumental, but in a huge-stone-monolithic-box-on-a-hill-in-Pretoria kind of way. They clearly didn't understand the angst and heartbreak that Anneline had been trying to convey to the world and me; using a subtle subtext and Shakespearean undertones.

The song was all about taking off her Romeos (*I'm assuming this meant under-broekies. Naughty*), down at the bar (*Ladies' lounge, I think she meant*).
Then she couldn't wash her car *(After ten double Klippies and Coke it's never a good idea to perform manual labour, especially late at night on Voortrekker Road and especially not in high heels and wearing a Miss SA tiara)*
When a pretty, pretty boy tuned her howzit. *(Me, obviously, but I think she meant ruggedly handsome but it didn't rhyme too well)*
Then she had no desire to go back to the bar and drink some Old Crow *(A bit like Virginia wine. An acquired taste)*
Then she took off her Romeos again.

Nobody had ever written a song about me and I was truly honoured. It was a masterpiece and my heart ached whenever I heard it on the radio. Which I think was once.

In my effort to get her some exposure on *Pop Shop*, I sold my collection of second-hand hankies and bought thirty copies of the single. The song immediately rocketed up the charts to number 523, then stalled and disappeared without a trace. I've still got twenty-two spare copies in the loft and just like Bitcoin they've fluctuated wildly in value. I'm willing to sell some for a grand, or maybe a beer or whatever you've got, really.

Sadly, like Rodriguez, Anneline's musical genius has been ignored for decades but I'm currently filming a documentary that will once again place her at the pinnacle of World music. I decided that as soon as I got back to Cape Town I would rescue her and bring her back to my old suburb of Thornton. Maybe we'd rent a bachelor flat in Rifle Range Court. How could she resist?

Chapter Thirty-two
Don't Spare the Horses

Elated to be free we were soon on the N1, steaming back to Cape Town. Glen drove and we got drunk. Upon reaching the bridge marking the border between the Orange Free State and the Cape, we got out for a smoke and contemplated our newfound freedom. We saluted the Free State, then pulled our pants up and went on our way. Somehow, we'd made it. The longest two years of my life. I was almost twenty-seven. Life had sped past and I needed to catch up but first I needed to celebrate; South African Breweries ramped up production, Klipdrift planted more vines, and the pubs of Cape Town started hiring more staff.

Me, Mike and Glen on a bridge over the Orange River. Showing our appreciation for the Free State after klaaring out.

A year later, national service was reduced to eighteen months, then a year and in 1994 it was stopped completely. Bastards!

I was assured that this was due to us pulling out of Angola and SWA shortly after the battle of Cuito Cuanavale. I'm not sure what happened at that battle, I've heard conflicting reports about whether we won, lost or drew but it seemed to be the catalyst for our withdrawal. It signalled the beginning of the end for the war on the border.

Negotiations began and the UN Security Council Resolution 435 was passed. The SADF started pulling out of Angola and SWA as the peace process rolled on to independence for the newly named Namibia on 21 March 1990. (Bloody hell, I should've failed a couple of years at college and I'd have been fine. Loads of my mates had sneaked out of doing their national service. I didn't blame them. They headed to the UK, Australia or the USA, or stayed at college and university. Some only went overseas to do a weekend pottery course and ended up becoming professors of Ancient Greek history – that'll teach them.)

Apartheid was also coming to an end. The rise of the alternative Afrikaans movements encapsulated by the Voelvry Music Tour showed the Big Crocodile that many of the next generation of the Volk weren't going to accept the status quo anymore. Johannes Kerkorrel, Bernoldus Niemand, Koos Kombuis and many other rebels lit the way for young Afrikaners to reject Apartheid and demand reforms. The genie was out of the bottle and it wasn't going back in.

So where are the generals and ministers who sent us off to war?

Probably sat in their cushy coastal holiday homes, counting their lovely pension money and bitching about the New South Africa, while the countless troeps they'd sent into battle got badly injured, physically and mentally. Even today, many former troeps are out there battling to survive, stuck in rehabilitation homes if they're lucky, or out on the street if they aren't so lucky. Many have major anger issues that are often fired up by alcohol, drugs or a troubled conscience. Some have committed suicide, become alcoholics and died an early death. Consequences like relationship breakdowns, mental illness and self-harm are often invisible and hard to measure, but even today they're still out there.

Fortunately, I'd escaped fighting on the border or the townships but even I've lost it a few times since my army days; especially when I'd just got out. Two years of pent-up anger at our daily humiliations were stored up in our minds and fists. I was *gatvol* of being ordered around. Anybody telling me what to do or giving me kak was liable for a blast. Once at the Koeberg social club I threatened one of Speedy's customers with a broken tomato ketchup bottle – he'd insulted me about being a soutpiel – Speedy quickly jumped in before the man-mountain strangled me. On another occasion, I drunkenly pulled a knife on the poor barlady at the Underberg Hotel in KZN after she refused to serve me any more booze late at night. She patiently calmed me down and put me to bed. Fortunately, good people surrounded me.

The sports centre still stands proudly, possibly the most expensive building in Kroonstad, and definitely the heaviest; if there's ever a nuclear war, the aliens that come to inspect humanity's self-destruction will probably find it intact.

Your army ID number was programmed into your brain, tattooed onto your heart and seared into your soul.

Even after many years, every soldier remembers his number. I have no idea what mine is – selective amnesia, maybe.

What happened next?

Sneezer: He went on to become a lieutenant – a good one, I heard. After the army, he became a hippy and ran an aloe products factory. Eventually, the lure of cement dust dragged him back to the construction industry and he joined Afrisam, a leading supplier of superior quality construction materials. They made him COO of Aggregates and Readymix (a COO is like a CEO but has to impersonate a dove in board meetings). After years of hauling gravel around, his back gave in, but then he scored a *moerse* luck by joining Jojo Tanks as the Managing Director just as the drought hit. I hope he's got shares.

He's married to a Yorkshire lass, who keeps him humble and has two kids, who keep him poor.

Suggsy: After basics, he fled to Ireland before finally ending up in Brighton, England where he creates bespoke furniture. Even today the army has its claws in him; heading to South Africa for a visit, border control informed him that he'd be denied entry as he was still listed as AWOL. He had to change his name and get a new UK passport to see his family again.

Slab: As a proper civil engineer Slab started a road construction company which lasted for a few years. Later he immigrated to Australia where he is married with kids.

Speedy: Upon completing his six months' national service he'd acquired a taste for life on land, so he left his merry career on the oilrigs and went into business. While checking the form on a horse race in the *Cape Times,* he came across an advert promising him untold wealth and happiness. It was a franchise that offered software to teach people the science of trading stocks and shares. He didn't have a clue about trading shares but it would impress the girls so he bought the franchise with his savings. Surprisingly, it worked. There were enough gullible fools to buy into the promise of easy money and he soon moved into fancy offices in Green Point. He even presented a financial advice show on radio from the call box at Seagulls Bar in Green Point; the desperate cries of *suipgats* pleading for the barman's attention fortunately resembled the feeding frenzy of the JSE trading floor.

Financial independence and a glittering career beckoned but so did the pub. Eventually the supply of gullible fools dwindled and so did Speedy. Stock exchanges around the world breathed a sigh of relief.

He briefly flirted with the renewable energy industry but is now deeply embedded in the military industrial complex.

He resides in Durbanville, is married to one lady, has two kids and is still allowed in three pubs.

Colin Bardsley: My dad died in my arms two years later at St Lukes Hospice in Kenilworth. He was riddled with cancer.

Cape Town, 1989.

I was having a braai with all my chommies at Clyde Pinelands Sports Club and as often happens the chat moved onto politics. I was now *gatvol* of apartheid and its effects on the country and its citizens. I was ready to have my say. I'd done my two years. I'd earned it.

As I looked around at my best mates, the people I loved and respected most in the whole world – Beans, Pik, Moose, Speedy, Dougie, Stinky, Sean, Janet, Greg Thorne, Rory, Whitey, Mart, Pete, Daisy – two years' of pent-up frustration erupted.

"It's a load of kak. Bugger the Nats and PW"

Silence. All I could hear was the crackle of burning *rooikrans* and the sharp intake of breaths.

"Your *moer*," someone laughingly chirped. "When you've done your camps, then you can have your say,"

In the darkness, I couldn't help but crack a smile.

The Big Crocodile

18 January 1989: PW Botha suffers a mild stroke.

2 Feb 1989: PW Botha resigns as leader of the National Party.

March 1989: The NP elects FW De Klerk as state president but Botha refuses to resign.

14 August 1989: Botha resigns from the state presidency abruptly on. Complaining that De Klerk hadn't consulted him over his scheduled visit to see president Kenneth Kaunda of Zambia:

He said he had asked the cabinet what reason he should give the public for abruptly leaving office. "They replied I could use my health as an excuse. To this, I replied that I am not prepared to leave on a lie. It is evident to me that after all these years of my best efforts for the National Party and for the government of this country, as well as the security of our country, I am being ignored by ministers serving in my cabinet."[1]

De Klerk was sworn in as acting state president and immediately declared the need for change.

2 February 1990: De Klerk gave an address to the country's parliament in which he announced plans for sweeping reforms of the political system. He announced that a number of banned political parties, including the ANC and Communist Party of South Africa, would be legalised.

February 11, 1990: Nelson Mandela was released from prison after 27 years.

The Big Crocodile and his wife Elize retired to their home, *Die Anker*, in the town of Wilderness. It was widely believed that he remained opposed to many of F. W. de Klerk's reforms.

PW Botha refused to testify at the new government's Truth and Reconciliation Commission (TRC), which was chaired by his nemesis, Archbishop Desmond Tutu. The TRC found that he had ordered the 1988 bombing of the South African Council of Churches headquarters in Johannesburg, he was fined and given a suspended jail sentence for his refusal to testify in relation to the human rights violations and violence sanctioned by the State Security Council (SSC) which he, as president until 1989, had directed.

June 1999: PW Botha successfully appealed to the High Court against his conviction and sentence. The Court found that the notice served on Botha to appear before the TRC was technically invalid.

Tuesday 31 October 2006: PW Botha died of a heart attack at his home on, aged 90. His death was met with magnanimity by many of his former opponents. Former President Nelson Mandela was reported as saying "while to many Mr Botha will remain a symbol of Apartheid, we also remember him for the steps he took to pave the way towards the eventual peacefully negotiated settlement in our country".

President Thabo Mbeki announced that flags would be flown at half-mast but the offer of a state funeral was declined by Botha's family, and a private funeral was held on 8 November in the town of George, where Botha's body was buried. Mbeki attended the funeral.

The private research group The Indicator Project of South Africa has stated in a report entitled Political Conflict in South Africa that unrest in the country between September 1984 and June 1988 was the worst in its history, in view of the number of people killed (more than 3,500), injured, and imprisoned (over 55,000), and the socio-economic losses sustained.

June 1989. The side of the N1 Highway. Goodwood.

It was freezing cold and my 'Ridesafeman' powers of autosuggestion had failed me for the past thirty minutes; nobody had stopped to give me a lift. That morning I had pulled on my army uniform for the first time since klaaring out of Kroonstad, six months before. I'd decided to hitch to Johannesburg to find my fame and fortune – I'd decided to get into the television industry. I had no qualifications, no experience, no contacts and no bloody idea.
What could go wrong?

Glossary & Abbreviations:

ANC: African National Congress. The liberation movement founded in 1912 and led by Oliver Tambo, Nelson Mandela and others.
Baas (Afrikaans.): Boss
Babelas (Afr.): Hungover.
Bakkie (Afr.): Utility vehicle. Used for transporting sheep, sacks of grain and children.
Ballas bakking (Afr.): Baking your balls; sun tanning, relaxing.
Balsak (Afr.): Ball sack. A kitbag, for storing your military kit or your testicles.
Bandiets (Afr.): Bandits, convicts, prisoners.
Bietjie (Afr.): A bit, a small amount.
Bietjie vry (Afr.): A bit of fooling around, usually with the opposite sex or not.
Biltong (Afr.): Dried spiced meat. A South African delicacy and now the favourite snack of customs officials around the world.
Bliksem (Afr.): To punch, to beat up. Also an exclamation like dammit!
Bliksem/s (Afr.): A gentle insult. Rascals.
Boshoed (Afr.): Bush hat.
Braai (Afr.): A barbecue, but for real men.
Chommie (Afr.): Chum, mate.
Choop-stil (Afr.): Very quiet. Especially when hiding under your bed during the parade.
DB : Detention Barracks
Dagga (Afr.): Marijuana.

Die Stem (Afr.): The South African national anthem. 'The Voice'.

Dik gesuip (Afr.): Extremely drunk.

Dof (Afr.): Stupid.

Doibie (Afr.): A plastic helmet, or an inner for a metal helmet.

Dom (Afr.): Dumb.

Dominee (Afr.): Pastor.

Donga (Xhosa/Zulu)): A dry gully.

Dop (Afr.): An alcoholic drink.

Doos (Afr.): Idiot.

Fok (-ken; -ol) (Afr.): Fuck. Fucking. Fuck-all.

Gat (Afr): Hole/asshole.

Gatvol (Afr.): Exasperated.

Gerook (Afr.): High on dagga.

Gesuip (Afr.): Drunk.

Grootjas (Afr.): Big coat or jacket.

The Groot Trek (Afr.): The great trek/journey.

Hardegat (Afr.): Hard-arsed, opinionated.

Hokkie (Afr.): Hut.

Houding (Afr.): Military bearing.

Hou jou bek (Afr.): Shut your mouth.

Hou my vas, Korporaal (Afr.): Hold me tight, Corporal.

Jas (Afr.): Coat.

Jol (Afr.): A party, a good time.

Kak (Afr.): Shit.

Kak off/out (Afr.): Shit off.

Klaar in (uit) (Afr.): The process of checking in or out of the army.

Klaar (Afr.): Finished.

Kaserne, kaserne aandag! (Afr): (Lit.) 'Bungalow, bungalow. Attention!'. (An order for all troeps in the bungalow to come to attention.)

Kiff (Afr.): Cool, excellent.

Klap (Afr.): A slap.

Kleinkas (Afr.): Small cupboard.

Keurraad (Afr.): Selection board.

Laaitie (Afr): Youngster, kid.

Majat: Low-grade marijuana.

MK: (Umkhonto we Sizwe). (Lit.) The Spear of the Nation. The armed wing of the ANC.

Moeg (Afr.): Tired.

Moer/Moer-in (Afr.): To hit. Pissed off.

Moerse (Afr.): Huge.

Moffie (Afr.): Derogatory term for a gay person.

Naai/naaier (Afr.): Fuck/er.

NGK: Nederlandse Gereformeerde Kerk. The Dutch Reformed Church.

Nogal (Afr.): As well.

Opvok (Afr.): To fuck up, abuse.

Ou (Afr.): A guy. As in: "He was a good ou."

Paraat (Afr.): A well-disciplined, enthusiastic soldier.

Perdestal (Afr.): A horse stall.

PF: Permanent Force. Defence Force members who were on contract. Usually doing more than three years' service.

PFP: Progressive Federal Party. The liberal opposition party in parliament.

Poes (Afr.): A lady's naughty bits.

Poesklap (Afr.): A hard slap.

Poes-in (the) (Afr.): Very angry.

Poppie (Afr.): A young woman.

Roef/Roefie (Afr.): A new recruit.

Roer jou gat! (Afr.): Move your ass.

Rooi gevaar (Afr.): (Lit.) 'Red danger'. Communists.

SABC: South African Broadcast Company (Propaganda tool for the government of the day)

SADF: South African Defence Force.

Skerp (Afr.): Sharp.

Skelm (Afr.): To cheat.

Skietbaan (Afr.): A shooting range.

Skollies (Afr.): Rascals, troublemakers.

Skop (Afr): To kick.

Slaapgat (Afr.): Lazy.

Sluip (Afr): To skulk.

Smaak (Afr.): To enjoy or like.

Strek (Afr): (Lit). 'To stretch'. A military salute to Non-Commissioned officers. Putting your arms down by your sides.

Stukkend(e) (Afr.): Broken.

Suipgat (Afr): Big drinker.

Swart gevaar (Afr.): (Lit.): Black Danger: A phrase coined by the National Party making reference to the threat of being overthrown by the black population.

Swerf (Afr.): To swerve.

Tik (Afr.): Low-grade crystal meth.

Tree aan (Afr.): To form a squad.

Troepie (Afr.): Troop. The lowest rank in the army. Private.

Tune (Afr.): To tell.

Varkpanne (Afr.): Pig pans.

Vasbyt (Afr.): (Lit.). 'To bite fast'. To hang in there.

Veld (Afr.): Field, plains.

Verklaaring (Afr.): Deposition, request.

Voetsak (Afr.): Get lost.

Wag (Afr.): To wait.

Wakker (Afr.): Awake.